ON BEING A WRITER

INTRODUCTION BY
WILL BLYTHE

Edited by Bill Strickland

Concept Development by Jennie Rosenthal

Writer's
Digest
Books

Cincinnati, Ohio

93   92   91   90   5   4   3   2

Library of Congress Cataloging-in-Publication Data

On being a writer.
    1. Authorship. 2. Authors, American—20th century—Interviews. 3. American literature—20th century—History and criticism. I. Strickland, Bill.
PN149.048   1989   808'.02   89-16501
ISBN 0-89879-366-1

Design by Clare Finney

The following page is an extension of this copyright page.

CONTENTS

INTRODUCTION

When you are trying to write well, it helps to find out what you and authors such as Ernest Hemingway have in common. He, of course, is a dead writer who wrote *The Sun Also Rises.* You are not. On the other hand, you are alive and scrawling and there may be some consolation in that. You will probably be pleased to discover (as I was) that Hemingway preferred to compose his first drafts with a #2 pencil. Such a homely fact can form a bridge from you to Papa. After all, you may own such a pencil. You may have already used it! And if you and Hemingway have shared the wonderful and increasingly archaic feel of tracing words on paper by hand, can it be long until you also write a lovely sentence or two?

The interviews in this book will put you in touch not only with exalted notions of art but also with the endearing arcana of a writer's life—the preferred pens and pencils, the paper, cups of coffee, shots of bourbon, and household pets. Don't scoff at these particulars of the writing life. This is not mathematics. The humble and specific are a writer's stock-in-trade. Writing well remains a mysterious endeavor, resistant to blueprints and outlines (thank God) and it is reassuring to establish connection with the masters, even if the link is as slender as a pencil.

So what if this smacks of voodoo, of talismans, of fetishistic objects? An author's routines are as propitiatory as a rain doctor's. To read about writing habits is to realize how assiduously, how slyly the muse must be courted. In this context, interviews serve as reliquaries of authorial wisdom, what writers, especially aspiring ones, may resort to rather than saints' bones or hanks of hair.

Culled from the past three decades of *Writer's Digest*, the interviews here feature a remarkably catholic array of writers. Rarely, if ever, have Rod McKuen, Norman Mailer, Red Smith, and Erica Jong, to name just a few, shared so cozily the same forum. The "popular" writers in this anthology generally come off as no less insightful about their vocation than their more literary peers. Most of the writers appear quite at ease with their earnest interrogators. Nearly all of them talk well, sometimes almost as well as they write.

That gentleman farmer, William Faulkner, for instance, known for his truculence and shyness, displays a forthright eloquence in a 1962 interview, although a few of his remarks resound with a rather Nobel ring. Still, his analysis of the genres of fiction is admirably concise and colloquial—and, I think, exactly right: "All the trash must be eliminated in the short story, whereas one can get away with some of it in the novel." Now that's a cagey Mississippi farmer talking.

It may surprise you that even a professionally reticent writer such as Faulkner should chat so freely about his novels and the process of composition. But who among us can resist a chance to hold court occasionally? Furthermore, most writers at work spend their days cloistered in their rooms. "I think the most important thing for a writer is to be locked into a study," says Erica Jong. To write successfully requires stamina and concentration and solitude. No writers I've known have been able to burnish reputations for wild life when actually writing. No doubt it comes as a relief for them every once in a while to leave the monastery and blabber on like normal office workers. When they are not pretending to be woodsmen and criminals, writers occasionally find it pleasant to talk shop and, given a choice between shop talk and the higher abstractions of aesthetics, I'll usually take the former.

So what do they talk about when they talk about writing? The writers here are neither dogmatists nor theoreticians. They speak in the grand American tradition of the engineer, the handy-man, the jack-of-all-trades. "Let's just write this thing," they seem to mutter, tinkering away inside their stories, "then we'll figure out how we did it." In an age of French metababble and semiotic sludge, their pragmatism is refreshing. "A story can do anything as long as it's effective," says John Steinbeck. "There's no recipe for passing good story writing on."

But these writers' heritage partakes of more than the handy-man. They are adherents to another sturdy American tradition—the Puritan work ethic. They trudge daily to their typewriters and computer terminals, displaying the stern-faced stolidity of assembly line workers, certain that success comes first to those who only sit and wait. "Write everyday, keep a schedule," exhorts the playwright Arthur Kopit. I certainly sympathize with those who exclaim, "If this is the bohemian artist in full cry, we might as well become accountants." Rod McKuen rises early every day to write, and when his powers of invention flag, switches from one poem to another. Similarly, the poet James Dickey rambles through his house, hammering at one typewriter, then another, slamming out several poems at a time.

But if getting to the writing table is often the first order of business, then arising from it with an honest, personal piece of work is the ultimate aim. This demands that you trust in your own impressions, your own inklings, above all others. "You alone must become the final measure of things. Find something that only you could say," suggests Dickey. Such self-reliance means that you write first and foremost for yourself. A writer, says Allen Ginsberg, must "express himself completely without worrying about what it looks like in public."

These are wise comments on the craft of writing, and for better or worse, this is an epoch of literary craft, a time when sentences often shine more brightly than the books they make up. The Great American Novel—remember that?—has come to seem the laughable relic of ludicrously ambitious writers. How dare anyone attempt to sum up so much of a maddened century in a single work of fiction? The egomania of it all. Such books require more energy and intelligence, more nerve and vision than many writers possess. Or so the story goes.

These days, aspiring writers flock not to newspapers, not to freight trains and infantry battalions, but to the university writing programs that have sprung up around the country like triplex movie theaters. I've been there myself. Since the teachers in these programs understandably regard it as presumptuous, beyond their ken, to teach "passion" and "vision," their students end up learning technique, the machinery of writing. Really, it's writing as applied auto mechanics. The sort of novels Henry James

called "loose, baggy monsters" have been rounded up, caged, and fed a starvation diet to turn them into sleek, aerobicized volumes.

But the application of craft alone is never enough to summon forth a memorable story, novel, poem, play, or column. The novelist Kurt Vonnegut says that writers ought to have a passion for and an engagement with something beyond the page:

You should have something on your mind. You should have opinions on things. You should care about things . . . Of course, a lot of creative writing courses teach you how to counterfeit energy, sincerity, and involvement. It's a little like going to modeling school to learn how to put on your make-up and always be beautiful.

"You have to care," says columnist Ellen Goodman. "That's the most important thing." Fortunately, what you care about is your own business. And even in this credential-crazy era, you don't need to go to school to have passions, to be obsessed, to be hurt or shattered or moved or amused into writing. Life takes care of that. This book of interviews, of pencils and paper, advice and inspiration, is a fine place to start taking care of the rest.

—Will Blythe

HARLAN ELLISON

*You're a writer. And that's something better than
being a millionaire. Because it's something holy.*

When I wrote the following essay in
1960—it was published in 1961—I was
26 years old, and had been a professional at my craft for only four years.
Now, almost three decades later, with 45
books written, more than 1,400 stories, essays, articles
and columns published, a dozen movies and three dozen
teleplays turned out, and an embarrassing number of
awards listed after my name in Who's Who, I am called
upon to face that bombastic tot who careered across the
pages, shooting off his mouth with such *obiter dicta*
about the holy chore of writing. I re-read that essay, and I
wince. How filled with hot air and looniness that kid was.
Like a banjo player who had a big breakfast.

I find the bravado and hip-shooting of that 26-year-
old Ellison a matter for to blush. But, astonishingly to me,
I find that what he had to say, flensed of all the rodomon-
tade, quite a testament to the nobility of spending one's
life at the writing rigor. I'd say it less flamboyantly now,
perhaps, but I'd very likely say the same things. But it's
not to justify where I was nearly 30 years ago that I write
this update.

Here are a few things I learned later. They may help.

First, is the big secret. The one no one ever tells you.
And it is this: *any*one can *become* a writer. (If you doubt
it, consider Judith Krantz. If someone who writes that
badly can become a writer, then even the dippiest of us
can become a writer, chacma baboons can become writers, sludge and amoeba can become writers.) The trick is
not in *becoming* a writer, it is in *staying* a writer. Day
after week after month after year. Staying in there for the
long haul. Because, at final moments, when they plant us,
and Posterity takes a scrinch-eyed look at what we've
done before deciding to remember us or forget us, it is
not a single book or story or play that wins or loses the
day, it is the *totality* of what has been produced. Not a
single hill, but a mountain range that stretches and rises
and dips, and has sweep that can be judged. Through all

the fads and successes and times when the critics ignore
a writer, it is the work that goes on unabated. And, finally,
it is all that sustains us.

Second, success is a killer. It twists you, and bends
you, and lies to you. When you are in the public eye, you
are treated like Athena sprung fullblown from the forehead of Zeus, and you get used to the praise. When the
vogue passes, and all that remains is the quality of the
work, you must put the cheap pleasures of celebrity behind you, and keep producing. Eventually, if you live long
enough and keep working well long enough, they find
their way back to you, and new generations of readers
find you, and it's better, warmer, much better indeed.
Trust me on this one.

And last, and most important, if you want to be the
writer that you confront 30 years later without shame,
then learn to ignore your readers. They mean well, and
for the most part they are terrific people. But they *know*
what they like from you, and if they have their way they'll
demand it again and again—as reflected in the demands
of the market and the editors and the reviews—and 30
years down the pike you'll find you've written the same
book 11 times. So thank your readers and the critics who
praise you, and then ignore them. Write for the most intelligent, wittiest, wisest audience in the universe: write
to please yourself.

And *never* let mere money be an influence. A good
writer can always make money, even if he or she has to

---

*Harlan Ellison, known as a tough negotiator, drove a
characteristic hard-but-easy-to-take bargain in allowing us to reprint this inspirational piece: We could
use the essay only "if I can write," Harlan said, "an
update sidebar that will precede the original, which
reads both goshwow and raw to me now. Agree to that,
and we gotta deal."*

We had a deal.

drive a truck or lay brick or work in the steno pool. Money is never a reason to sell out the holy chore.

That ought to sustain you. Ibsen said to live is to war with trolls, and I promise you that if you write well, and your words become popular, there will be trolls a-plenty trying to give you an enema with a thermite bomb. Be tough, be contained, be very very good at the keyboard and perhaps, 30 years down the line, you can face yourself and grin at the kid.

* * *

Lautrec once said (or so Jose Ferrer leads us to believe), "One should never meet an artist whose work one admires. The work is always so much better than the man." This is as true of me as it was of him (Lautrec, not Ferrer), though I hasten to explain I am in no way comparing myself with Henri de Toulouse-Lautrec.

It's just that I find rapport in what he is alleged to have said, because though my stories often reflect goodness and truth and subtlety and courage, I'm incapable of being good and honest and subtle when writing about my writing. (You notice I said *my* writing, not just Writing in General or The Art of Writing, because as far as I'm concerned, when it comes to Harlan Ellison's Writing, I'm a hell of an authority—and I think I'm good. I admire Malraux and St. Exupéry and Hemingway and Schulberg and Hardy and Conrad and Ed McBain and William Goldman, but they're authorities on themselves [and don't believe any of that flapdoodle about a writer being unable to estimate his own work; if he's anywhere near talented, he knows better than anyone else] so all I can speak, for or about, is what *I* write, what I am. And since I've got to believe I'm something, I've got to believe I'm good. I'm not as lean and hard as Hemingway, and I'm not as bittersweet punch-in-the-belly as Goldman, because I'm me and they're they, and I'd never want the twain to meet. When I was 17, I wanted to be another James Joyce. I wised up. I settled for being the first Me. Not only is it less strain, but it stays within the limits of possibility.) But, I digress.

Stick with me, I've got a point.

Writing isn't a game with me. Neither is it "a job" as it is with many of my friends in "the trade" who work from 10 to 4 with an hour off for Beaujolais and biscuits. It is my life. Now snicker all you wish, that happens to be the plain and simple of it. And it not only offends me, it disgusts, short tempers, and enrages me to see people *playing* at being writers.

There are the poor, damned souls who must write, who haven't any more choice in the matter than whether or not they breathe.

I'm not saying anybody doesn't have the right to tinker with the greatest gift in the world; I'm not saying you can't go out and have your swill put between hardcovers by an ego press, or donate your stories free of charge to a little magazine that can't afford to pay but *can* afford to steal; I'm not saying you can't write 300 novelettes and hide them in your trunk because you're too frightened to show them to anyone, under the pretext that you "write only for yourself"; I'm not even saying you can't sell a few pieces to a reputable magazine, and settle down to calling yourself a writer.

I'm not saying you can't do it.

I'm just saying you can't stop me from looking on you with contempt.

In short, this article is a statement of purpose . . . a declaration of my place in the Universe and my thoughts about what I set down and what it's worth. To me. So if you are a fat little old lady in Mashed Potato Falls, Wyoming, with an antimacassar hat and a penchant for astrological poetry, if you are a dewy-eyed college student who accepts everything they tell you in creative writing courses without compunction or cerebration, if you are (in other words) a phoney, a dilettante, an imitator, a hack or a humbug, pass on to the articles that tell you what words to put into your characters' mouths or how to lick the mailing label, because this thing I'm writing will offend you.

And that would be just what I'd want to do; and you wouldn't want to give me any satisfaction, now would you?

But if you *know* you can write, if you *have* to write, if you spell like an aborigine and phrase like a longshoreman but have *something to say*, please, for God's sake! stay with me, because you aren't alone . . . there are many like you. I'm like you . . . we think alike, we suffer alike, and we want to go—where?—*there*, alike! This is for you.

You're a writer.

Credentials, first. Why listen to a guy if you don't think he's been where he's sending you?

I'm 26, I've sold 11 books and 300-odd stories published all over the lot. I've never sold to *The New Yorker*, *Saturday Evening Post* or *Ladies' Home Journal*, and I don't have to downgrade their editorial practices because they wouldn't buy *my* kind of stories, and I won't write *their* kind, so we have a nodding acquaintance—I say nodding and they say nodding. I started writing when I was old enough to spell kat, and I haven't stopped. I've got a big mouth.

I sold my first story to Larry Shaw in 1955 when he was editing *Infinity Science Fiction*, and it was a very bad story by my standards today. That was my first and it tasted good, Lord how good it tasted! It was like jumping with all my clothes on, into the ocean and catching that first, freezing crash right in the face. It was like loving all the best-looking girls in the world at once. It was like making a muscle and finding one! Hard and smooth and just right because it was all mine, nobody else's just mine. And I ran through the streets of New York, so help me, I ran and waved the check like it was the standard at the front of a B-movie cavalry charge. And I cried. Because now somebody else believed. Now somebody else said, "Okay, kid, you can stop screaming, I believe you can write. And I'm willing to give you a penny a word to back up my faith."

You're chuckling at that penny a word?

Don't, brother, because I'll bust you right in the jaw. That was the sweetest penny a word I'd ever known. Before or since. It was the birth and the puberty and the having it all, wrapped up in one check. So don't laugh; that's a warning.

If you're wondering when I'm going to get down to it—the point—then turn on, because you aren't a writer. You may be an author, but you certainly aren't a writer. If you understand what I've been saying, that I have *been* saying it since I started, about what it is to be a writer, and how it's got to be—at least for me—then you, too, are a writer.

That's the difference. There are writers, and there are authors. *Any*body can be an author. With the demand for material as great as it is today, any poor slob who can write without bumbling over his syntax can sell. But it's one thing to get your name under a title and get it set in type, and quite another to be a writer. Many of the latter never see print. That's a crime, but it's the way the world is run, unfortunately. Some guys write because they have found a relaxing, nonstrenuous way to beat the hard work system. Others do it because it's catharsis; these are the gut-spillers. Still others do it because they like to keep eating . . . regularly or gluttonously, it doesn't matter which. Then there are the poor, damned souls who *must* write, who haven't any more choice in the matter than whether or not they breathe.

That's me. I *have* to write. When I was younger (last week) I was wont to say, rather melodramatically, that I wrote from the gut. This led to all manner of clever ripostes from my contemporaries who compared my effusions with the more advanced stages of gorge-buoyancy. Since then I've tempered my semantics and relocated the source of my work. It comes from the heart and the soul and the head and the index fingers of my right and left hands which are the only ones (poor slobs) that ever learned to type.

But that's the gut, too.

When you start out, and you don't quite know how or what to write, and all you know is that you *must*, it's easy to get led astray. So you write penny-a-word blood-and-gore mystery stories, you write science fiction novelettes at 30,000 words around a bad cover idea, you write anything and everything, because it's all pouring out of you and the heat is so great that if you stop it up you'll split wide open like a pumpkin out of a tenth-story window.

So you write.

And you write.

It's training. It's learning the basics of plot structure and characterization and dialogue in the only vineyard that counts: before the editors and the professional critics and your fellow writers who know the roots and background of the field—not the nice folks you've let read your story in hopes they'll bolster your ego. Now you aren't a chipmunk on a treadmill, running after a sprig of parsley. Now you're out in the open where they can belt you . . . or applaud you. The pulps were a great training ground for many of the valuable writers of today; you've heard that before. Don't pay attention to the snobs who tell you it's "commercial" and art it ain't. Guys like F. Van Wyck Mason, Marquand, C.S. Forester, Dashiell Hammett and too many others to go into here, got their starts and their basic training in the commercial pulp markets.

Though the pulps are with us only shadowedly these days, and fiction outside hardcovers is divided nastily into warring camps of bland *Cosmopolitan* fiction with its "average boy and girl" stick figures, and of "pastiche" fiction without destination in the arty periodicals, the writer of fiction can still find markets for his work. If it's good. That's all it has to be. Guys who beg off for their bounce notes with comments about how they're ahead of their time, or how the editors buy only from their relatives, or how they write only to purge themselves . . . these are not writers, these are the Mollusks. They aren't hungry enough. They don't want it as badly as you or I.

Writing for the detective magazines, the science fiction magazines, the sophisticated men's field, these are all reputable backgrounds for a conscientious writer; they may be sneered at by the sybarites, but I'll take one solid Charlie Beaumont to three dozen pudding-gutted one-story wonders in the "little" magazines. The former is a man capable of writing octagons around the herd of the latter.

But there are dangers in the pulps, too. You have to know when your apprenticeship is at an end. You have to recognize when you're writing for the buck and not because you have to write and you don't care what it is as long as it broadens and deepens you.

And then one day you find you aren't saying anything. You're running the backside off your hero and getting him sapped over the head at regular intervals to meet the word requirements, and you stop. Just like that.

You freeze. And then you know for sure you're a writer. You're a writer who has flown up his own tail like the *sakahachi* bird, but you are, sure as God made little green apples, a writer. Abruptly you realize that you are tired of conning your readers and, worse, conning yourself. You find you've got things to say about the nature of life and the inevitability of loneliness for the sensitive person in our times and the stench of prejudice and the transitory nature of success . . . and you curse yourself.

You are a liar.

You are a cheat and a thief. You've cheated yourself and stolen from your talent. You've deprived them of what you have and what you could tell them. They need it, you need to give it to them, you've got to make your stand. Because all you are, all I am, is what I write. Away from the typewriter I'm a man, but behind it I'm something else entirely.

I'm something more than a man. I can say what I believe, what I truly believe, and it will be read and understood by *someone, somewhere*, and I'll have communicated. Do you understand what I'm saying? Do you realize what a feeling that is? It's creating the Heaven and the Earth in less than seven, and being God to yourself. That's what it is.

Laugh at Kerouac all you like for his trickery and his self-deceit, but *he* feels it. All you have to do is *read* the man, let him talk to you in his own voice, and you'll know he feels it. Not when he's tinkering for a buck, but when he's joyful and true and completely with it. Then he is only slightly less than immortal, and I've been that way, and if you understand what I'm saying, you have been, too.

You're a writer. And that's better than being a millionaire. Because it's something holy.

Over my typewriter I've got a few Words to Work By. They work for me. They might not work for you. I'll give them to you, with the understanding that I'm not trying to be lit'ry or pushy. They just help me, and what the hell . . . maybe you, too. Like so:

There is no use writing anything that has been written before unless you can beat it. What a writer in our time has to do is write what hasn't been written before or beat dead men at what they have done.

That was Hemingway in 1936. He's right, too, you know. And if for a moment I had to believe it's all been done, I think I'd shrivel like a spider web in a flame. Then Matthew Arnold said it all just right about what it takes to write. He said:

Produce, produce, produce . . . for I tell you the night is coming.

Which is the whole story. Guys who give me the old line about how they're "thinking it out" or "living it up" before they can get to the pen or the typer, give me the coolie-jams, because the only way to write is simply . . . to write. And the last thing I write by (though I've found it's the hardest of the three to live up to) is something Flaubert said, as translated by Budd Schulberg in "The Disenchanted":

Art is a luxury. It needs clean hands and composure. If you make one little concession, then two, then five . . .

I've also got up a quote from Brendan Behan, but what that old tosspot has to say is more in the nature of an antisocial way of *living* for a writer and doesn't really have anything to do with the practice of same, so I'll just taunt you with its obscure reference.

Yet no amount of quoting or philosophizing can say it for you. I was motivationally researched the other day by a gentle little woman who came to my door asking me to look at a presentation folder of ads and then tell her why I didn't flip my nut when I saw a photo of a Hammond organ, and when it was all done, she asked me—rather timidly, as most nonwriters who consider Writers something supernatural are wont to speak—whether writing courses would make a person a writer.

I had to answer honestly, because I have neither the patience nor good sense to lie, that as far as I was concerned, if you're a writer, you know it when they drag you squawking out of the womb. You may be able to fake it by attending writing classes, but you haven't got it *here*. I know a couple of writers who make close to 30 grand a year doing nothing but pounding a machine, but they aren't *writers* by my definition. They are nice, sweet guys and wonderfully competent authors who can write in any style you designate, at any length you set, for any market and with whatever viewpoint you require. I despise their writing. I try to get them to lose money by writing what they feel, not what they reason out for story-value.

They ignore me.

And a damned good thing. They'd go broke in a week if they tried to be writers. They're authors, the same way some people are bricklayers or die-stamping press operators. There are men with talent and perceptivity and empathy who write commercially, who turn out fiction that doesn't really live within them—Harvey Swados, Herb Gold, Charles Beaumont, R.V. Cassill, to name four that come to mind—but they do it well. They do it on a level few "quality" writers can match, and they do it with the inherent flair for knowing the right thing to say in the right way that makes them writers, not authors, in the manner no amount of articles on how to be a writer can tell you. It's something in the genes. Not the intellect. These men may not *like* writing pure moneystories (though I suspect they derive the same aesthetic pleasure out of a well-turned commercial piece as they get from their more feeling works) but they *can* do it when they feel they must . . . and they know the difference. It makes for a schizoid personality in a manner of speaking, but it also tones up the blood, brings apples to the cheeks and improves the complexion.

If you can do it, you're not expected to be judged on that sort of work, those stories. Every working writer has to learn to do it.

Just know what to do with your emotions once you've learned.

I've done it, and I can't go back to read those pieces.

So I froze. I didn't write for a while. And those who had tagged me as a writer on juvenile delinquency (because of my first novel and book of short stories on the subject), and those who had tagged me as a writer of science fiction (because of my ditto and my ditto) wondered what had happened. They wondered if I'd hit a slump. Which was nonsense. No writer ever hits a slump. As Algis Budrys (who is a helluva writer, and who taught me about half of what I know) once said to me: You don't slump, you just reach a plateau. Then you have to get your wind, and readjust your thinking and your synapses, and get set to write better, with more maturity, with greater passion and purpose. He was right.

I'm nothing. Nothing at all without writing. Without truth, my truth, the only truth I know, it's all a gambol in the pasture without rhythm or sense.

(An explanatory note: Earlier I said writing could not be taught, and above I said Budrys had taught me about half of what I know. This is not, though on the surface it may seem to be, dichotomous. Budrys—who is, in case you haven't discovered him, one of the few writers of the past ten years in the field of science fiction to demonstrate memorable qualities of true literature in his work—taught me intangibles. How do you estimate the education of a writer in things like GET OUT OF COLLEGE AND START WRITING or even FAWNING PRAISE CAN KILL YOU: GET YELLED AT MORE OFTEN, IT'LL TOUGHEN YOU? How do you estimate their value? You don't. You just realize years later that the most valuable training you had was watching a writer like Budrys plotting a cover story, or having Budrys turn you on to Cozzens before the mass got hold of *By Love Possessed*, or being shocked and terrified at how much Budrys could blue-pencil out of a 3,000-worder you could have sworn was tight as a Chianti cork. Get taught how to write? Not on your life. But a mentor—even a reluctant one—can often work the embolisms out of your talent. Schools . . . uh-uh.)

I started writing stories that I reread and stared at

with astonishment. What the hell are you *writing*, Ellison? I asked myself.

In "Daniel White for the Greater Good," I tried to say Negro prejudice stinks, by making a strong case for the necessity of lynching a Negro.

In "Final Shtick," I psychoanalyzed my own childhood from the focal point of anti-Semitism in an Ohio town.

In "Lady Bug, Lady Bug" I propounded the theory that love can only uplift and cleanse, thus destroying the safety of mediocrity, loneliness and bastardliness.

In "May We Also Speak?" I presented four views of the not-so-beat generation, and discovered to my horror, pleasure and satisfaction that I was talking about a new breed of human being, The Hung-Up People. All my stories were examining the moral, ethical and physical attitudes of the Hungry Ones, who have come into being in the past 15 years. Who would buy these stories?

No one, that's who.

But I *had* to write them. I didn't have any choice.

Throw myself at the typewriter. Pound away at it for six and eight and even eleven hours straight, with nothing but pack after pack of cigarettes, and my gut started to feel cold and misty the way you feel the next day after waking all night on No-Doz and hot, black coffee. And when they were done, exhausted, drained, lying back with no means of expression, an empty thing, all of it there, down, set and right and the way you wanted it. That was the way it had to be.

Then along came Bill Hamling at *Rogue*, and he was another one of the important ones, another of the ones who said, "You write it, and I'll publish it, because you've got it. You're saying things your own way." So he published "May We Also Speak?" and about 20 others, and Knox Burger at Gold Medal will be figuring a way to market a whole book of stories about my hung-up generation I want to call "No Doors, No Windows." (But which will get bounced because Knox has enough sense to know he can't really market the thing to the mass, but what the hell do I care, he's got the novels, and they're good and Knox knows it, and he's about the best goddamn editor I've ever had.)

You see, they're important. The editors. You have to say something to them. You don't have to write for them, "slant" for them—oh, that goddamn odious phrase. All you have to do is write true. And anybody who writes for the fat man with the cigar, behind the big editorial desk, is a cheat and a liar and not worth the type fonts to set him up. He is stealing from the people, and from himself. He's writing other people's stories, other people's ideas. But the editors are important: the real ones, the good ones, the ones who want to buy books and stories, not just material to fill their pages or meet their schedules.

And guys who sell themselves out, who lie and make it to Hollywood or Book-of-the-Month Club or big-time TV, those guys are cannibalizing themselves, and I weep sad and long for them. Because they are killing what they had to offer. And I swear to myself that if I get lucky and somebody bites on one of my stories, and I make a potful in H'wood, I won't let myself get suckered into the solid gold trap. To hell with the swimming pools and balling the starlets and impressing everybody.

Because, you see, I'm nothing. I'm nothing at all without the writing. Without truth, my truth, the only truth I know, it's all a gambol in the pasture without rhythm or sense. It's empty. God gave it to me (so help me, Deist or no, I believe that!) and I can't cheat myself or you or them or anyone by not doing it the best way I know how.

That's the heart and head of the writer, to set it all down before they put him down the hole. To get it all out the right way, the best way, the truest way you know how.

Do you feel it?

Do you know what I mean?

Then you and I are family. We can meet at the phony cocktail parties where the buffoons say, "I've led this real wild life, see. It would make a great story. All you got to do is write it and I'll split with you fifty-fifty," so that you want to give them a rap in the mouth, and you and I, we'll go over in the corner and talk, because you and I have a sacred trust. We aren't authors, we're writers and we live off what we do, not where we appear. We see some of it, and we dismiss Isherwood's "Camera" theory because we've got to live it as well as write it. So we'll talk.

You and I.

You and me.

The both of us writers.

I'll talk to you.

You talk to me.

I'll understand you, and you'll understand me.

We're the blessed ones. We're the damned ones. We're the ones who can do one thing in this world but oh God how well we do it! We can write.

Talk to me.

BY MICHAEL SCHUMACHER

RAYMOND CARVER

*It really comes down to this: indifference to everything
except that piece of paper in the typewriter.*

For nearly two decades, Raymond Carver was one of the best-kept secrets in the literary world. His short stories and poems, generally published by literary magazines and small presses, were read with great enthusiasm by a solid cult following interested in the wonderful kind of work that never seems to gain a lot of attention, but a large national following was slow in coming. His work won awards and prizes and was considered almost a staple in anthologies and "best of" collections. He was at the cutting edge of a resurgence of interest in the short story, but he was hardly a literary presence caught up in either book-biz glitz or the halls of academia.

Today, Raymond Carver is both "bankable" and well honored. Large, high-paying magazines solicit his work, while students, writers and interviewers solicit his time and opinion. He is considered one of the best—if not the best—of the modern short story writers. He is in constant demand on the lecture, teaching, and writers conference circuits. His papers and manuscripts are gaining value with collectors and university libraries.

To escape the brouhaha and constant work interruptions, Carver and Tess Gallagher, the poet and short story writer who has been his companion, critic and inspiration for the past decade, have moved from upstate New York to Port Angeles, Washington. But even there, they have to unplug the phone or hang out a hand-painted "No Visitors" sign to elude the attention and get down to real work.

Carver admits that his past and present are two different lives, and his success has only sharpened his focus and perception of the past. He is lucky to be alive, he says, adding that his stories and poems "bear witness" to his past and, unfortunately, to all too many people's presents.

His life story, in fact, reads like one of his fictional works. Born in Clatskanie, Oregon, in 1938, Carver was the product of a father with a penchant for wandering and drinking—a sawmill worker who moved from paycheck to paycheck; Carver's mother supplemented the family's income by working as a waitress or clerk. Art and literature weren't discussed at the Carver dinner table.

Still, Junior (as Carver was called) wanted to be a writer, but it wasn't going to be easy: Carver married his high school sweetheart and had two children before his 20th birthday. Though he followed his father into the sawmills, Carver and his wife shared dreams of escaping their blue-collar tedium—"marginal lives of quiet desperation"—as *Newsweek* described those lifestyles.

Carver's writing career began when he moved his family to California and enrolled at Chico State College, where he took a creative writing class taught by John Gardner, the late novelist, essayist and teacher who became a vital influence on Carver. From then on, Carver worked menial jobs to support his family, stealing time to write. He published plenty of his work—much of it to great critical acclaim—but there was little or no money in it.

If this interview didn't celebrate survival, the "locomotive, iron-will" that rekindled a writing career that was, in Raymond Carver's own estimation, "flat-out extinguished," the words would read too raw:

"I'd be happy if they simply put Poet *on my tombstone.* Poet—*and in parentheses,* and Short Story Writer."

But in this last major interview before his death in August 1988, the modern master of the short story offered his past and current lives as testament to the power of creation. Carver seemed settled, interviewer Michael Schumacher recalled, working steadily on what would become the collection of stories Where I'm Calling From, *and comfortable with his realization that "Every day now is a bonus. Every day now is pure cream."*

"We had great dreams, my wife and I," Carver wrote years later, remembering those hard times. "We thought we could bow our necks, work very hard and do all that we set our hearts to do. But we were mistaken."

Their marriage ended and Carver took to drinking. Not even the 1976 publication of his first collection of short stories, *Will You Please Be Quiet, Please*, could reverse his slide. As his first life was reaching its end, Carver, like one of his fictional characters, was powerless to alter his life's direction. Discussing this period with *The Paris Review*, Carver's assessment was brutally honest: "You never start out in life with the intention of becoming a bankrupt or an alcoholic or a cheat or a thief. Or a liar."

Carver's survival is testament to the resilience of the human and creative spirits. His second collection of stories, *What We Talk About When We Talk About Love*, (1981) was a sort of catharsis, a compilation of works stylistically stripped to the bone, an anthology of the pain and despair his life had become. At the core of the stories was Carver's modern version of Sisyphus—the working stiff, perched near the summit of the mountain, shoulder to the boulder, unable to push it to the top, too proud or stubborn to let it roll to the bottom, frozen in a seemingly endless test of strength and endurance. The book, like his first, was greeted with overwhelmingly favorable response, and Carver became recognized as one of the most powerful forces in short fiction since Hemingway.

Carver's second life fell into place two years later, with the publication of *Cathedral* and his receiving the prestigious Mildred and Harold Strauss Living Award by the American Academy and Institute of Arts and Letters; the former allotted Carver still more critical acclaim—a nomination for a National Book Critics Circle Award—while the latter afforded him, to the tune of $35,000 annually, the opportunity to devote all his time to writing. With this newfound freedom, Carver left his creative-writing teaching post at Syracuse and turned his writing skills to poetry, publishing *Where Water Comes Together With Other Water* in 1985 and *Ultramarine* a year later. Like his stories, Carver's poems are dynamic and compressed, with each word a carefully chosen tool used to stretch tension to near-breaking point.

Today, Carver is working on another compilation of short fiction, to be published later in 1988. There's been

talk of a novel over the years, but Carver is clearly in no hurry to write it. He has written one screenplay—for director Michael Cimino—and he hints that he would like to write another. He was guest editor for the annual *Best American Short Stories* anthology in 1986, and in 1987 he and Tom Jenks collaborated to edit *Short Story Masterpieces*, an ambitious collection of what they consider to be the best American short stories published between 1953 and 1985.

Despite the demands placed on his time, Carver is a warm and cooperative man who doesn't seem caught up in all the hoopla surrounding his work and literary reputation. He is soft-spoken, even when talking about projects he cares about passionately. He is modest, yet confident in assessing his present status: "I feel that I *am* going to survive—I'll not only survive, but I'll thrive. It hasn't been easy, but I'm sure other writers have had it as hard or harder. But this is my life and my experience."

Because Carver is rarely asked more than a few passing questions about his poetry, and because his last two books were poetry collections, I began my questioning in that area, and saved the discussion of short fiction for later. I was glad I did.

> *Blue-collar life put a premium on directness and being straightforward. There wasn't a whole lot of room for the Henry Jamesian kind of indirection.*

You've published more volumes of poetry than short fiction. How did your career as a poet evolve?

Back when I began to write and send things out, I gave an equal amount of time to short stories and poems. Then, in the early '60s, I had a short story and a poem accepted on the same day. The letters of acceptance, from two different magazines, were there in the box on the same day. This was truly a red-letter day. I was writing both short fiction and poetry in a more-or-less hit-or-miss fashion, given the circumstances of my life. Finally, I decided, consciously or otherwise, that I was going to have to make a decision as to where to put the energy and strength I had. And I came down on the side of the short story.

You continued to write poetry, though.

Yes. For many years, I was an occasional poet, but that, to me, was better than being no poet at all. I wrote a poem whenever I could, whenever I had the chance and wasn't writing stories. Those earlier books of poems were small-press publications that are now out of print. The best of those poems are preserved in the collection *Fires*, which is in print. There are, I think, about 50 poems that I wanted to keep from those earlier collections, and those poems went into *Fires*.

For the last couple of years, you've been more than an occasional poet. Your output of poems during this period has been prodigious. How did that come to be?
After the publication of *Cathedral* and the attendant hubbub, I couldn't seem to find any peace and quiet or a place to work. We were living in Syracuse. Tess was teaching and there was a lot of traffic in the house, the phone kept ringing, people were showing up at the door. And there was her school business, and some socializing. But there was little time to work. So I came out to Port Angeles, to find a quiet place to work. I came here to this little house with the intention of writing fiction. I had not written any poems in well over two years and, so far as I knew, I felt it was conceivable I might not ever write another poem. But after I'd gotten out here and had just sat still and was quiet for about six days, I picked up a magazine and read some poems, and they were poems I didn't care for. And I thought: "Jesus, I can do better than that." [laughs] It may not have been a good motive to begin writing poems, but whatever the motive, I wrote a poem that night, and the next morning I got up and wrote another poem. This went on, sometimes two or even three poems a day, for 65 days. I've never had a period in my life that remotely resembles that time. I felt like it would have been all right, you know, simply to have died after those 65 days. I felt *on fire*.

So I wrote all of those poems, many of which went into *Where Water Comes Together With Other Water*, and I didn't do anything for a few months. But then I thought: what if the book comes out and it gets a good pasting [laughs] and I'm told I should never write any more poems, that I should stick to my fiction? Whatever the reasons, I began writing poems again, and by the time *Where Water Comes Together With Other Water* was published, I had a new book in the drawer. When I look back on this period of time, when I wrote those books of poems, I can't really account for it. This is the truth! All the poems seem now like a great gift—the whole period seems a gift. Right now, I'm back writing stories, and in a way it's almost as if that time never happened. It did, of course, and I'm glad it did, and I don't want to make more of it than it is—but it *was* a wonderful time. It was a high time. I've written a few poems since the publication of *Ultramarine*, but mainly now I'm concentrating on fiction. I hope that when I finish this collection of stories I'm working on, I will go back to the poems because, for me, when I'm writing poems, I feel there's nothing in the world so important. You know, as far as I'm concerned, I'd be happy if they simply put "Poet" on my tombstone. "Poet"—and in parentheses, "and Short Story Writer." [laughs] And way down at the bottom someplace, "and Occasional Anthologist."

And "Teacher?"
And "Teacher," yes [laughs]. "Teacher" would be at the bottom.

When I talked to Jay McInerney about his having you as a teacher, he spoke of you in much the same way as you've talked about having John Gardner as your teacher. Did you enjoy teaching?
I did. Never, in my wildest imaginings, could I have seen myself as a teacher. I was always the shyest kid in the class—any class. I never said anything. Coming, as I did, from a family where nobody had gone past sixth grade, the idea of being around the university in such a capacity, as a teacher, was important, I suppose, to my self-esteem. Most important was the fact that I had summers off, and I was earning a more-or-less decent living while I was doing it. A lot of writers who teach badmouth the schools, but I never got into that situation; I was glad to have a teaching job.

My teaching role model, of course, was John Gardner. But there was also another fiction writer, at Humboldt State University, named Richard Day, and a poet, in Sacramento, named Dennis Schmitz. I tried to teach a writers workshop class the way they did. I tried to give people a lot of personal attention. There was a literature class that Jay took from me in which I might have been, you might say, a little ill-prepared, so I'd always call on Jay to get the conversation going [laughs]: "So what do you think about this book, Jay?" And he'd take off and talk for ten minutes [laughs].

Do you think it's a good idea for aspiring writers to attend these schools or workshops?
Obviously, it's not for everybody, but I can't think of any writers or musicians who have just sprung full-blown without some kind of help. De Maupassant was helped by Flaubert, who went over all his stories and criticized them and gave him advice. Beethoven learned his business from Haydn. Michelangelo was an apprentice for a long while to someone else. Rilke showed his poems to someone early on. Same with Pasternak. Just about any writer you can think of. Everybody, whether it's a conductor or composer or microbiologist or mathematician—they've all learned their business from older practitioners; the idea of the maestro-apprentice relationship is an old and distinguished relationship. Obviously, this is not going to guarantee that it's going to make a great—or even a good—writer out of anybody, but I don't think it's going to hurt the writer's chances, either.

If nothing else, the encouragement is important.
Yes, exactly so. I don't know, frankly, what would have happened to me had I not run into John Gardner when I did. A writer can see that he's not in this alone, that there are other young writers around who care passionately about the same things he cares about, and he can

feel heartened. Once you're out there in the world, on your own, nobody cares. I think a writers workshop situation is a shared endeavor, and an immensely important endeavor. It can be abused by students or teachers, but for the best teachers and students, it's a good thing.

Do you encourage your students to read a lot? How important do you see reading being to the writer?
I think writers—especially young writers—should want to read all the books they can get their hands on. To this extent, that's where it's helpful to have some instruction as to what to read and who to read, from somebody who knows. But a young writer has to make a choice somewhere along the line, whether he's going to be, finally, a writer or a reader. I've known good, bright young putative writers who felt they couldn't begin to write until they had read *everything* and, of course, you simply cannot read everything. You can't read all the masterpieces, all the writers that you hear people talking about—you just don't have the time. I mean, I wish there were two of me—one to read and one to write—because I love to read. I probably read more than many people, but I don't read as much as I'd like when I'm writing full time. Then I read very little, if anything. I'm just writing and that's all. When I'm not actively writing, I tend to read anything—history books, poetry, novels, short stories, biographies.

What do you encourage your students to read?
Flaubert's letters—that's one book I'd recommend. Every writer should read those letters. And Chekhov's letters, and the life of Chekhov. I'll recommend a great book of letters between Lawrence Durrell and Henry Miller, which I read some years back. What a book! Writers should read, yes, to see how it's done, for one thing, how the others are doing it; but there's also the sense of shared enterprise, the sense that we're all in this together. It's been my experience that poets, especially, are helped by reading books on natural history, biography in addition to the usual reading they do in the area of poetry.

You write in the American idiom and pay close attention to details, which brings to mind William Carlos Williams and William Blake. Were they influences?
William Carlos Williams certainly. I didn't come to Blake until a good long while after I had started writing my own poetry. But Williams—very definitely. I read everything of Williams's that I could get my hands on when I was 19 or 20 years old. In fact, I started a little magazine when I was at Chico State College. It was a little magazine that ran for three issues, and it was called *Selection*. I published an original poem by Williams in the magazine. I wrote him a fan letter and said I was starting a little magazine (of course, I couldn't promise anything but contributor's copies), but he sent me this wonderful poem.

He scrawled his signature across the bottom of it. It was one of the great thrills of my life, and it happened shortly before he died. It was called "The Gossips," and it was included in that posthumous volume of his, *Pictures From Brueghel*.

How about his short stories? There's quite a similarity in his and your styles in short fiction.
I like his stories a lot, but I can't say for sure how much of what he was doing—the way he was doing it—got into my own stories. They may have, you know, because at that time it seemed like I was influenced by almost everything. I was just 19 or 20 years old, and John Gardner was my teacher. He was directing me to authors—people I *should* read, books I *had* to look at—so, consciously or otherwise, Williams's poetry influenced me, and maybe the stories did, too. But he was a more direct influence on my poetry. I suppose the influence on my fiction would be the early stories by Hemingway. I can still go back, every two or three years, and reread those early stories and become excited just by the cadences of his sentences—not just by what he's writing about but the way he's writing. I haven't done that in two or three years, and I'm beginning to feel like it's time to go back and reread Hemingway.

When you're writing a lot of poetry, does your mind work like a camera, where you see things like a snapshot—everything's taken in instantly, and you see the importance of what's before you?
I think so, yes. A lot of my poems begin with a visual image of some sort, like what you're talking about, a snapshot. These snapshots happen often. Most writers have trained themselves to be alert to these moments, but some of us, myself included, aren't always as alert as we'd like to be. Still, when these moments do happen, either at that moment or not too long afterwards, there might be a few words or a line that attaches itself to the image and brings this picture back again. That line often becomes the first line in the poem. Nothing that I write is inviolable—I often change virtually every word that's in a story or poem—but usually that first line, which is the thing that set me off to write the poem or story in the first place, that line remains unchanged. Everything else is up for grabs. But I like the idea of the picture because there's a glimpse of something that stays fixed in your head.

When you have that first line in your head, do you know right away whether it's going to be in a poem or a short story?
I'm not making a conscious decision to use a line in a poem or story. When I'm writing poems, it's invariably, inevitably going to become a poem, and when I'm writing stories, it's going to become part of a story. Some writers write poetry and fiction at the same time; they can move

easily from this to that, but I don't seem to be able to work that way. When I'm writing fiction, I'm only writing fiction; when I'm writing poetry, everything I touch seems to turn to poetry. So if that first line comes when I'm writing poetry, it's going to become a poem.

Some lines in your poetry have also appeared, almost verbatim, in your fiction.
I know. There's been a crossover like that in at least three or four stories and poems. There's a poem of mine in *Fires* called "Distress Sale," where people haul all their gear out on the sidewalk and somebody witnesses this, and then that's in my story, "Why Don't You Dance?" It's happened in a few other instances. There's a poem called "Mother" that has some lines that come up in a story called "Boxes." In every case, it was dealt with first in the poem. Then I must have felt it making such a large claim on my emotional life that I felt somehow it was unfinished business and went back to it and dealt with it in a larger, fuller way.

The poem "Mother," works very well by itself, but that incident—the idea of the mother calling on Christmas and saying she's going to kill herself if it doesn't stop snowing—was interesting when it was part of "Boxes." It seemed to heighten the tension you established earlier in the story. I don't know if this is conscious or not, but in "Mother," the narrator's thinking of seeing a psychiatrist, while in "Boxes," the narrator is thinking of having his mother see the psychiatrist.
There's a different kind of spin to it, yes. Most of my stories and poems have a starting point in real life, in reality, but I'm not writing autobiography. It's all subject to change—everything is—in a story or poem. Whatever seems to suit the work best, that's the direction I'll go in. The stories and poems may have, as their genesis, some lines of reference to the real world, but, as I've said, I'm not writing autobiography by any account.

Still, it appears that you're getting closer to the bone, more autobiographical, when you're writing poetry.
I think so. The poetry gives me a chance to be intimate or open or vulnerable—or even surreal sometimes—in a way that I don't often engage in when I'm writing fiction. I'm more removed, more at a distance when I'm writing fiction. I feel I'm much closer to the center, the core, in the poetry.

> *There are significant moments in everyone's day that can make literature. That's what you ought to write about.*

Let's turn to your work as a short story writer. Interest in the short story seems to be resurging lately, with more and more story collections published every year. How do you account for this?
I think it's the single most eventful literary phenomenon of our time. I don't think there's ever been a time like it for the short story, or for short story writers. Many short story writers today are not even interested in writing novels. As you know, some short story writers can command advances that are every bit equal to some of the advances being paid for novels. The bottom line is always how many copies are being sold, and books of short stories are being sold these days like never before. It's a most remarkable thing. There was a time when, by and large, the commercial presses looked on publishing short stories as an enterprise that would be better left to the small presses and the university presses, but now that situation is completely turned around. Short story writers figure prominently on publishers' lists. Their books are reviewed prominently and supported in important ways by the publishing houses.

You, of course, have been mentioned as one of the main reasons for this trend.
Well, anything I can say to that sounds a little self-serving, and I feel a little awkward talking about this. I feel that a number of other good writers began working more or less at the same time I was starting out writing stories; and any success that might have come my way, or someone else's way, has helped all this along. But, sure, the good things that have happened to me have been good for every other short story writer as well. But don't forget that the publication of John Cheever's short stories in 1978 helped things considerably, too. I think maybe a lot of young writers saw what was happening and felt heartened: they felt it was all right to write short stories exclusively and not worry about writing novels. This gave license to lots of short story writers. There were a number of short story writers at work, and I feel I'm one of many.

Who, of the story writers, do you like?
Oh, I like Toby Wolff—he's a wonderful writer. Joy Williams is another. Richard Ford. Charles Baxter has published a couple of good collections. I like Ann Beattie's stories. Alice Munro, the Canadian writer, has to be one of the great story writers. Jayne Anne Phillips. Andre Dubus. Mark Helprin is first-rate as a story writer. Barry

Hannah. I like many of John Updike's stories and Bobbie Ann Mason's stories. Joyce Carol Oates. We're talking about living writers now; there are the great dead writers, too, like Chekhov and Tolstoy, Hemingway and Frank O'Connor and Flannery O'Connor. Isaac Babel. And there are so many others.

In addition to this interest in the short story itself, there's been a growing interest, even on the part of the literary elitists, in tales of survivors, whether they're found in the stories by writers such as yourself, Charles Bukowski, Wolff, Thomas McGuane, and so forth. Why do you think that is?

Well, in part, of course, it simply has to do with the fact that these people are bearing witness to what they have experienced; they're able to talk about it. There's a fascination with somebody who's been there and come back—lived to talk about it, as it were. You know: "I'll tell you what it's like. This is my song, this is my poem or short story. Make of it what you will." I think there's a rock-hard honesty about what many of these writers and musicians are offering, which is of more than passing interest to the public, so the public is paying more attention.

When you wrote about your father in "My Father's Life" for Esquire, *you mentioned the time you told him you wanted to be a writer, and his advice was "write the stuff you know about." Can you explain how your blue-collar background helped you with your writing, both in terms of subject and approach?*

For certain I had a *subject*, something to write about, people and events that I knew well. I never had to go around looking for material. Also, I think that blue-collar life put a premium on directness and being straightforward. In that life, there wasn't a whole lot of room for, or patience with, the Henry Jamesian kind of indirection.

I guess the reason I mention this is I've been to too many creative writing classes and workshops where you have people with backgrounds similar to your own, and they were writing about being college professors or students.

Yes, I know. They ought to be writing about what they know about. There's a lot that they know about, other than the college campus scene and the professor-student situation. God knows, that's a subject matter all right, and

some people can make art out of it. But a writer, young or old, can't fake it. He's got to write with authority, and he'd do well to write about something he's acquainted with and about the things that move him—not the things that *should* move him, but the things that *do* move him. There are significant moments in everyone's day that can make literature. You have to be alert to them and pay attention to them. That's what you ought to write about.

A poem in Ultramarine, *"What You Need For Painting," really struck me. It's a list poem taken from a letter by Renoir, but taken in the context of writing, it seems to be your advice on the ingredients needed to write a good poem or short story.*

Especially those last three lines.

Which read: "Indifference to everything except your canvas/The ability to work like a locomotive/An iron will."

In the beginning, when I was trying to write, I couldn't turn off the outside world to the extent that I can now. When you're writing fiction or poetry—or when you're painting or performing or composing music—it really comes down to this: indifference to everything except what you're doing. Your canvas, as it were. Which, translated to writing, means indifference to everything except that piece of paper in the typewriter. As for the ability to work like a locomotive and an iron will: by God, that's what it takes. Anyone who has written anything knows all of these things are necessary—requirements. A young writer could do worse than follow the advice given in those lines. I think all of those things are necessary. If the car needs to have an all-important service job but the Muse is with you, so to speak, you just have to get to your typewriter and stay there and turn the rest of the world off somehow, forget about everything else. That is my philosophy of writing, if I have one. You could put those words on my tombstone, too [laughs].

In discussing technique in your introduction to The Best American Short Stories 1986, *you listed the five elements you consider important in the short story: choices, conflict, drama, consequence and narrative. Do you have those things mapped out in your head before you start writing?*

No. I begin the story and it takes a natural course. Most often I'm not aware, when I start a poem or story, of where it's going until I get there. Not while I'm writing it.

> *Had I been able to do something else . . . maybe I would have done something else . . . The flame went out . . . but, yes, I did survive.*

The drama enters the story, and the consequences and choices present themselves. I guess I tried to separate them in the essay, but they're all connected.

Often when reading one of your short stories, I get the impression that something very important has happened just before the story begins—or will happen after the story ends. Your stories, like Hemingway's, really deal with the tip of the iceberg. When it works, it's wonderful, but a lot of beginning writers have problems in this area: they assume their readers know what's going on—occurrences that are never mentioned in their stories. What's the cutting edge to you? How do you teach that to your students?

Well, you can't keep necessary information from the reader. You can assume that the reader can put a face on some of these characters—you don't *have* to describe the color of their eyes, and so forth. Insofar as the stories are concerned, you have to presuppose some kind of knowledge on the part of the readers, that they're going to fill in some of the gaps. But you can't leave them drifting around without enough information to make them care about these people; you can't obfuscate what's going on. To this extent, I had problems with some of the post-modernist writers of the '60s. You'd sometimes read the work and you never knew what the problem was—just that there *was* some kind of problem or difficulty. Everybody was out of sorts in the story, but the fiction was divorced from reality in every way, shape and form. I'm much more interested in stories and poems that have some bearing on how we live and how we conduct ourselves and how we work out the consequences of our actions. Most of my stories start near the end of the arc of the dramatic conflict. I don't give a lot of detail about what went on before; I just start it fairly near the end of the swing of the action.

Your stories begin at crisis point.

Yes. But there *is* a fine line—the cutting edge, as you put it—where you have to give the reader enough, but you don't want to give him too much. I don't want to bore the reader, or bore myself.

Kurt Vonnegut wrote that short story writers should just write their stories and then toss out the first few pages when they were done.

There's something to that. D.H. Lawrence made a remark to the effect that you finish your story and when it's all finished, you go back and shake the branches of the tree, prune it again.

Some of your early stories have really been overhauled between the time they were originally published in little magazines and their eventual publication in your later collections. Sometimes the endings and even the titles were changed. In explaining these revisions in

your "Afterword," to Fires, *you wrote that "maybe I revise because it gradually takes me into the heart of what the story is about. I keep trying to see if I can find that out. It's a process more than a fixed position." Could you explain that a bit further?*

There was a time when I revised everything, and they were often quite extensive revisions. I don't know, maybe I didn't know what was around the corner, if *anything* was around the corner, so I was just more interested in messing around with the work I had on hand. At that time, I didn't feel that the stories were in any kind of fixed place, and I wanted to get them there—wherever that was. Now I don't feel this need to do all the revising that I once did. Maybe I'm feeling more secure with the stories I'm writing, or more satisfied, or more confident. Something has happened, at any rate. Now I tend to write the stories and for the most part lose interest in them after they're written. In some way, after they're published, they don't seem to belong to me any longer. I don't mean to make out more out of it than there is, but I guess I feel now like there's everything to do and little enough time to do it in, so I tend not to be so keen on revising the stories. Now I do all the revisions when I'm writing the story.

When you're revising, what are you looking for? What do you tend to change?

I want to make the stories interesting on every level, and that involves creating believable characters and situations, along with working on the language of the story until it is perfectly clear, but still a language capable of carrying complex ideas and sophisticated nuances.

A number of your stories have been written in the first person from a woman's point of view. Do you believe that the stories' impact—their "rightness"—is strengthened by the woman's point of view? Was it difficult to write a story this way?

The first time I ever attempted to write a story from the point of view of a woman, I was nervous about it. It was a real challenge to me. When I brought it off, it was like a rush. I was excited. I like to be able to write with authority in either gender. Now when ideas for stories come to me, they seem to present themselves to me with the point of view as nearly an inevitable thing. But, again, I think the choices are being made for me because of the nature of the material, and because of the way I'm approaching it. I just gear up and do it, and I like it.

Point of view is so important to a story. I've heard of people who have changed from first to third person in a story after it's been written.

Well, my friend Richard Ford changed the point of view of one of his novels. He worked on it for two years, and he felt it wasn't right, so he spent another year changing the entire point of view. That's dedication. And real seriousness in what you're doing. You want it right and you don't have that many chances at it. I don't know how many books a person's going to take to the grave with him, but you want to have it right, or else what's the point?

When you're writing steadily, what's your typical work day like?
I get up early, somewhere between 6 and 6:30. I'm always at my desk by 8. If it's a good day, I'll just stay at my desk until at least 11 or 12, when I'll break. On a good day, I can stay at my desk and do something all day, because I like to work; I like writing. When I'm working, I put the phone on the answering machine and unplug the phone upstairs, so if it rings downstairs, I can't hear it ring. I can check in the evening to see if there are any messages. I don't watch much TV—I watch the news usually—and I go to bed fairly early. It's a pretty quiet life, generally.

Do you prefer to write a story from beginning to end in one sitting?
Yes, I'm afraid of interruption and losing the story, whatever it was that made me want to write the story in the first place. I don't think I've ever spent longer than two days writing the first draft of a story. Usually only one day. I spend lots of time after that typing it up and reworking it, but I think it's good to try to get that story down before you lose sight of it. It might not look so good tomorrow. So on the first draft, you have to put your trust in whatever, just hope and assume that something's going to come of it, just barrel on through and try to get the first draft quickly before you lose it. Then you can be slow and thoughtful with it.

I remember reading somewhere that, in the early days, you used to steal away and write in your car.
That's true. I wouldn't recommend it as a place to work [laughs] but it was necessary for me at that time of my life. I don't know if I got anything lasting out of it, but at least I was working on *something*. I was trying to do something and I had no place to go. I was young and there was just no room in the house. I didn't want to have to go out in the car—it wasn't that I wanted to go for a quiet drive in the country and park next to the river. No, I'd just go out and sit in the car in the parking lot, just to be away from my kids and the turmoil and confusion in the house.

Do you warn your students about how tough the writing life is?
Oh, I talk about it a little sometimes, but you can't tell them how hard it is. Not really. You can't truthfully tell a young poet or fiction writer they have to have not only the utmost seriousness in regard to their writing but that they're going to have to devote the rest of their lives to it if they intend to be any good at it. But you can't tell them

what they're going to have to go through. You can sort of tell them, but they'll have to live through it themselves; they'll have to survive that themselves. You don't have to say much to the best of them. If they're smart, they have an idea of what it's like, and they know it won't come easy to them; if they're not smart and they're not hard on themselves, then they won't be writing very long after they graduate.

I've always been curious about the relationship between the hunger to publish and the hunger to create. What do you think that relationship is? Is the hunger to publish a good motivating factor?
I think it is. Even when I was teaching, I always felt it was too much of a hothouse and rarefied atmosphere if there was never any talk about the young writers submitting work to magazines. And on occasion I'd take in some bound galleys, or show them page proofs I was working on, so they could actually see this stuff. They don't know the first thing about the process a book goes through from inception to manuscript, from letter of acceptance to copyedited manuscript and galley proofs. So I'd show them these things and talk about possible markets for their stories. I don't think it diminishes the work to talk about publishing that work. Quite the contrary: there's literary creation and there's literary business. Art and commerce do sometimes go hand in hand. When I first got something accepted, it gave my life a validation that it didn't otherwise have. It was very important to me. I think I got paid a dollar for the first poem I ever published, but that didn't dampen my enthusiasm. No, I was thrilled with that one-dollar check.

There are, however, a lot of serious writers out there who have to try to balance art with budget: you want to write good, strong work, but you also have to feed your family. Sometimes you feel like you're playing Beat the Clock: *if you don't get something out, you don't pay the rent next month. Did you find that happening to you?*
My situation was similar *and* different. I knew I was never going to get rich writing poems, not when I was getting paid $1 or $5 or else being paid in contributor's copies. And, for years, I was writing short stories, of course, and if I got paid at all, it was $25 or $50. The first story in *Esquire* brought me $600; but then I didn't publish in *Esquire* for a very long while after I started writing, so I knew I wasn't going to get rich writing stories, either. So, in truth, I never faced the same dilemma. The problems were similar, in that the kids were there, eating me alive, and I had to make all those monthly payments— some of which we didn't make—but the fact that I was writing stories and poems didn't make any great financial difference to us. Had I been able to write them any faster and still take the time that was necessary for them, I would have done so, but I seemed to be teaching or work-

ing or raising a family and so forth, so I simply did the best I could, on what I could.

When you were thinking about becoming a writer, did you hope just to publish your work in the types of magazines you had around your home, publications like True *and* Argosy? *And what made you decide to devote your work to the more serious markets?*

Until I met John Gardner, I had no concept of serious literature. I simply knew I wanted to be a writer and, of course, nobody in my family did any reading, so there was no guidance of any sort whatsoever. I just had to continually follow my nose, whether it led to a historical novel or an article in *True*. Everything was more or less of equal merit, or value, until I met Gardner. This is one of the most important things about our meeting: he'd say something like "I'm not only here to teach you how to write, but I'm also here to tell you who to read." That was immensely important to me. I began to read Joseph Conrad and Isak Dinesen, along with so many other important writers. For the first time in my life, I had some direction. I was introduced to the little magazines by Gardner, and I became interested in the stories and poems they were publishing, so that's what I set out to do: to write well and publish what I wrote. I don't want to seem snobbish about the other magazines—it wasn't that I turned up my nose at things like *Argosy* and *True* and so forth—I simply didn't have enough time in my day to read everything and write everything.

One of your big breaks was meeting Gordon Lish, your longtime friend and editor. How did that happen?

Our relationship goes back to the mid-1960s. He was working for a textbook publishing firm across the street from the textbook firm where I was working in Palo Alto. That's how we became acquainted. Then he went off to become the fiction editor for *Esquire*. The next I heard from him, he was writing a letter on someone else's stationery. It was from *Esquire*, and he'd crossed off the old editor's name. In the note, he said, "I've taken over the fiction editor's desk from the above-named good gentleman. Send me whatever you have." I was still working at the publishing company, and I proceeded to dispatch all the stories I had in the house—four or five stories—and by God, they all came back [laughs] with a message saying "Try me again, these are not right." I didn't know

> *There's literary creation and literary business. When I first got something accepted, it gave my life a validation it didn't otherwise have.*

what to make of this. If my close friend becomes the fiction editor at *Esquire* and I still can't get a story in, what chance do I have? You're in real trouble then [laughs]. But I pulled up my socks, sat down and began writing more stories, and he finally took one. It was a story called "Neighbors," and that was one of the turning points in my life. And then he took another one, and so forth. Then he left *Esquire* and became an editor at Knopf. He gave me a contract there for a book of stories. So we go back a long way.

He was always a great advocate of my stories, at all times championing my work, even during the period when I was not writing, when I was out in California, devoting myself to drinking. Gordon read my work on radio and at writers conferences and so forth. He was like Gardner in the sense that he offered encouragement. He was also like Gardner to the extent that he would say that if you could say something in 20 words instead of 50 words, say it in 20 words. He was very important to me at a time when I needed to hear what he had to offer. He's still championing the work of young writers.

There seems to be a trend in the publishing business for greater writer-editor relationships.

I was talking about this with Tess the other night, as a matter of fact. We were talking about Robert Gottlieb and his move from Knopf to the editorship of *The New Yorker*. As we talked, I realized that this is probably the first age in literary history where editors have become public personalities, in some cases, even greater personalities, or figures, than many of the writers they are involved with. Gottlieb goes to *The New Yorker* and it's a front-page piece in *The New York Times* and news in papers and magazines all across the country. And the distinguished editor, Gary Fisketjon: they've written an article about him in *Esquire*, and he's been profiled in other magazines. I know any number of writers who will go with their editors when they move from one house to another. Writers have established close relationships with their editors, and they will go wherever their editors go. The first editor I ever heard of was Maxwell Perkins, and he had that relationship with Thomas Wolfe, Hemingway and so many other writers. Editors play a larger role in a writer's life these days, and I don't know whether this is a good or bad thing. I don't know what conclusions to draw from it, but it's a fact that they have become public personalities in their own right, and this is quite remarkable.

Your survival as a writer has been a source of inspiration to a lot of struggling writers. Somehow, you've been able not only to work your way past a number of imposing barriers, but also to translate your experiences into universal stories. How do you feel about all this today?

I just feel like an instrument. It *has* been a question of survival, and had I been able to do something else, I don't know, maybe I would have done something else. But I *had* to write. You know, the flame went out: I think it was flat-out extinguished there toward the end of my drinking days. But, yes, I did survive. In fact, after I got sober and had quit drinking entirely, there was a period of time, for a year or so, when I didn't write anything, and it wasn't even important for me to write anything. It was so important for me to have my health back and not be brain dead any longer that whether I wrote or not really didn't matter any longer. I just felt like I had a second chance at my life again. And then, when things were right, when I was well again, I taught for a year in El Paso, and suddenly, I began to write again. And that was just a great gift, and everything that has happened since then has been a great gift. Every day is a bonus. Every day now is pure cream.

BY EDWARD P. STAFFORD

ERNEST HEMINGWAY

*The hardest trade in the world is the writing of
straight, honest prose about human beings.*

Havana was still free that summer—and hot, as it will always be. They still served you frozen daiquiris during the wait for customs at the airport. Castro was a remote shadow in the eastern mountains, and Ernest Hemingway was still alive and working.

Papa lived and worked at his Finca Vigia in the suburb of San Francisco de Paulo. It was necessary to stop at the gate just off the main road and get an old man who lived nearby to open it. Then there was a straight road through the woods for perhaps a quarter-mile, a curve to the left—and the Finca. It had broad steps, columns, and a feeling of spaciousness, informality and comfort. It was of not recently painted white stucco, un-airconditioned and a little over-grown. From the back there was a view of the rooftops of Havana with the sea beyond; there was a rectangular pool where each day Mary Hemingway swam her mile, in the nude for freedom of movement, and fired the gardener if he watched. A few yards from the house, but matching it in materials and appearance, was the squarish, three-story tower in the top of which Hemingway did his writing. There were also cats—about 15, mostly kittens, which lived in the tower's first floor—the "cat house."

Inside, the Finca was laid out like a short-legged H—a long living room capped by smaller ones at its ends. One of the smaller rooms was a den-office-library, another a dining room, another a library. The first room was the most interesting, with an incredibly piled and cluttered desk, heads of buffalo and kudu high on the walls, two zebra-covered scrapbooks of Hemingway obituaries published prematurely at the time of his double plane crash in Africa more than three-and-a-half years ago, and books. Everywhere, in all rooms, there were books. A writer, Papa believed, had to read: for pleasure, for knowledge, for experience, but most importantly, to see what the competition is.

"There is no use," he explained, "writing anything that has been written before unless you can beat it. What a writer has to do is write what hasn't been written before or beat dead men at what they have done. Only dead men are useful as standards, as competitors, because only their work has been tested by time and has proven value. It is like a miler running against the clock rather than simply against whoever is in the race with him. Unless he runs against time, he will never know what he is capable of attaining."

Papa picked his dead milers with discrimination. On his shelves were books by Tolstoy, Dostoevski, Stendhal, de Maupassant, Mann, Joyce, W.H. Hudson, George Moore, Stephen Crane, Turgenev, Flaubert and several dozen others, similarly disparate as to era and nationality, having in common only their greatness.

Perhaps I was prejudiced in advance by my knowledge of his lifetime of artistic discipline and integrity—whatever his personal problems and foibles—and of his single-minded, undeviating search for his own conception of literary perfection, but, for whatever reason, his own greatness seemed immediately apparent.

White-bearded, wearing a long, white, Cuban shirt, he came down the front steps with "Miss Mary" to greet

---

The novelty of this 1964 piece is not its classic Hemingway advice—write true and work hard—but in the almost reverent description of Edward Stafford's unforgettable afternoon: meeting not just a mere idol—which many people do—but an idol who also happens to be one of the best writers in history.

The two met for a single afternoon in 1958. "I did not see Papa again," Stafford remembers. "Yet, whatever I write will be partly his." There may be too much worship of the Hemingway myth in that—and in this story—for some people.

But they've probably never met their idols.

us. I had recently achieved brief attention as a successful contestant on a television quiz show by answering (without assistance) a series of questions on American literature, a number of which had concerned Ernest Hemingway; and I had unashamedly made use of my moment of glory to arrange this meeting with him. During the introductions, Hemingway was warm and cordial, his handshake strong and good, but he wasted no words, made no small talk.

I had been secretly worried that Ernest Hemingway, the man, would be given to the sort of brusque, Anglo-Saxon dialogue that is found in his books. After a decade and a half at sea and ashore in the Navy, I could speak and understand that language as well as any, but I have never been a man for four-letter words in mixed company, and I knew that my liberal but convent-bred wife would be in agony—and I with her. My worrying could not have been more groundless. Whatever he may have been in other times and at other places (and I doubt if he were very different), the Hemingway who talked with us in the long living room of the Finca Vigia was candid and direct, but a kind and hospitable gentleman to whom it would have been inconceivable to offend a guest.

Naturally I was interested in talking about Hemingway and his work. He was not. He was interested in my experience on the quiz show and the sort of questions that were asked—which brought us onto common ground with a discussion of the Hemingway questions. As I talked, his level brown eyes never left my face. He listened completely, fully concerned, with an absolute lack of self-consciousness, without thinking of what he was going to say next; and when I was through, he gave me back, with utter candor, whatever response had been elicited in the clear, cool mind behind those eyes.

Papa enjoyed hearing the questions that had been asked about his work, and answering them himself, slowly, thoughtfully; thinking back and relating events to each other.

What two plays had he written and what were their dates of publication?

The Fifth Column was easy because he remembered writing it during the late fall of '36 and early winter of '37 in the Hotel Florida in Madrid, which was being hit repeatedly by Franco's artillery. It took longer to remember when the little three-page *Today Is Friday* was published but he thought back, logically, and got it.

Work every day. No matter what has happened the day or night before, get up and bite on the nail.

We had drinks, which Miss Mary mixed. Papa was on the wagon, except for light wine, since the African crashes.

What book had he published in October of 1926 and what was its English title?

Papa remembered there had been two books that year; *Torrents of Spring* had come out, appropriately, in the spring and that left *The Sun Also Rises* for October. In England, it was called *Fiesta*.

We discussed the sources of the titles of *The Sun Also Rises*, *A Farewell to Arms*, *For Whom the Bell Tolls*, and *Across the River and Into the Trees*, then the nationalities of the heroines (English, Scotch, Spanish and Italian), which had been other questions. Gradually, we turned to the subject I most wanted to develop, Hemingway's thoughts on the profession in which he had made himself a giant, to which he had given his life and all his energy and talent: writing.

My wife needled him. "Is it true," she asked, "that you take a pitcher of martinis up into the tower every morning when you go up to write?"

"Jeezus Christ!" Papa was incredulous. "Have you ever heard of anyone who drank while he worked? You're thinking of Faulkner. He does sometimes, and I can tell right in the middle of a page when he had his first one. Besides," he added, "who in hell would mix more than one martini at a time, anyway?"

Having been guilty of that heresy any number of times, but recognizing his mastery in that field also, I let the question remain rhetorical.

"What about hours?" I asked. "How long can you actually be productive on a daily basis? How do you know when to stop?"

"That's something you have to learn about yourself. The important thing is to work every day. I work from about seven until about noon. Then I go fishing or swimming, whatever I want. The best way is always to stop when you are going good. If you do that you'll never be stuck. And don't think or worry about it until you start to write again the next day. That way your subconscious will be working on it all the time, but if you worry about it, your brain will get tired before you start again. But work every day. No matter what has happened the day or night before, get up and bite on the nail."

This was the kind of thing I had come to Havana to hear.

I became more specific. "I was never in the *Enterprise*," (a World War II aircraft carrier I was basing a book on) I confessed. "I'm not sure I've ever even seen her except maybe once, at sea, several miles away. Is that going to hurt the book?"

"Have you ever been on other carriers?"

"Yes."

"Okay. Then I'm glad you weren't aboard the *Enterprise*. If you've been in a street fight on one block, one city, you can write about a street fight in another block or city. And if you had been aboard, you would have been in a particular department or unit and it would be hard not to write from the viewpoint of that unit, or overemphasize it or the people in it.

"But," he went on, "it's getting kind of late to write about World War II. Timing is important. At first it is too fresh and you are too close to it, then there is a good time to write, and after that it begins to get too far away."

I thought about that and said I felt I could still write about that war. I remembered it well, I had kept a careful journal to help the memory, and I had been in almost all the places and several of the actions in which the carrier had been.

That was important, Papa said, because one of the things you had to have to write was an exact, detailed and specific knowledge of what you were writing about. The other "absolute necessities," he said, were a "a real seriousness in regard to writing, and talent."

"What about the very first draft?" I asked him. "How do you do it? Pencil, pen, typewriter, dictation? How?"

"When you write," he said, "your object is to convey every sensation, sight, feeling, emotion, to the reader. So you have to work over what you write. If you use a pencil, you get three different views of it to see if you are getting it across the way you want to. First, when you read it over, then when it is typed, and again in proof. And it keeps it fluid longer so that you can improve it easier."

"How do you ever learn to convey every sensation, sight and feeling to the reader? Just keep working at it for 40-odd years the way you have? Are there any tricks?"

"No. The hardest trade in the world is the writing of straight, honest prose about human beings. But there are ways you can train yourself."

"How?"

"When you walk into a room and you get a certain feeling or emotion, remember back until you see exactly what it was that gave you the emotion. Remember what the noises and smells were and what was said. Then write it down, making it clear so the reader will see it too, and have the same feeling you had. And watch people, observe, try to put yourself in somebody else's head. If two men argue, don't just think who is right and who is wrong. Think what both their sides are. As a man, you know who is right and who is wrong; you have to judge. As a writer, you should not judge, you should understand."

I felt as though I was monopolizing the conversation and I wasn't even sure Papa was enjoying it. But there was so much I wanted to know.

"Is it a good thing to talk over your work with other people, other writers? Is that a way to learn? It has often seemed to me that most of the great talents of the century were living in Paris in the twenties when you were, and you all knew each other. You must have talked about writing—and it must have helped."

"Good conversation with good people is always stimulating, especially *after* work. You can talk about writing generally, about words, and when you are learning and trust or respect another writer, he can help with the blue pencil and in other ways—but never talk about a story you are working on. If you tell it, you never write it. You spoil the freshness, you mouth it up and get rid of it in the telling instead of the writing. Writers should work alone, then talk."

In the course of the talking, we had lunch. I remember a delicious cold soup made with lots of vegetables and a clear water, which Miss Mary explained was an Andalusian peasant dish. It was perfect for the hot climate.

The talk turned to other writers. My wife defended Graham Greene, whom Papa good-naturedly thought was "a jerk" because he "traded on his religion" and was a convert. But, as if to prove his lack of bitterness, he went to the library and came back with a copy of Greene's latest book and the only one my wife had not read, and inscribed it for her: "From her friend, Ernie (Graham) Greenaway." Kathleen Winsor he did not consider a professional writer. Alan Moorehead, in Papa's opinion, was great. He insisted that I read *Gallipoli*, which I said I would do, but that was not enough.

"Don't just say that," he said, holding me with his eyes across the table. "Really get and read it."

In his humility, he was not aware that an apprentice writer like myself needed no such urging when he recommended a book. It was already branded onto my memory and, of course, I would read it.

During lunch, and when the strangeness had worn off a little, Miss Mary, in her forthright way, chastised me gently for having addressed Papa as *Ernest* in the letter I had written him before our visit. I tried lamely, if truthfully, to explain that I had considered any number of salutations before using that one, but that no other seemed right; and that probably, the wrong one seemed right because of my long familiarity with everything he had written and which had been written about him. I wasn't making very much sense when Papa cut in.

"Oh hell. It was one writer to another."

When the time came to leave, it was still hot and humid, with no breeze. The sweat glistened on all our faces and emphasized the old bullet groove on the left side of Papa's forehead. Miss Mary walked us out to the car and we were both in when my wife missed her purse. I went back for it, and was turning to leave again when I saw Hemingway, solid, scarred, grizzled and completely naked at the other end of the living room. It was hot and his guests had left. We grinned at each other and I ducked out, glad it was I and not my wife who had returned.

I never saw Papa again.

BY LOIS ROSENTHAL

MARSHA NORMAN

*I was from a working class family—my father sold insurance.
I thought people like me don't become playwrights.*

I never imagined that I could make a living as a writer when I was growing up in Louisville," says Pulitzer Prize-winning playwright Marsha Norman. "Though I won essay contests in high school and I had an incredible English teacher who was always after me to use my writing skills, I didn't know any writers, and I certainly had no local playwrights as role models. Kentucky's writing tradition was mainly a mountain one, I thought. And I certainly wasn't part of that.

"I was from a working-class family—my father sold insurance. I figured playwrights mostly came from wealthy East Coast families who had big libraries in their homes and whose children went to prestigious colleges. I thought people like me don't become playwrights. I was 29 years old before I finally believed I could have a life as a writer."

It was during the time she spent "not being a writer" that Norman picked up the experiences that have fueled her work. After graduating from Agnes Scott College with a major in philosophy in 1969, she worked with emotionally disturbed children in a Kentucky state mental hospital, taught gifted children, worked for the Kentucky State Arts Commission, and wrote a newspaper column for children for the *Louisville Times* (where she also acted as book editor).

"Since my philosophy degree didn't qualify me for anything, for ten years I worked at all sorts of jobs—anything anyone would hire me to do," says Norman. "During that time I didn't view the world as a writer, and I do think writers look at life with a different eye, as if they are writing it all down. I spent ten years simply living, and I think now that all of my writing comes from that period."

But Norman was also becoming frustrated with her life in the world. Nothing seemed hard enough. She was changing jobs too often. She was finally ready to face the desire to be a writer she had harbored for so long. But finding out whether she had the talent to fulfill her dream frightened her. Could she face the consequences if she wasn't good enough? If she tried writing and found she just couldn't make it, was she prepared to spend the rest of her life in some other way? She felt she had to give herself completely to writing or forget it altogether.

"To me, concentration is the key to writing," says Norman. "Focus is so important that you have to be able to work for 48 hours straight if that's necessary, have nothing standing in your way. There should be no excuses like, 'Well, my writing would be better if I didn't have to work full time.' People who hedge their bets, who write in their spare time, may never know the answer to the question, 'Could I be a writer with a capital *W*?' "

To finance her try at serious writing, Norman spent a year working three jobs: teaching during the day, writing for the newspaper and working on scripts for an educational television series. Her goal was to save enough money to take the next year off.

That was in 1977, when she was 29. By late winter of that year, she began writing her first play, *Getting Out*, which she finished by the end of the summer. It was produced by the Actors Theatre of Louisville in the Second Humana Festival of New American Plays, then was produced off-Broadway at the Phoenix Theatre in 1978, and at the Theatre de Lys in 1979. *Getting Out* was heralded

---

Ignoring for a moment the sheer power of her survival story, what sets this 1988 profile apart is the lyrical beauty of Marsha Norman's voice: How, for instance, can her "machinery" and "map" descriptions of playwriting sound more artistic than technical? The answer lies in the same gift that created such plays as 'night, Mother and Getting Out.

But don't let her words overshadow her survival tale. Because stories like this are rare. Especially when told by Marsha Norman.

by critics and established Norman's reputation as a playwright of importance.

Where did such a strong first play come from? "When I was working at Central State Hospital, there was an 11- or 12-year-old girl who was extremely violent. I followed her career and knew that she wound up in a federal prison. I wondered what would happen to someone who was locked up and couldn't get out. I wanted to write about this violent kid and the consequences of her imprisonment."

Norman researched what life in prison does to inmates. She talked with prison authorities across the country and found that people in long-term solitary confinement come out of prison withdrawn, cold, passive and distant. This describes Arlene, the central character of *Getting Out*.

"Still, I figured it would be a dull play if I had my main character so passive, and withdrawn, and fearful, and sad. The audience would never guess she had been a violent kid, so I created Arlie—Arlene as she was as an unpredictable and incorrigible teenager—and put them both on stage together. Arlie is Arlene's memory of herself; Arlie changes during the play to become the adult Arlene. This was the technique I used to tell their story."

Norman says she chooses to write about people up against extreme obstacles and how they respond with courage to the crises that confront them. If Arlene hadn't just been released from prison, Norman wouldn't have been interested in her. Her fascination with a character results from the event that jolts the character's life and how she handles the change. This is why Norman's plays always have one strong central character.

"In *Getting Out*, Arlene performs an act of great courage when she tears up a matchbook and goes upstairs to play cards," says Norman. (Arlene destroys the phone number of a man who could seduce her back to a lifestyle that would once again put her in prison.) "Another example—and the world may not agree with me— is that I think Jessie performs an act of great courage when she commits suicide in *'night, Mother*. Though Mama is on stage with Jessie during the entire play, there is no question that Jessie is the most important character. Mama's whole function is to stop Jessie from killing herself."

The theatre is a communal event, like church. The playwright constructs a mass to be performed for a lot of people. She writes a prayer, which is just the longings of one heart.

Norman suggests that as you learn about your characters, you should master their language, become versed in how they sound, to produce true-to-life dialogue. For instance, when Arlene says in *Getting Out*, "I ain't eatin' no more scrambled eggs," it's a line *only* Arlene could say. If her mother wanted to communicate the same information, she'd say it differently. The language characters speak should be theirs, not the playwright's, because *how* characters talk is an important part of *who* they are.

Norman likens the speech of her characters to the music made by an orchestra. The combination of instruments produces the sound of the whole composition—just like characters' voices in a play.

Once Norman has the central character and the situation she wants to write about fixed in her mind, she writes a two-sentence version of her play. She believes this is crucial because if you aren't able to produce a synopsis, your structure isn't solid. You must create a map so you know exactly where you are going. "My map in *'night, Mother* was: A woman and her mother live together for many years. On page 8, the daughter says, 'I'm going to kill myself, Mama,' and the play is the next 90 minutes until she does. My new play, *Sarah and Abraham* [a workshop version was performed in 1988 at ATL's Humana Festival], is the story of a small theater company improvising their way toward the classic, tragic drama of Sarah and Abraham. The first scene takes place on the first day of rehearsal, and the last scene is the final, full-performance version of Sarah's death.

"Once you have the beginning and the end of the play fixed, you can construct the most direct route between the two. Say you decide you want to drive from Louisville to Omaha—you have to consult a map to figure out how to get there. If you'd like to go by way of Mammoth Cave, that's fine, but is the detour worth the extra time? You may decide to take a more direct route. Because a play is very much like a piece of machinery, you can have a mechanical approach to it and it doesn't hurt a bit. Writing plays is an orderly process. It helps if you have a logical mind."

During this time of mechanical constructing, Norman chooses the two hours of her focal character's life during which the play will be set. In *'night, Mother*, Norman believes that the boldest moment, the time when the character's whole life is most visible, is the period right before Jessie kills herself. If she chose an earlier two-hour period, the audience would miss the developing conflict. If she set the play at Jessie's funeral, she could use the flashback method to tell Jessie's story—but would it have the same impact?

The time period of the play also helps determine which characters will appear. In *'night, Mother*, only Mama appears on stage with Jessie in the hours before her suicide. If the play had been set in Jessie's childhood, Jessie's father, brother, and playmates would have parts.

One way Norman believes writers can ease the complex task of constructing a play is to set it in an environment in which the author feels familiar. She will know how characters behave in this situation, and how they speak, so the writing will be more natural and a great deal easier.

As an example, *Sarah and Abraham* is about a little acting company, and the scenes are set in a rehearsal hall. The result: a facile peacefulness in the writing because you know Norman is at home here.

Though she does not know what being incarcerated is like, Norman says she is familiar with the feeling of entrapment Arlene experiences in *Getting Out*. She knows about living in grimy apartments, feeling locked up with people during long drives in cars. These are powerful, emotional connections to the idea of prison. "It's not enough to just research a play's environment. You must write about what is close to you. That's why I advise people to pick something from their past—an event that happened at least ten years ago. That's enough time for all the insignificant experiences to have fallen away and for you to have perspective about what really occurred.

"Think about situations in which you were terribly frightened, were badly hurt. Ten years is enough time to be able to confess, 'I was hurt; I was scared.' And chances are, something you remember being frightened or hurt by ten years ago is extremely important to you. You are remembering it vividly because your mind is still working on it in some way."

Norman thinks playwrights are obligated to expose their private worlds; if you have knowledge no one else has, that's what the subject of your play should be. She cites Harvey Fierstein's *Torch Song Trilogy* as an example, because it was the first piece of its kind to tell what life is like in the backroom bars frequented by the gay community. *'night, Mother*, which won a Pulitzer Prize for Drama in 1983, exposes a mother-daughter relationship in the same private, behind-closed-doors way.

"I have a little piece of paper at home that says, 'Have I written something that will humiliate me?'" says Norman. "This is a note I wrote to myself after I finished *'night, Mother*. I thought it was a very strong possibility since the play is so risky. I had no idea who would want to read it, or direct it, or even see it.

"But this is exactly the kind of abandon you must write with. You must not care if anyone wants to see your play. You must write it for yourself. That way, there's a force, a drive behind your writing that gets into the script. The need to know is the driving force behind *'night, Mother*. Why does Jessie want to do this? The audience keeps asking that question all through the play."

Norman says that something quite serious must be at stake in a play or people will be angered by being imprisoned in a theater for two hours. They want to see the outcome of important situations that matter very much to them, so that at the end, they will feel good about being in the audience. No one wants to watch inconsequential events; audiences want to see heavyweight bouts.

"But your play can be about anything," says Norman. "You can imagine the most dull circumstance in the world. If you tell us clearly, and accurately, and passionately, what makes it work, audiences will pay attention all night."

Passion is the key. Norman cautions against writing about something just because you think other people will be interested in it. You must choose subjects *you* truly care about. Take time to dig deep, find out what really matters to you.

She remembers a college professor expert in pre-Socratic philosophers, a subject most students found boring. Yet this professor had such a passion for these philosophers that Norman remembers her lectures about the alteration of earth, air, fire and water—the elements the philosophers said composed the earth—with excitement. Norman says her professor's ability to transfer passion is the definition of real art, and transferring passion is exactly what great pieces of theater should do.

To make sure your finished play sounds true to you, Norman advises asking someone to read it aloud while you listen. Even better, if you have access, ask a community theater group to read your play. Norman likens writing a play to designing a dress. You want to see if the person who is going to wear it can sit in it easily, can walk freely. When your play is read to you, you can see what needs fixing. You can test the veracity of the dialogue against your internal knowledge of the world you are writing about. Note whether you have made your intentions clear. And because every second counts in the theater, make sure your lines perform the function you've intended.

Also listen to the rhythm and pace of your lines. A play must work like—again—a piece of machinery: begin slowly, then feel comfortable while picking up speed. A play must move forward constantly. When you hear your play read, you can tell if you've stopped and pulled off the road for a while. Your aim should be that everyone in the theater arrives—at the same time—at a destination they all find agreeable. Then everyone hops out to get a look at the view.

As heartily as Norman encourages reading play drafts aloud, she discourages *talking about* them while you're still writing. "It's dangerous, because you are apt to take people's opinions so seriously, so personally. You can be diverted from your purpose if someone you care about says he doesn't like what you're doing. Plays should be the product of a single point of view, and if you can talk about a play, you shouldn't be writing it. Save writing for only those things you can't talk to anyone about."

What to do when you find yourself stymied at a silent typewriter? To ease herself into a scene when it doesn't seem to come, Norman writes about what she wants to accomplish rather than trying to write the scene itself. By scribbling out, for instance, that the milkman comes to the door and when he does, the person inside the house will respond in a certain manner, you can work in a piece of dialogue that you can base the scene on.

"I make notes to myself," says Norman. "I fool myself, in a good way, into dodging the pressure. I tell myself that I'm not trying to write a scene, I'm just making some notes for the day when I really do want to write it. One friend of mine just starts typing a scene he's already written until something new occurs to him. We all have to adopt techniques to prime the pump in some goal-oriented way when we hit a dry spell."

Another way Norman suggests to keep your pump primed is to read at least four hours a day. It's important to be well versed in classic and contemporary theater so you can pick up vocabulary and craft, so you can study the best writers at work.

It's particularly important to note the difference between a written play and the way it is performed on stage. If a play is being performed in your city, Norman suggests reading it, then going to a performance, then reading the play again, so you can see what is the playwright's real work. You may also find it valuable to take the written play to the theater and look at the pages while viewing the production.

Norman also believes that reading anything that interests you will help develop the pleasure of exploration that is crucial to a writer. Pay special attention to the subjects that hold your interest over a long period of time. Get good at selecting topics you'll still be fascinated with two years in the future, so that you'll still be intrigued when you're in the fifth draft of your play and its third regional theater production.

Asked what kind of living playwrights can expect to make after all the work, the agonizing, emotional investment, Norman answers carefully and thoughtfully. "I look at writing plays as a kind of hobby and I don't expect it to support me. In fact, I think you must find a way to be free—emotionally and financially—to write for the theater. You can't start depending on it for anything, or need it, because when you do, you'll begin to second-guess the audience. You'll cater to them, try to figure out what

they'll want to see, which will destroy your creativity. You must write out of absolute freedom.

"To support myself as a playwright, I write movies, which is what most successful playwrights do to earn a living. When you have gained national success in the theater, it's like being awarded a gold medal in the Olympics. If you're a skater, you can look forward to a job with the Ice Capades. It's the commercial version of the art.

"But I think the art of screenwriting is developing. It's not work good writers condescend to do anymore. And the movie industry is well aware that the better written a movie is, the better it works.

"Many playwrights who have not had national success do teach. Whatever you have to do to support yourself, you must buy the freedom to write plays. I buy back time for myself whenever I go to California to work on a screenplay. I do it in order to have time that I don't have to account for—to anyone—so I can write a play."

What if, after so much sacrifice, that play is bashed by critics? How can any playwright protect herself from such public hurt?

"You can't," says Norman, "unless you're the kind of person who loves to be knocked around. I don't believe any writer when she says she doesn't care about reviews. I don't look at my writing as something separate from myself. My soul, my spirit, my heart are out there. I'll only get to write ten or so plays in my lifetime, so when one of them is crushed, I'm just devastated.

"You can give yourself a place to go to recover from the hurt. You can try to keep in mind that the real verdict doesn't come in for 50 or 100 years. This thought is coming on me with age because nobody really knows whether I'm important, or Sam Shepard is important, or whether David Mamet is important—any of us. We won't have a clue for a long time. Arthur Miller says that many of the playwrights who were thought to be the queens and kings of the American theater when he was growing up are unknown now. You can take comfort in that.

"When you've been hurt and you think you'll never have the courage to write another play, you must wait until a subject comes along that interests you enough to make you forget that you might be hurt again. It's like having a baby or falling in love. You must wait until something or someone comes into your life and calls you back. Then you say: 'I really love this material. I really want to tell this story. This time it doesn't matter whether or not they hurt me.'

"When I wrote *Getting Out* in 1979, it was wildly acclaimed. But early success doesn't mean you're always going to be successful. I wrote *Third and Oak, Circus Valentine* [which was disastrous] and *The Holdup* [which has been occasionally performed] between *Getting Out* and *'night, Mother*. [Norman has written *Traveler in the Dark* and *Sarah and Abraham* since *'night, Mother*.] People were ready to say I was finished, that I had written one wonderful play—*Getting Out*. I had some learning to do during those years. It's ridiculous to think I could go directly from *Getting Out* to *'night, Mother*.

"You can't ever believe your best work is behind you. You can't ever believe you've already written the play you're going to be known for, which is what people were telling me between *Getting Out* and *'night, Mother*. You begin to feel set up, like the critics are going to watch to see how bad your next play will be. But then, with all of these experiences, I'm living the only life I know how to live.

"Theater is so critical because it has always been able to release people from their isolation. They can say, 'We all feel that way' or 'We're all in trouble about that.' A novel may sweep you up in its story, but it is a very private experience. The theater is a communal event, like church. The playwright constructs a mass to be performed for a lot of people. She writes a prayer, which is just the longings of one heart."

BY JOHN KERN

RED SMITH

Any sportswriter who thinks the world is no bigger than the outfield fence is not only a bad citizen, but also a lousy sportswriter.

*A*nd he noticed how the wind was blowing, looked at the portrait, poured another glass of Valpolicela and then started to read the Paris edition of the New York Herald Tribune.

I ought to take the pills, he thought. But the hell with the pills.

Then he took them just the same and went on reading the New York Herald. He was reading Red Smith, and he liked him very much.

—Ernest Hemingway,
Across the River and Into the Trees

If sports reflect our culture and values, Red Smith must be recognized as having been one of the leading arbiters of our national character.

Apart from demonstrating one craftsman's affection for another, the Hemingway passage is an example of the impact Smith has had on journalism. In the 30 years since the publication of that novel, Smith emerged as the dean of American sportswriters. Syndicated in more than 500 newspapers around the world, his column was as important a part of the sports page as the box scores. His wit and perception enlivened and ennobled such annual rituals as the World Series and Kentucky Derby, and no sports event was an event without him.

Curiously, Smith claimed that he had no particular affinity for sportswriting. His only ambition, he insisted, was to be a newspaper reporter. He was born Walter Wellesley Smith and raised in Green Bay, Wisconsin. After graduating from Notre Dame with a degree in journalism, he landed a job as a cub reporter at the *Milwaukee Sentinel*. It wasn't until he joined the *St. Louis Star* in the late twenties that he moved to the sports department.

Early in his career, Smith was surrounded by characters who seemed lifted from the pages of a Damon Runyon story. The race tracks, ball parks and boxing arenas where he plied his trade contained a lively and often no-

torious cross-section of prohibition America. Aside from the usual assortment of jockeys, ballplayers and fight managers, his beat was peopled with bookies, bootleggers and gangsters, many of whom had more than just a rooting interest in the sports scene.

As a reporter for the *Star* and later the *Philadelphia Record*, Smith spent the next two decades in the shadow of legends. He was in the press box when Seabiscuit matched up against War Admiral, when Joe Louis slugged his way to the heavyweight championship, and when Joe DiMaggio was compiling his record 56-game hitting streak.

In the mid-1940s, Smith began a 20-year stint at the *New York World Herald Tribune*. At the behest of his editor, Stanley Woodward, he left the daily beat and began writing his own column. His tenure at the paper encompassed the most controversial period in American sports. He was one of the first sportswriters to speak out about such topics as baseball's color line and the undermining influence of television coverage. In fact, his judg-

---

Among writers, it's nearly a photo-finish as to whether Red Smith is more admired for his legendary definition of writing or for his legendary column Sports of the Times.

Whichever, the Pulitzer-Prize winning "Dean of American Sportswriters" opened his vein at least four times a week for more than 55 years and 500 newspapers. This interview, given just before his death in January 1982, finds him reminiscing about the golden era of baseball and other sports, the state of current sportswriting, and the obligations of all writers.

His last column appeared only four days before his death, and told of his plans to write only three columns a week. He ended the column with his hope that "someday there would be another Joe DiMaggio."

Someday there may be another Red Smith.

ment was so respected that he was called before a Congressional committee to testify on baseball's reserve clause.

Despite his long and distinguished career, Smith did not begin to receive widespread recognition until he moved across town to *The New York Times*. In 1976, he was honored with a Pulitzer Prize. Four years later, Smith was again thrust into the spotlight when he became one of the first to suggest an American boycott of the 1980 Moscow Summer Olympics as an appropriate response to the Soviet invasion of Afghanistan. His column drew worldwide comment and was instrumental in advancing the cause of those who favored the sanction.

Although he worked on newspapers for well over a half-century, Smith's pre-eminence was due less to his longevity than to his impeccable prose style. "Writing a column is like opening a vein and letting the words bleed out, drip by drip," he once said, in a variant of his famous quote. "Get it right, get it fast, not too much 'Gee Whiz!' and keep plenty of 'So What!' "

At his best, Smith transcended the reportorial aspects of the sports contest and offered a poetic evocation of time and place. A column he wrote about the Travers Stakes horserace in Saratoga Springs is a testament to his mastery. Titled "A Lovely Morning under the Elms," it begins:

Through the fragrance of wood fires burning under the elms in the stable area behind Saratoga's main track, wreaths of morning mist curled up to be burned away by slanting rays of sunshine. Hot-walkers led horses in lazy circles between the barns, while other horses stood relishing the flow of cool water from garden hoses trained on their forelegs. Grooms swabbed horses with soapy sponges and rubbed them dry. The rhythmic throbbing of hooves could be heard from the track itself, where horses were working.

Just before Smith's death, I visited him at his summer home. The white-haired journalist stepped from his station wagon in a slightly rumpled tan suit and walked across the tree-shaded pebble driveway of his summer home on Martha's Vineyard. He was carrying a sheaf of papers under one arm and had a wry expression on his weary face. When he reached the front steps, he gave me a hearty handshake and apologized for being late. (Our interview had been scheduled for 1, and by the time he arrived it was well past 2.) Moments later, as we settled into a pair of redwood chairs on the porch, he sipped a bottle of imported beer and explained that he had only just returned from covering the Travers Stakes.

It seemed ironic that a man who had spent his life meeting deadlines would be late for his own interview. But Smith could be forgiven if he had lost a step or two over the years. Even at 76, he maintained a schedule that would exhaust a man half his age.

Smith was never comfortable with his celebrity status. He believed that a reporter should not allow his notoriety to overshadow a story, and he took a dim view of such journalists as Howard Cosell. "A guy like Cosell doesn't broadcast sports," he said contemptuously. "He broadcasts Cosell." When asked about all the awards and acclaim he has received, Smith simply shrugged his shoulders and said, "I'm just a newspaperman trying to write better than I can."

Keeping his discomfort with the writing name he had built for himself in mind, I began our conversation by talking about another name.

How did you get the nickname "Red?"
You might find it hard to believe, but it was because of the color of my hair. When I was young, the girls used to describe it as spun gold. I actually grew up with the nickname "Brick" and carried it throughout college.

When I went to work for the *St. Louis Star*, I was known as Walter W. Smith. We were very formal at the *Star*. But when I moved over to the *Philadelphia Record*, I discovered that they were quite casual and had bylines like Bill Dolley, Joe Fallon and Herb Good. My first assignment was to cover a Phillies game and, since I didn't know the *Record's* policy, I just sent the piece in unsigned. The slot man on the copy desk made it read "by Walt Smith," and when my wife Kay saw it, she screamed bloody murder. To her, "Walt" was a hick name. So, the following day, I shamefacedly went to my editor and told him my wife wouldn't allow me to use that byline. The next time I sent in a story, the slot man took his best shot and came up with Red.

You started your career in 1927 as a cub reporter at the Milwaukee Sentinel. *How did you become a sportswriter?*
After I left the *Sentinel*, I faked my way into a job as a copyreader at the *St. Louis Star*. Nobody openly accused me of being a fake, but I was the most dispensable copyreader on the paper. One fall, the managing editor fired about half his sports department. He was desperate, so he asked me if I knew anything about sports. I told him I knew what the average fan knew. He then wanted to know if I was honest. If a fight manager offered me a $25 bribe, he asked, would I take it? At the time I was only making $40 a week, so I said, "Twenty-five dollars is an awful lot of money." He said, "Report to the sports editor on Monday."

Early in your career you became disillusioned with sportswriting.
When I was in St. Louis, there were two major-league baseball teams, two college football teams, relatively few boxing matches and no professional hockey. I would get awfully bored in the winter. All I ever did was cover basketball, which bored the hell out of me. Also, I was young

and full of the romance of journalism. I had the feeling that empires were crashing all over the world while I was stuck in St. Louis covering roundball. So, with the consent of my editor, I went back to rewrite and special assignment and stayed there until I went to Philadelphia.

When did you get back into sports?
In 1933. I had gone to the *Philadelphia Record* not knowing whether I would be on the local side or sports. I didn't really care because I just liked the newspaper business. The boss told me he was going to put me in sports and keep me there. I didn't mind because sports were much livelier in the East. I got to cover the Penn-Yale and Army-Navy games, boxing, Eagles pro football and the two baseball teams.

What was the first important sports story you covered?
The heavyweight initiation fight between Jack Sharkey and Young Stribling in Miami Beach in 1929. Sharkey and Stribling were the two outstanding American contenders for the heavyweight crown. At the time, I was stationed in Florida covering the St. Louis Browns on my first spring training trip. Gene Tunney had retired undefeated and Jack Dempsey was the nominal promoter of the match. Sharkey won it on points and it was a dull fight. But it was exciting for me because of Dempsey and all the major fighters involved. Also, sitting right next to me at ringside throughout the match were Al Capone and his henchmen.

What was it like to be a sportswriter during the twenties and thirties?
It was lovely. Of course, I didn't begin writing sports until 1928, so I missed most of the so-called golden age of the twenties. But I saw Babe Ruth play and knew Jack Dempsey, although I never saw him in a fight. I saw Walter Hagen, Gene Sarazen, Byron Nelson and Bill Tilden as a pro. I also knew Bobby Jones but never saw him hit a ball.

In boxing there was a whole company of wonderful rogues with names like Jack Hurley and Jack Kearns. Archie Moore once said of Kearns, "Give Jack a hundred pounds of steel wool and he'll knit you a stove." Well, that was a bloody good description of the characters you had in those days. They're all gone now. Today boxing is run by people versed in electronics and Harvard-trained lawyers who know how to put a closed-circuit television show together. In many cases, they even manage the fighters.

During the thirties you traveled with Frank Graham and a man who was the most famous sportswriter of his day—Grantland Rice. What are your memories of him?
Pure love and affection. I have had luck going for me all my life. But by far the greatest piece of luck I ever had was the privilege of traveling as part of a threesome with Frank and Granny. Neither drove, so I was always behind the wheel. But that was a privilege because all I had to do was listen and I was never at a loss for a column.

But Granny, apart from being the most generous, modest and courtly gentleman in the world, was also mighty talented. People jeer at his stuff today because of its Boy Scout enthusiasm. But Granny was just exactly right for his era. And if he were around today, he would be just exactly right for this era because he was a genius.

You also knew Ring Lardner.
I met Ring Lardner in the old Phillies ballpark, Baker Bowl, in 1930. I was sitting in the press box, which had a dozen desks and was narrow and deep and set into the second deck. At one point I looked around and saw the Western Union chief Stu Boggs greet this tall, dark, heavy-browed man I had been reading since childhood and just worshipped. Boggs brought him down the aisle and planted him right next to me in the front row. Lardner had a show opening in Philadelphia and had come out to see Bill Hallahan pitch for the Cardinals. We sat together for the entire doubleheader and chatted. He was my hero and I was thrilled. It was a big afternoon in my life.

Sometime later in New York, I got to be very friendly with his son John, whom I loved. I actually think that John wrote funnier than his father when it came to writing sports. He was brilliant. Of course, he didn't do his old man's fiction, which is what really made Ring Lardner famous.

Did those writers influence you?
When I was just starting out as a sportswriter, I deliberately and unashamedly imitated whoever was my hero at the time. There was a succession of them—Damon Runyon, Westbrook Pegler and Joel Williams, who was then at

> *You just have to sit down and write. I never saw myself as a literary figure. The phrase "writer's block" would sound a little pretentious in my mouth.*

the top of his game at the *New York World Telegram.* After a while, I realized that I was no longer imitating. In fact, I would go to extremes to avoid saying something the way it had been said before. I felt I had to say it my way.

I never boasted about imitating. I never said, "Didn't I write that one the way Pegler would have written it?" In fact, I never confessed until long afterwards that I consciously imitated other sportswriters. But I think that by imitating them I picked up some of their "moves"— in the sense that a boxer has "moves." And they have stayed with me until now.

How has sportswriting changed over the years?
Recently, a young journalist interviewed Blackie Sherrod, who is a veteran sportswriter for a Dallas paper. He asked Blackie about the differences and changes that he had seen in the business. Blackie said that it used to be you moved into a hotel and the first thing you check was the bathroom and if there was a bottle opener on the wall it was an acceptable hotel. Now the first thing you look for is a three-prong outlet for your electric typewriter.

But the one thing that has really made a difference is the airplane. We used to travel from places like St. Louis to Boston by train, which took all day and all night. We played cards with the ballplayers and got to know them intimately. There was plenty of leisure time because they played in the afternoon. If you worked on a morning paper you had all night free, and if you wanted to, you could go drink beer with the ballplayers.

Now you finish a ball game in Detroit at midnight and don't have time to write a decent story for a morning paper. In an hour you have to make the team plane and everybody falls asleep and ends up in a place like Los Angeles or Anaheim. A.J. Leibling once said of himself, "I can write faster than anybody who can write better than me and better than anybody who can write faster than me." Well, I can't write faster than anybody. I simply can't write as good a story at midnight to make a morning edition as I could in the old days after an afternoon game.

What are the differences between reporting and writing a column?
If you are reporting the news, your job is to get the facts

> *I have known writers who paid no damned attention whatever to the rules of grammar and rhetoric and somehow made the language behave for them.*

into the paper as swiftly and as accurately as you can. If you have the chance to write in a fashion that is readable or entertaining, that's a bonus. It puts a great burden on you. Anybody can get the facts right if he waits for history to guide him. But a reporter has to get them in time for the next edition.

The columnist expresses his own personal view of a situation. I remember the time I was covering a World Series game and said to my editor, Stanley Woodward: "Look, we have someone writing the lead, a guy for each clubhouse, someone doing crowd reaction and someone covering the feature angle. What's left for the columnist?" And Stanley said, "You've got to try and get the smell of the cabbage cooking in the corridors." The columnist tries to capture the color, flavor and electricity of an event. It's not an easy assignment.

Which do you prefer?
I would rather be a columnist. It's harder. But I have complete freedom of choice of subject and approach to subject within the libel laws. If you are doing a column, you have that freedom.

A sportswriter has an obligation to deal with the broader implications of sports. Doesn't a certain responsibility come with that?
Listen, I believe that any sportswriter who thinks the world is no bigger than the outfield fence is not only a bad citizen of the world but also a lousy sportswriter because he has no sense of proportion. He should be involved in the world in which he lives.

I have had an argument or two with sports editors on this point. One once complained about something I wrote not being, in his view, strictly sports. He said, "We're hired to cover sports." I told him, "I'm not. I'm hired to write my column." Which was true. I wasn't hired to write a column about sports exclusively. I feel free to branch off into politics or the theater or whatever else is relevant.

How much influence do you think you have as a sportswriter?
None. I never believed in this stuff about the power of the press. I really don't think that newspapers have that much influence. For instance, during most of the [Franklin] Roosevelt years, 95 perent of the newspapers opposed him and he got elected four times.

You received a Pulitzer Prize in 1976 for commentary. [laughs] In other words, that means: We can't think of any other reason to give it to you.

How did you feel about the award?
Pleased. But it didn't come as the surprise it should have been. A friend of mine, who was a member of the jury, called me up about six weeks ahead of time and told me I had won. So, by the time the sports editor broke out the pink champagne, it was old hat.

The award solidified your position as the "dean of American sportswriters." How does that make you feel?
Old! That's what makes you the dean. I remember once in festivities before the Kentucky Derby, Grantland Rice chose me as his junior dean to share some of the responsibility. Well, I wasn't all that deanish at the time, and there wasn't any responsibility to share. Of course, I was flattered that Granny invited me to be his junior dean. The point is it was a joke and being a dean is a joke. It just means you're the oldest.

Has the fact of your celebrity—the fact that you are Red Smith—hindered you in your work? Can you still be just another reporter asking a question in a locker room?
Sure. I must say I was amused by the report that Morley Safer did on me on *60 Minutes*. They showed me going down to the clubhouse and getting into a crowd of reporters standing around Pete Rose. The director must have pushed people aside and nudged me up to the front, because then you hear Morley's narration say, "But the others quickly part to make room for him when he comes in. . . ." Nonsense.

Do other reporters ever defer to you?
I should say they do not. There is no reason in the world why they should. They're just trying to do their job.

Which sports do you enjoy covering the most?
I always said the one that gave me my most recent column is the one I like the most. But I find that the meat and potatoes sports of the sports page—baseball, football, boxing and horseracing—are the ones I like best to cover. I also enjoy covering big championship golf and tennis. I never saw an ice hockey game I didn't enjoy, but I don't find that it writes very well.

What makes hockey and basketball difficult to write is the fact that they are running games. The flow of the game goes up and down. They shoot at the goal and either score or miss. That's all there is to it. Whereas in baseball the drama of the situation can build the way a really fine dramatist would construct the plot of a play. You can reach the climax with the score tied, the bases loaded, two out, three and two on the hitter, and everyone running with the pitch. Where can you find a more thrill-ing moment? Or a fellow running out a triple in itself is a beautiful thing. That's what I mean by writing well.

Also, there are more good stories and colorful people to be met on the backstretch of a race track than anywhere else. Now, I don't mean the rich owners. I am more interested in the trainers, grooms, hot-walkers, exercise boys and jockeys. There is hardly one of them who doesn't have a rags-to-riches or riches-to-rags story, or both.

Is it hard to come up with a fresh angle for each event, especially with a sport like baseball, which has 162 games in a regular season?
When I was on the daily beat, some young guy asked me, "Doesn't this become dull?" And I said, "Only to dull minds." Because today's game is always different from yesterday's, and tomorrow's game will be different from today's. All you need is the interest and wit to perceive that difference and the ability to express or describe it. They all mean something different, even to a last-place club.

When do you know the approach you will use in a story? Is it during the game?
I hope so. At least you pay attention and know what's writable about that particular game. You probably won't know how you are going to approach it until after the game is over.

But often even when the game ends I don't know. I have known times when I went pretty empty to the clubhouse or football dressing room hoping and praying that God or somebody would deliver the right manna into my hands. And I must knock on wood because it's always happened.

Do you think that athletes—as a class of people—must be treated in any special way when you interview them?
No. I suppose that when somebody has just lost a tough one, he doesn't necessarily welcome a lot of stupid questions and might be a little touchy. If I have to interview someone, I try to be diplomatic. But I would just as soon let him cool off first. You see, seldom do I feel that I have to interview somebody. This is the lucky part of my job as a columnist. If I were on daily assignment, I would have a rough job.

How do you get your subjects to open up—to reveal something that they might not ordinarily admit?
I am not really trying to do that, which is possibly why some people who know me will confide in me. They know I'm not really trying to dig. I have always found that the notebook, pencil or tape recorder was to some extent an obstacle. I have always felt that if a fellow talks into a tape recorder or sees his interviewer scribbling notes, he is constantly reminded that he is talking for publication

and had better be careful of what he says. However, if we just sit and chat and I hold up my end of the conversation—whether it's germane or not—I think we get along a lot better. I think that people will sometimes unload in casual conversation as they would be reluctant to unload if it's stamped on the interviewer's brow, "for Publication."

One of your columns was made up almost entirely of direct quotes. You can do that without a tape recorder?
I can do that easily. I used to be better at it than I am today. In fact, Frank Graham was better at it than anyone else I ever knew.

Do you take notes or rely on your memory?
Memory. After the interview, I may sit down and reconstruct the sequence of the conversation in sketchy notes. But I learned from years ago that if I listened attentively, I could recreate the conversation almost entirely. And sometimes I take the extra trouble of listening for the characteristic turn of phrase—which all of us have—and remember it verbatim and put it where it belongs. Then, if there has been a third party listening in on the interview, he reads the column and recognizes that turn of phrase and thinks that I have quoted the whole conversation verbatim without taking notes.

You discard what you know will be of no use to you and make a point of remembering the things that are possibly useful.

Do you take notes when you are covering a game?
If I don't have anything else to write down. I'll write down the important plays, scoring plays or the key plays where I think the game turns over. But every time I go to a game to write a column, I hope that a beat man will be there to cover those aspects of the game. I don't want to poach on his territory if I can possibly avoid it. I hope I can find another approach, whether it be an interview with somebody connected with the game or—and I hate to use this expression—a mood piece that tries to capture the special character of the event.

When taking notes, what aspects of the game do you concentrate on?
If I begin to get some idea that I'm going to hang the piece on Reggie Jackson because he did something important in the game, I may take notes on how he stands at the plate, crouches, and how he faces the pitcher. I may take fairly detailed notes on a single aspect of the game like that because that's where I'm going to have my focus. Of course, that is something I have to discover during the game while there is time for me to take those notes. But you have to go to a game with a soft brain prepared to take an impression like wax.

How do you handle the pressure of meeting four dead-lines a week?
I used to meet seven deadlines a week. So this is a vacation.

The daily deadline is something you learn to accept when you come into this business. It's something you never question because newspapers must have deadlines and they must have daily deadlines or else they can't be daily newspapers. Sure there's pressure. You have to get your work done by such and such a time. It still makes me sweat if I am right on deadline and trying to do a decent job. I can't be calm about it because I work hard. That's the only way you can handle the pressure.

Do you ever have days when the words won't come?
Of course. The first time I met publisher John S. Knight, we were both belly up to a bar at Arlington Park in Chicago. When we were introduced, he said "Nobody can write seven good columns a week. Why don't you do three? You want me to fix it up?" I said, "Look Mr. Knight, suppose I wrote three stinkers. I wouldn't have the rest of the week to make up for it." That was the end of that conversation.

But you have to console yourself. You never settle for less than the best you can do with the circumstances that day. If you manage a stinker, your consolation is that tomorrow will be a better day.

How do you define a stinker?
A column that I don't enjoy reading. Or a column that I read and think is dull. I don't think it would be fair to say that I wish I hadn't done a particular column, because I know I had to do it—that on that day I needed a column and this was the best I could do. But I would describe a stinker as a column that if somebody else wrote it and I picked it up, I might not finish it.

How do you overcome a block?
You just have to sit down and write. I never saw myself as a literary figure. I've heard about writer's block. And, of course, there have been times when it was more difficult to write than others. And it's never been easy. But the phrase "writer's block" would sound a little pretentious in my mouth. It would sound as though I thought of myself as an artist or something. It would seem to be laying claim to an inborn talent.

Writing is very much like bricklaying. You learn to put one brick on top of another and spread the mortar so thick. As E.B. White wrote, "Writing all those sentences hoping to get one right."

Where do you work?
I have a barn behind my house in New Canaan in which I built an office with shelves for my books and reference material. I do a lot of my work there. The rest of the time I do it at the ballpark or the fight camp or the race track or wherever the job takes me. It almost never takes me

into *The New York Times* office.

I try to get started at a reasonably early hour in the afternoon. I'm unhappy if I get started after 4 p.m. And it's a rare afternoon when I start as late as 5. I think that 6 p.m. is supposed to be a kind of prevailing deadline for everything but last-minute stuff in sports. But I am unhappy if I don't have at least two hours when I sit down at the typewriter. If you give me four hours to finish a piece, I will take it.

Your column runs about 900 words. Do you write the entire piece in one sitting?
As a rule. But then it's blacksmithed out, word by word. You hammer it out on the typewriter one word at a time. I have never done a second draft. However, I have torn up leads and thrown them away by the bushel basket.

Early in my working newspaper life, I was half of a two-man rewrite staff on an afternoon paper that put out an edition an hour, all day long. I had to keep the typewriter smoking all day. There was no time for second drafts or anything else. You had to get the damn thing written and on the city desk and pick up the next thing fast.

But you take the time to tear up leads.
Oh yes. I was never by nature a fast writer. I became a fast rewrite man out of necessity. But that changed as soon as I stopped being a rewrite man and took to writing a personal column. It's quite a different thing. With a column, you're expressing yourself, your own personal ideas and views, and, though I shrink at this, to some extent your personality. You don't like to do it hastily.

Is a lead the most difficult part of a piece?
Generally speaking, I would agree with that. You'd have to make some exceptions. Now and then you come upon obstacles elsewhere. But if you get a satisfactory lead, you should be able to go on from there.

What is your advice to someone who wants to become a sportswriter?
Get all the formal schooling you can. Also, read as widely as you can—everything from the Bible to the telephone directory. When it's time to go to work, go pester the hell out of some city editor for a job on the local side. I have known only one really fine sportswriter who did not

> *My advice to an aspiring sportswriter would be: don't be a sportswriter. Learn what the newspaper business is about before you become a specialist.*

spend an apprenticeship under the discipline of the city desk. Learn what the newspaper business is all about before you become a specialist.

I have known sports departments that were just gentleman's clubs—little backwaters off the main stream of the newspaper itself. They didn't have any idea of what was news. They only knew that if the home team won, it was worth a banner headline on the front page of the sports section. And that's too bad. That makes for bad sports sections and bad sportswriters.

I have had so many kids say to me, "Oh boy, I love sports so much I know all the batting averages back to Ty Cobb." Well, that's the last possible recommendation. Love the newspaper business. It's all right to enjoy sports. However, a detached, but not unfriendly view of sports is the most desirable one. But above all, the dedication should be toward the newspaper business. So, my advice to an aspiring sportswriter would be: Don't be a sportswriter. If you want to specialize later on, that's fine. But you might change your mind after you get a taste of the other side.

What are the elements of a good sports story?
Precisely the same as the elements of any good piece of writing or good story. For one thing, the subject matter must hold some interest on its own. To make it a well-told story, it should be constructed logically and thoughtfully and be presented in a tidy or efficient fashion.

The writer should have some respect for the mother tongue. The grammar, syntax and rhetoric ought to be acceptable—and I mean acceptable by some established standard. I have known writers who paid no damned attention whatever to the rules of grammar and rhetoric and somehow made the language behave for them. I don't know how they managed it, but they did. For example, my late friend Doc Greene, who wrote a sports column for the *Detroit News*, absolutely ignored the rules of grammar and rhetoric. But at the top of his game he could write as good a column as could be written.

What do you think of the current state of sportswriting?
The overall level of sportswriting in this country is greatly improved. There are fewer papers and fewer jobs for total incompetents. But I can't think of a single sportswriter who I would put on a par with John Lardner, Frank Graham or Westbrook Pegler.

Why?
My contemporaries today don't laugh enough. They're too damned serious. I need a little laughter. I certainly got it from people like John Lardner and Westbrook Pegler. They had wit and humor, as well as many other fine qualities.

Would you agree that many current sportswriters are prone to overstatement and questionable syntax?
That's a generalization, and I don't believe in generalizations. Yes, some sportswriters are prone to overstatement and bad syntax. Some sportswriters are prone to vulgari-ties that turn me off. Other sportswriters are prone to childishness and ineptitude. Every sin that can be committed is committed by sportswriters. Some are happily free of those crimes. Some of us find other crimes to commit.

You have been covering sports for almost 55 years. How much longer do you plan to continue?
Until I stop enjoying it, which I think is improbable. Or till the *Times* chucks me out, which can happen anytime. Or till I snuff it at a typewriter, the way Grantland Rice did. I'd just as soon have that happen, because I think that's as good a way for a sportswriter to go as any.

BY MICHAEL SCHUMACHER

ALLEN GINSBERG

Follow your inner moonlight; don't hide the madness.

Allen Ginsberg blended in well with the rest of the people eating lunch at the small, crowded luncheonette section of the drugstore. The store, within walking distance of the university where Ginsberg was to read that evening, attracted a college crowd looking for a reasonably priced sandwich. Book bags littered the limited floor space, while their owners chatted about classes, sports, the opposite sex, and a variety of campus topics.

Ginsberg could have been a university professor, as far as these kids knew. He looked the part, with his gray suit and tie, round wire-rimmed spectacles, and neatly trimmed beard. He also had a book bag nearby. His choice of topics was poetry.

"Music and poetry have been together from the very beginning," he said in answer to my question about his recent involvement with recorded music. The night before, I had listened to a rough cut of *First Blues*, Ginsberg's two-record album combining his poetry with popular music forms. He had previously recorded two albums of William Blake's poetry set to music.

"My poetry has come to a point of refinement where song tones emerge," Ginsberg continued. "I practiced on Blake, to extract melodies from the vernacular or idiomatic tones, and then I began writing my own songs in the mode which is common to my nature: blues, rock 'n' roll and new wave. I think it's just a normal extension."

Ginsberg paused for a bite from his chicken-salad sandwich. Here was a poet who had solidified his reputation as a major writer before most of the kids around us were born, a man whose involvement with the Beat Generation of the fifties and the Flower Power movement of the sixties had thrust him to the front of the tremendous social changes taking place in those times, yet he seemed younger in spirit than the college set. His poetry and lifestyle defied the concept of aging. Instead, they constantly evolved, challenged all ages, and remained—like the works of Walt Whitman—a spirit of the people now.

But was the country ready for a rock singer who belonged to the American Academy of Arts and Letters?

It's not even easy to keep up with Allen Ginsberg's activities, let alone try to understand him through those activities. He rarely lights long enough to be categorized into the neat little pigeonholes that make Americans comfortable, and you get the feeling Ginsberg likes it that way.

For more than a quarter of a century, Ginsberg has been a moving target in the literary world. An essentially self-educated man, he has lived in India, Mexico, Africa, Paris, and too many American cities to name. His wide-ranging political interests have included ecology issues, the decriminalization of marijuana, war protests, gay liberation and a number of others that he describes as "human lib" issues. He conducts classes and seminars on meditation, sings on records with rock bands, and participates in political rallies and protests.

All this would qualify him as an interesting study in a history text examining this century's bohemian or leftist political behavior, yet these activities only underscore

---

Once, defining Allen Ginsberg might have been a simple matter of talking about Jack Kerouac, Neal Cassady, William S. Burroughs and other Beat figures. Today, the 63-year-old established rebel poet has left much of the Beat behind, while still carrying its roots with him.

That change—and the energy that brought it and many others about—is what Ginsberg, and this 1984 interview, are mostly about. You'll find plenty of poetic advice, but you'll also see the National Book Award Winner (for The Fall of America), *the National Institute of Arts and Letters member, the author of the astonishing* Howl *and* Kaddish, *stretch the bounds of poetry. And have fun doing it.*

his main activity, writing poetry. It is in poetry that Allen Ginsberg has secured a place in history. All his experiences seem to find their way into print.

Allen Ginsberg writes poetry in the same manner that he lives his life, combining his emotion, experience and literary tradition with a fresh, spontaneous style accentuating the importance of the present. Over the years, he has been criticized for his commitment to spontaneous poetry, especially by those who believe poetry should be worked and re-worked until it shines from the polishing. Ginsberg, though, believes spontaneity enhances a work's sense of time and place. "If you capture a moment perfectly, you capture eternity," he explains. "If you're present there in a moment, you're present there in eternity. Say you're writing with the idea that you're not really 100 percent present, that you can always come back and fix it up later to look like you were present. Your mind is split in a schizophrenic time gap.

"Ageless art has always been spontaneous. *Ozymandias*, Shelley's poem about time and eternity, was written in ten minutes as an exercise to show that he could do it right. The idea that spontaneity is something that's newfangled, bohemian, or abstract expression of modern, strange ideas is ridiculous. It's the oldest thing in poetics, just like vocalization is older than print."

Ginsberg credits Jack Kerouac, author of *On the Road* and one of the principals of the Beat Generation, as being the major influence on his spontaneous style. The two were close friends, and their early works revealed two young men heavily influenced by other writers, Kerouac by Thomas Wolfe, Ginsberg by Blake and John Donne, among others. Neither had found a voice until Kerouac decided to ignore the restraints of tradition and speak with the voice of his experience. The results were novels like *Dr. Sax*, *Visions of Cody*, *Maggie Cassidy* and *The Subterraneans*—works praised and damned by critics for the raw, unpolished style.

Ginsberg applied the same method to his poetry. In the early 1950s, he worked on a number of short manuscripts, learning and practicing the style, and then he began the huge, far-ranging poem that would establish him as a major writer:

I saw the best minds of my generation destroyed by madness
starving hysterical naked

> *I didn't intend to publish* Howl. *It was just too private. I thought my father would be embarrassed by it.*

Dragging themselves through the negro streets at dawn looking for an angry fix . . .

Howl was one of those rare poems that exploded on impact. People knew of the work before it had even been printed, the legend beginning when Ginsberg read it at San Francisco poetry gatherings. Even people who never read poetry had an opinion of *Howl* and its author. And when it became the subject of a sensational obscenity trial in San Francisco in 1957, the press flooded the courtroom. The poem beat the charges, and Allen Ginsberg had achieved the dubious status of celebrity poet.

Ginsberg's success—and the poem's impact and notoriety—may not have ever been realized had Ginsberg stood by his initial gut feeling about the work. "I didn't intend to publish it," he says today. "It was just too private. I thought my father would be embarrassed by it. In the writing, I figured I could say anything I wanted since it wasn't going to be published. That gave me a freedom to be frank, which I wouldn't have had if I'd thought that I was writing for publication. This is always a sort of trap that a writer, painter or musician has, to actually express himself completely without worrying about what it looks like in public."

Howl challenges a writer's concept of honesty and a reader's acceptance of the poet's intentions. Ginsberg and his fellow writers were suggesting that art is beautiful when it reflects the human; that the human is not always attractive, and therefore that beauty can be found beneath the warts and moles, scars and blemishes, of something outwardly plain or ugly. A poet's responsibility is to be totally truthful to himself and his reader, regardless of the physical beauty of the subject matter and the finished product.

This type of writing permits little revision, which strips away the honesty of the emotion present at the time of the writing. In his essay, "Essentials for Spontaneous Prose," Kerouac urged the writer to avoid revision except to correct obvious mistakes or to make what he termed "calculated insertions."

Allen Ginsberg follows this system, though he admits to revising more than Kerouac did. "I always did a little more blue-penciling, getting rid of saying the same thing twice. It's a matter of paying attention to the laxness of my first composition and blue-penciling syntactical excessiveness."

Of calculated insertions, Ginsberg clarifies: "If you're writing about a big, long trip and you forget to include a whole episode—you just forget it—then you can put it in. It wouldn't be a recasting of the whole rhythm or tone of the sentence. Nor would it be trying to make it better in a miserly way because you held back in your first writing. Nor would it be going back and retracing your steps for inspiration, because that would disturb the original organic rhythm."

In the past, many Beat Generation writers—Ginsberg included—compared this style of spontaneous composition to the improvisational jazz solos played by the bop musicians of the fifties. A player would take center stage and form his spur-of-the-moment feelings into music, knowing full well that he risked a sour note by performing with such reckless abandon. When the solo worked, it was the ultimate expression.

One of Ginsberg's highest points came in 1958, when he published *Kaddish*, another lengthy poem written in the spontaneous spirit of *Howl*. In *Kaddish*, however, Ginsberg took even greater risks, since the poem was a public rendering of the poet's feelings about his mother's death. Naomi Ginsberg had spent a large portion of her life being treated for paranoiac schizophrenia, and *Kaddish* lay bare all the pain that Ginsberg had kept to himself through the years:

Back! You! Naomi! Skull on you! Gaunt
immortality and revolution come—small
broken woman—the ashen indoor eyes of
hospitals, ward greyness on skin—
    "Are you a spy?" I sat at the sour table, eyes
filling with tears—"Who are you?" Did Louis
send you?"—The wires
    in her hair, as she beat on her head—"I'm not
a bad girl—don't murder me!—I hear the ceiling—
I raised two children—"

As with *Howl*, Ginsberg held back nothing in the writing of *Kaddish*. Boiling within the poem was all the anger, love, resentment, tenderness and confusion Ginsberg felt toward his mother's existence. Like *Howl*, the poem was shocking in its frankness, somewhat repulsive with its warts and blemishes—and successful. Robert Lowell called it a masterpiece.

Unlike *Howl*, *Kaddish* was intended for publishers. Ginsberg had found his voice and was comfortable having the world hear it.

Finding one's voice is the most important aspect of writing for anyone, and Ginsberg believes the key to success for novice poets is patience—not striving too hard for national attention, both in matters of gaining an individual style and in terms of having it heard. "To gain your own voice, you have to forget about having it heard. Renounce that and you get your own voice automatically.

Try to become a saint of your own province and your own consciousness, and you won't worry about being heard in *The New York Times*."

Many young poets, Ginsberg claims, work too hard to achieve a national voice and wind up writing generalizations that apply to no one. Striving too hard to be published, then, can become one of a poet's biggest obstacles. "It's more important to concentrate on what you want to say to yourself and your friends. Follow your inner moonlight; don't hide the madness. Take [William Carlos] Williams: until he was 50 or 60, he was a local nut from Paterson, New Jersey, as far as the literary world was concerned. He went half a century without real recognition except among his friends and peers.

"You say what you want to say when you don't care who's listening. If you're grasping to get your own voice, you're making a strained attempt to talk, so it's a matter of just listening to yourself as you sound when you're talking about something that's intensely important to you." Over the years, Ginsberg has chronicled his times through works addressing a wide variety of topics, from his travels, to politics, to his friends. The poems are able to bring forth that most important aspect of poetry—reader identification—in even his most personal writings, and he has been able to do so by using his own voice.

Ginsberg thinks this method of writing poetry not only captures a poet's times, but also offers the reader a clear look at who the poet is. "The sorts of things I see are the sort of guy I am," he offers in self-definition. "What I'm noticing is where I'm at. I'm pursuing a single line from Williams, which is trying to stick to objective, imagistic fact—including objects inside and outside the mind—and trying to do a sketch of that. If you look at the world and describe it, you have a whole field to write about that is more or less objective. Then, proceeding from there, it's just a matter of extending those descriptions outward, whether you're writing about a little beggar on the street or the movie in your head."

Gaining one's voice and a sense of identity is important—if that voice is heard. But in these times when even small presses are becoming choosier about what they publish, the already-starving poet may grow frustrated trying to break into print. Ginsberg's solution: "Publish your own. Mimeograph it with a few friends and send it out to all your friends. There's a flood of photocopying and mimeographing now. Cultivate a whole community where you are. Every town has its poets. In San Francisco, for instance, they have their own movement and poetry. Then, when there's a shooting star out of that— somebody like, say Antler [more on him in a moment]— he's seen elsewhere. You make your ground where you are, which is the point of Blake and Williams."

This approach worked for Ginsberg when he moved from New York to San Francisco in the mid '50s. The city, known for its enthusiasm for bohemian culture and acceptance of populist poetry, became the unofficial birth-place of the Beat Generation when Ginsberg, Kerouac, Gary Snyder, Philip Whalen, Philip LaMantia, Lawrence Ferlinghetti and Kenneth Rexroth gave regular readings and published their poetry there. *Howl* was originally published in mimeograph form, a piece of history worth thousands of dollars to collectors today.

Once the small poetry network is established on a local level, expand it. "Go to a big bookstore that has a lot of poetry books. Look them over and see if you find any affinity groups that you like among the little magazines and publishing groups, people you dig and who might dig your mind. Send them your stuff, just to connect with people you feel affinity with.

"Send your work to poets you like, and remember that they get 20 books a week and can't read them all. They can only glance at them, and if they see something they like, they will read it and respond."

The odds of being "discovered" by a major poet are slim, Ginsberg concedes, but he cites a number of examples of poets whose work he read cold in the mail, work which, in Ginsberg vernacular, blew his mind. Such was the case with a former Milwaukee factory worker, a young poet who wrote under the name Antler. Ginsberg received *Factory*, Antler's book-length poem, in the mail and was impressed enough to encourage the poet and write a blurb for the poem. The poem eventually became part of City Lights's "Pocket Poet" series, the same series that has published Ginsberg from the beginning.

A long line of tables had been put up near the back of the huge room, in a location near both the entrance to the hall and the bar, where plenty of beer and wine would be sold that evening.

Students, representatives of activist groups, and various hangers-on busied themselves at the tables, preparing for the onslaught of people who would be passing them at the Ginsberg reading in a few hours.

Buttons, flyers, pamphlets and stacks of other printed materials, all advertising events or hawking political awareness groups, were piled onto the tables.

Outside, in the lobby of the university, an anti-war collage, its artwork assembled on the face of an American flag, was displayed for Ginsberg's benefit.

"Do you think he'll read *Howl* tonight?" one of the students asked a friend.

"I hope so," her companion said. "We had to get a babysitter so we could come to this."

It is hard to imagine Allen Ginsberg *not* active in politics. When he enrolled in Columbia College in 1944, Ginsberg hoped to become a labor organizer. His interest in politics was inspired by his mother, who was active in leftist causes. His interest in poetry came from his father, Louis, who was a poet and teacher, as well as from William Carlos Williams, the local "underground celebrity" who en-couraged Ginsberg's early writings. Poetry and politics married early in Ginsberg's mind, and while the relationship may not seem too stable in the eyes of the academics, Ginsberg believes the two are compatible.

"There have always been political cranks and nuts, activists and populists, as in the tradition of Williams and Ezra Pound," Ginsberg says. "Charles Olson was interested in politics in a geographical way, as I am. There probably is a tendency for conservative, 'art for art's sake' thinking in the academics. Then, on the extreme of the New American Poets, are radical, populist Buddhists in the line of Williams, who was very political. On the other hand, there are some people who are 'bridge poets.' Robert Lowell bridged the gap because he and I read together and were friends."

The past two decades have found Ginsberg active in a number of political concerns. A great bulk of the poetry he published in the '60s, collected in *Planet News* and *The Fall of America*, reflected his involvement in the politics of those volatile times.

Since Ginsberg's politics are so closely allied to his poetry, one must wonder if his strong political stance might tarnish his acceptability in the poetic field, that perhaps his art might not be taken as seriously as it could be. "I don't think the ultimate thing is politics," he argues, noting that any splits within the poetry community are likely to be the result of literary, not political, differences. "I think the line of demarcation—as before and as ever—is between those who are working in the San Francisco Renaissance Beat Black Mountain New York school and the people who are still working in a somewhat traditional idea form."

Ginsberg is not particularly eager to discuss the politics of poetics. Gaining formal acceptance from the poetry community took him nearly 20 years. Between 1956 and 1974, Ginsberg had amassed a huge volume of published work, including poems like *Howl, Kaddish, America, The Change,* and *Wichita Vortex Sutra*—all considered masterworks today and taught on college campuses across the country. The main reason for Ginsberg's slow rise to the top was probably a rift in the poetry community, a battle for recognition, awards and grant money. At times, the battle got quite ugly. Things have simmered down lately, though, and Ginsberg approaches the topic gingerly.

"The differences concerned an artistic question about whether you wrote directly about your own experience, place and idiom, or whether you wrote in more literary, traditional and conservative form, reflecting English manners and rhythms as understood in the early 20th-century anthologies." Ginsberg chooses his words carefully, noting at the onset of the discussion that he is not interested in starting another fight, that "everything is sort of healing itself."

"I can't complain personally," he says. "I'm in the American Academy of Arts and Letters, and I've got a National Book Award. *The New York Times* and others have treated my books nicely."

Still, he says, good poetry volumes, published by small presses, are getting little or no recognition, mostly because they are not coming from a New York or university press.

"It's slowly changing, though," he adds as an afterthought, putting the subject to rest.

Allen Ginsberg's strong interest in recording music should not surprise anyone who has followed the poet's career. His poetry, influenced greatly by bop jazz greats Charlie Parker and Thelonius Monk, has a lyrical quality that has in turn influenced musicians such as Bob Dylan and Jim Morrison of the Doors. (Ginsberg appears, beardless and wearing a top hat, in a photo on the back of Dylan's 1965 album, *Bring it all Back Home*.) Ginsberg was so impressed by the way the Beatles allied poetry and music on *Sgt. Pepper's Lonely Hearts Club Band* that he played the album for an aging Ezra Pound.

More recently, Ginsberg appeared—singing and playing finger cymbals—in the movie *Renaldo and Clara*. He wrote lyrics and sang on *Combat Rock*, an album by The Clash, a new wave band. And then there was *First Blues*, his own improvisational rendering of poetry set to music.

All this may seem unusual to a country that stereotypes its poets as severe people who write their visions in an indecipherable manner, but Ginsberg sees it as continuing the oldest tradition in the poetics—the minstrel tradition. "You have to remember that traditionally, in every anthology, the popular songs of the day are some of the most beautiful lyrics preserved in anthologies. Any anthology of United States literature in the twentieth century has got to include specimens of black blues, rock 'n' roll and popular song.

"When I was in grammar school and high school in Paterson, New Jersey, I heard a lot of Leadbelly and Bessie Smith. I went to black spiritual churches along River Street and heard preaching and singing, so I heard a lot of spiritual, popular music when I was young. My singing poetry seems to be a natural development, now that I'm getting old enough to recover my own person and enjoy my body, speech and mind."

Ginsberg places great importance on a person's incorporating as much of the mind, spirit and body into a

> *To gain your own voice, forget about having it heard. Become a saint of your own province and your own consciousness.*

work as possible. A longtime student of Buddhism, Ginsberg meditates daily, a practice he believes has helped him make the most use of his entire being. His poetry readings, featuring a combination of reading, singing, chanting and meditation, have drawn fire from traditionalists who believe in following a certain form, but Ginsberg shrugs off the criticism. "Poets usually read for an hour, or an hour and a half. I usually read an hour and a half with text, and then sing another hour. At my readings, I've arrived at a structure or system of using different voices, coming from different parts of the body. I read some poems for spoken poetry, some for conversational voice, some for oratorical voice, and some for heart voice, which are erotic poems.

"In 1963, when I got back from India, I went to a poetry conference in Vancouver with Robert Duncan, Robert Creeley, Charles Olson, Denise Levertov, and a lot of other great poets. I was chanting the 'Hare Krishna' mantra and Robert Duncan said, 'Except for one or two poems like *Howl*, you use your voice and body more when you chant than when you read your poetry.' That struck me: why didn't my poetry vocalize my whole physical and emotional body? My attempt in *Plutonium Ode*, a recent work in the oratorical form, was to make a piece of vocalization which mobilizes the entire body in pronunciation and vocalization."

Applying this to his improvisational style is not easy, Ginsberg goes on. "You have to be inspired to write something like that. It's not something you can very easily do just by pressing a button. You have to have the right historical and physical combination, the right mental formation, the right courage, the right sense of prophecy, and the right information, intentions and ambitions. But it is possible to get in a state of inspiration while improvising. I did that once in Chicago at a reading. It went on for 25 minutes, with my doing a description of the universe and its basic characteristics, beginning with the idea of suffering as being part of it, and emptiness and transitoriness, and going on to an exposition on how to meditate and what kind of virtues you derive from meditation. I had this scheme and I simply followed it out. I got quite inspired."

At 58, Allen Ginsberg shows little sign of slowing down. Poets don't retire to calm existences in Arizona and Florida, and even if they did, Ginsberg would undoubtedly buck the trend. He lives as if aging were something other people do.

How does a person like Ginsberg, who places such value on spontaneity, plan for the future? Is there anything he would like to accomplish yet in his lifetime?

"A thousand things," Ginsberg fires back without hesitating. "A long, epic poem. A couple of really new, personal blues. A poem or song with words so inevitable that people will be able to use it all the time, like they do with Dylan and Blake."

He lists projects and hopes for another five minutes. There is no particular order or priority to the items on the list, but you get the feeling that he is sincere about each entry. In conclusion, he says that he would mainly like to follow the path of meditation he has set in front of him.

"It's a workable goal," he says, as if he realizes that fulfilling all his goals is not possible. "One thing, incidentally, which refers to some of what we've been talking about, concerns something I heard form Mark Van Doren when I was a kid, something which is also parallel to Buddhist behavior. Van Doren was a good poet and teacher who wrote essays for the book review section of the *New York Herald-Tribune*. They were always enthusiastic, sympathetic, perceptive, and full of empathy. When he was asked what happened when he got a book he didn't like, he said: 'I only write about things I like. That's what engages my attention. Why should I waste my energy on something I'm not interested in?'

"It was so obvious! Why waste your energy on a put-down, bummer scene? Why have the complaining and resentment, when you should be liberating energy to go up the path you want, in the direction you want. It's not just a matter of looking at the bright side, either. It's looking toward what you're interested in and what you think will do some good, rather than feeling it necessary to go around knocking everybody all the time. A lot of critics do. They seem to take pride in showing how smart they are through put-downs. It's not helpful. You should be pointing arrows toward the road you want to be on. It saves you a lot of energy."

Energy is a key word to understanding Allen Ginsberg. There are times when he appears to be writing his life—in terms of poetry, journal entries, interviews, and lectures—as quickly as he lives it.

"This happens to certain writers and painters," Ginsberg admits. "At a certain point in the life of the writer, the works, the art and the life become identical. The person merges with his artwork, the order of activity of the life centers around the artwork, and the artwork becomes the main drama. Like Van Gogh: the mind of the painter and the subject matter of the printing are one unified seizure of illumination."

Allen Ginsberg looked exhausted. In less than a day's time, he had given a handful of interviews, attended a party thrown in his honor, practiced with a rock band on several songs he would be singing at his university reading, and toured an art museum. A two-hour question-and-answer session with campus students had reduced his already soft-spoken voice to a whisper. A man known for his seemingly endless supply of energy was clearly running on a low battery, and he had a sold-out reading still ahead of him.

Though he was already late for dinner at a local poet's home, Ginsberg patiently answered questions and signed books for the students staying on after the session.

One kid asked Ginsberg to sign a map. He would soon be leaving on a cross-country jaunt, and he thought that the poet might have a few kind words to stave off road-demons. Ginsberg smiled and scribbled something across the folded sheet.

Another student wanted information about an upcoming poetry conference at the Naropa Institute in Boulder, Colorado. Who was going to be there? How long was it going to last? Could someone without any money attend? Ginsberg reached into his shoulder bag and pulled out a stack of printed information on the conference. "It will be good," Ginsberg said, repeating the plug he had delivered earlier in the afternoon. "If you can find a way to get there, it will be worth the trip."

Still another student, armed with a manila envelope jammed with poems approached Ginsberg and asked him if he had the time to read his work. For an instant, Ginsberg looked like he might have run out of runway, but he agreed to take a look. "I've been awfully busy," he said, "so it might be a while before I get them back to you. Try to hold them down to six or seven poems."

The student started to open the unsealed, bulging envelope.

"That's all right," Ginsberg conceded, taking the whole thing and placing it in his bag. He looked around for the man responsible for his schedule.

"Where are we going next?"

BY FRANK FILOSA

RAY BRADBURY

He nails himself to the cross of his typewriter.
He must crucify himself in order to discover himself.

When Ray Bradbury opened the door of 610 and congratulated me on my punctuality, I got the impression that punctuality is important to him. His eyes, light blue in the bright California sunlight, were frank and ingenuous like those of a highly intelligent child. He wore his reddish blonde and still abundant hair long on the sides and top.

As I set up the tape recorder and the mike, I surveyed the room. Looking at me from a narrow black frame was the Illustrated Man in all his chromatic glory. Pictures on the walls drawn by UCLA students showed scenes from Bradbury short stories. On the large, polished wood desk stood an electric typewriter and in the corner of the room a gray steel filing cabinet, its drawers bulging with manuscripts. On a stand next to the typewriter was the fresh white manuscript of a screenplay adopted from *The Martian Chronicles*.

Books were everywhere in the room, many bearing Bradbury titles. They stood in piles on the floor. They filled the chairs and corners of the desk and covered the sofa cushions. With brisk movements, Bradbury cleared a space for me to sit down. He spoke energetically, smiling often with his eyes, and showing the comfortable sophistication of the well-traveled individual who insists on being exactly what he is.

Mr. Bradbury, I think we should first establish your actual area of literary operation—science fiction, fantasy . . . there seems to be some controversy on this point.
My field is myself, as it should be for any writer. I wouldn't have given the same answer years ago. I've only stumbled on it in recent years. We're all on a voyage of self-discovery when we move into any of the art fields. That sounds awfully fancy, but I can't see it any other way. In a lifetime of writing, now, since I was 12, I've been moving into various parts of my subconscious. Growing up I was fascinated by the Oz books, by Flash Gordon and Buck Rogers and Fu Manchu. The Chicago World's Fair was a marvelous experience for me. As I said, I was fascinated by all the vital, imaginative stuff of which childhood is compounded. In my work these memories emerge symbolically as in *The Illustrated Man*, or as, for instance, in the carnival in *Something Wicked This Way Comes*.

At the same time I've been purging myself of my personal nightmares. I bring them out in the open and have my own private Grand Guignol on paper. For instance, in my youth I was afraid of the dark and I've written about this in a little book for children I call *Switch on the Night*. I seem naturally to work in the area of fantasy, weird fantasy, and in science fiction, another kind of fantasy.

What is the secret to the universal response your type of science fiction draws?
That's a big question. Every field of art has its good and bad practitioners. I guess that science fiction is in the mainstream of world literature. It shares in the universal-

---

Ray Bradbury is a 69-year-old writer who put a hot dog stand on Mars. And got away with it. His renderings of space travel and robots are ludicrous. His backgrounds are implausible, his plots immature.

And readers love him.

He'd established his reputation well before this 1967 interview with works such as The Martian Chronicles, Something Wicked This Way Comes, Dandelion Wine, Fahrenheit 451, *and hundreds of short stories. The revelation of this interview comes not from the how and why of that reputation (although it is touched on), but in Bradbury's explanation that his "effortless" prose comes only through unyielding discipline and "terrifying" dredging of memories. Imagination—and Martian hot dog stands—are hard work.*

ity of the mainstream. Since we live in a science fiction culture, I write about it in science fiction terms.

But your writing seems apart from the field because it concentrates more on character and emotion than "science." And because of your grace in handling both. For instance, sensuality is everywhere in your writing—the descriptions of nature in Dandelion Wine, *the boyish vitality in* Something Wicked This Way Comes— *but nowhere do you mention, outright, sex.*

I'm bored limp—I was going to say "bored stiff," but somehow that doesn't seem appropriate—I'm bored limp by writers who think that by describing a thing realistically, they've described it. I'm not interested in the facts, the machinery, the mechanics. I'm interested in the interpretation of those facts.

When I went out to Cal Tech to lecture to all those bright, marvelous 18- and 19-year-old boys, I thought they'd crucify or at least pillory me because I'm no scientist and I know it. Science is a frame of reference in my stories, a launching pad for the imagination. But I was delightfully surprised. The boys said, "All right now, we have the facts. You, the moralist, you, the fourth-rate philosopher, tell us what to do about them."

Regardless of what tense I write in, past, present or future, to me that miracle of miraculous man upon a miraculous planet remains constant. It is only in the particulars of man's situation that changes occur. My stories are about those particulars and those changes.

What's true in science is true in the sexual field. I'm interested in what sex does to us as people. This is the fire at which we all warm our hands. My interest is in using my knowledge about sex creatively to help people understand themselves and each other. Why is it, for instance, that people stay together long after they have discovered they are destroying each other? Quite often, even with intelligent people, the truth is that the sexual satisfaction they derive from the relationship makes them willing to put up with the terror and denigration of it. Now here's a truth I'm willing to investigate. But it has little to do with the raw facts as they are presented in the average novel. I'd rather approach the mystery on another level and nail it down if I can.

You put death at the base of your stories in the same way, especially in Something Wicked This Way Comes. We all have in the background of the family one middle-aging Uncle who ran off to Alaska with a blonde. Now, my experience has taught me that sex has very little to do with such seemingly ridiculous and injurious acts. Death has everything to do with it. Death is saying, "Time is short; time is rushing down the glass. Enjoy! Be young again!" Not that the fabled Uncle wanted to be perverse, but he is frightened by the descending torrent of time. In the novel *Something Wicked This Way Comes,* the old man confronts Death squarely, and when

offered the choice between ugly dissolution and beautiful perversity, refuses both. Here is a man who had learned to grow old gracefully.

But I've noticed a distinct unwillingness in your stories to let people grow old and die. In Dandelion Wine, *Helen Loomis talks regretfully about youth and old age in terms of the dragon eating up the swan.*

This is strange to say, but one of the most marvelous occurrences for me recently was the death of Ian Fleming. His dying words were, "Oh, it was all such a lark." That's just what I wanted him to say. He couldn't have done better. He lived life to the hilt. The zest was still in him, even at the end. When I write about the death of my friends, I am not only exorcising my own nightmares, I am trying to help the reader find his own resolution of his nightmares or, at least, the capacity to grapple with them without being beaten by them.

I have no huge nostalgia based on a romantic image of the past. Childhood is a horror for most of us ... we wouldn't want to live it over if we had the chance.

Yet, you started writing in that "horror" period—prodigiously at the age of 12 in pencil on brown wrapping paper. Do you still write in longhand?

No, my handwriting is so dreadful my daughters weep when I visit at school on open house night and sign my name. At the age of 14 I learned to type and by now I've grown to be a very fast typist.

Do you write every day?

Every day of my life except weekends, which are for the family: my wife and my four lovely daughters.

Could you describe a typical day, your process of writing?

I do a first draft as passionately and as quickly as I can. I believe a story is only valid when it is immediate and passionate; when it dances out of your subconscious. If you interfere in any way, you destroy it. There's no difference between a short story and life. Surprise is where creativity comes. Allow your subconscious to come out into the light and say what it has to say. Let your characters have their way. Let your secret life be lived. Then at your leisure, in the succeeding weeks, months or years, you let the story cool off and then, instead of rewriting, you relive it. If you try to rewrite, which is a cold exercise, you'll wind up with all kinds of Band-aids on your story, which people can see. It's very important that a story have a skin around it just as we have a skin. A story must have the same sort of life we have though it is shorter. It has this fantastic entity to itself, a need to run to its end and you just have to let it go.

Any advice on coaxing the stories to dance out of the subconscious?

You just get . . . I say "you," I mean "I" . . . I get tremendously excited. I remember I read a line once in a poem by Robert Hillyer, or the time I read a line in an essay by Aldous Huxley and then sprang immediately to my typewriter and wrote a short story. Or it may be that I'll hear someone say something and I'll think, "yes, how fascinating." Or I'll sit down at my typewriter and try word association. I'll type the first two words that come into my head, such as "The Veldt" or "The Dwarf." Then I say to my subconscious, "All right, you're on your own. I believe in you implicitly. I don't doubt you for a moment. Now, subconscious, tell me everything you have saved up over the years that I don't know about dwarfs. Let me bring on some characters. I'll bring on one to speak for the subject of dwarfs and one to speak against the subject of dwarfs and out of this interchange let's see what kind of life experience we get." My subconscious takes over and says, "Here's my delight," and an hour or two later the story is finished.

> *You let the story cool off and then, instead of rewriting, you relive it.*

Hemingway said that he never liked to discuss his work before he had written it. How do you feel about that?
That's very important. Writing is like sex. You have to save your love for the love object. If you go around spouting about your idea, when it comes time to go to bed with that idea, there'll be no "charge" left. You can't father children that way.

Yet you often give lectures to young writers and students.
I'm the purest kind of hambone there is. In my teens I did a great deal of amateur playacting and this is still a frustrated part of my psyche. Two or three times a month I go out and fling my arms around and jump up and down and yell at the kids and have a great time. It's the same sort of process you go through with a short story. The students question you. They force you to explain yourself. And, resultantly, from hearing yourself talk, from listening to the surprises leap off your tongue, you develop your personal philosophy over the years. By lecturing I fill out the other half of my creative life. Writing is a living process, dynamic. Lecturing is an explaining process, analytical.

Do you feel there were any writers who influenced your work?
Yes, I've made up a kind of genealogy, a family tree. I often think of Robert Frost as my wonderful grandfather and Willa Cather as my grandmother. Eudora Welty is an eccentric cousin of mine and Edgar Rice Burroughs might even be my father. Jules Verne I remember as a marvelous Uncle who used to bring me fabulous toys that ran underwater and through the skies and off to the far planets. Somewhere along the line John Steinbeck is my older brother and Ernest Hemingway a still older brother than that. William Faulkner is a very wise old second uncle. A teacher would be Aldous Huxley. Going way back in the genealogy would be fairy tales, which I loved from the age of three on. I read all the Oz books religiously. Buck Rogers had a tremendous influence. I have one of the few complete collections of "Prince Valiant" in the country, which I've put away over the last 27 years.

You see I'm naming all my influences. If you ask me, and I hope you will, I think this is one of the troubles with the intellectual life in this country. We are damn snobs and I'm tired of it and I would put it down. "Peanuts" to me is a wonderful experience. Ian Fleming was a good writer and served our needs at a certain level very well. Sax Rohmer's *Fu Manchu* is great fun, great fun. Too often the intellectual is unpopular in this world because he's a spoil sport. Wide tastes, foolish and lovely and happy and silly tastes make the complete human and the complete writer. I feel sorry for the silly intellectuals who came upon Pop Art late. Most of us were fortunate enough never to have left it behind, so we don't have to discover or rediscover what we always knew and enjoyed.

You wrote, "Success is a continuing process. Failure is a stoppage. The man who keeps moving and working does not fail."
The average young person you meet today seems to have the motto, "If at first you don't succeed, stop right there." They want to start at the top of their profession and not to learn their art on the way up. That way they miss all the fun. If you write a hundred short stories and they're all bad, that doesn't mean you've failed. You fail only if you stop writing. I've written about 2,000 short stories; I've only published about 300 and I feel I'm still learning. Any man who keeps working is not a failure. He may not be a great writer, but if he applies the old-fashioned virtues of hard, constant labor, he'll eventually make some kind of career for himself as a writer.

Isn't this hard to do for most people? The rent has to be paid. You have to do mundane things like eat. In your teens you sold newspapers and between editions you wrote, but didn't you have to give up most of the things people feel they have to have?

Depends on what you have to have.

You can get along on a very small amount of money. You can give up clothes. You can give up movies and theater. You can eat Kraft Dinner every day of your life. I'm a student of Kraft Dinner. I'm a specialist in Campbell's Tomato Soup. You can go to the market today and for a few cents you can have a banquet. I still love Campbell's Tomato Soup. This is a free plug for them and I hope they send me a free can of soup. I'm the cheapest freeloader in the history of mankind. My idea of a real meal is to sit down with a can of tomato soup, a couple glasses of milk and a half a pound of crackers. I went through a record of expenses I kept during my first year of marriage. At that time I was making about $30 a week writing and my wife was making 35 at a job to support us so I could get my writing done. We'd go down to Ocean Park at night and have a couple of hot dogs and a Coke. We'd go through the penny arcade and for 32 cents we'd have a magnificent evening. If you have someone who cares about you, it's very easy to give up things. If you're alone, you buy things to compensate for your loneliness.

Money is not important. The material things are not important. Getting the work done beautifully and proudly is important. If you do that, strangely enough, the money will come as a just reward for work beautifully done. A tape recorder, an automobile, they don't really belong to you. What really belongs to you? Yourself, you. That's all you'll ever have. I am ruthless with anyone around me who doesn't think or create always at the top of his form.

Yet only about 1 percent of all writers make a living at it.

I'm sure the percentage is higher. There are more science fiction titles in print today than ever before. There are more paperbacks. TV is a place a writer can work once or twice a year to pay the mortgage and then go on to write that short story or that novel if he chooses. Most, however, will not so choose and will sell out and be lost forever.

You work in TV yourself, don't you?

Generally once a year. You see that's the trouble with many writers, they can't stop at once or twice. The money looks too good to them so they keep on, but a writer isn't remembered for TV or films. He's remembered

If you write a hundred short stories and they're all bad, that doesn't mean you've failed. You fail only if you stop writing.

for his play or his short story or his novel.

You've also worked in motion pictures—you authored the screenplay for John Huston's production of Moby Dick, *and you are now writing a screenplay from your novel* The Martian Chronicles. *Also, Francois Truffaut has done a cinematic treatment of your novel* Fahrenheit 451. *Do you find that screenwriting demands a different kind of talent than, say, fiction or playwriting?*

If I were to describe writing novels or short stories, I'd say: "The word is everything'; writing for the stage: "word plus action would be true; and when you write for the screen: "The less said the better." Poetry and motion pictures are closer together than novel and motion pictures because a good poem is automatically symbolic. It seizes a moment of time and freezes it in images. That's what films do. In writing *The Martian Chronicles* for film, I'm trying to write a silent picture as much as possible.

In adapting your short stories into plays as you've done for your production, The World of Ray Bradbury, *did you find yourself in the position of a novice having to start all over again in a new medium?*

Before I answer your somewhat complicated question, let me go back a few years to the time I was collaborating with Charles Laughton on several projects (one, a science fiction opera), which were stillborn. During that time I'd go over to his place and swim in the pool or sit around listening to one of the great theatrical children of our time quote Shakespeare and Shaw. He'd float majestically around the pool and try out his ideas on me. When he was preparing to do Lear at Stratford, he'd say, "Now this is the way I see Lear." I was his audience of one whom he was corrupting in the right way. Well, listening to him talk about Moliere and Jonson and other great writers, I learned a new respect for language. This is a long way round to your question, but I took only the concept from the short stories as originally written and created new characters and situations suitable to stage action.

I learned what every playwright must learn—to play off the minds of the audience. They become the character, they become the setting, they become involved directly in the situation. Their imaginations are put to work. This is a use of language I had begun to understand by listening to my friend Charles Laughton, and which I was able to put into practice in the writing of these one-act plays. It seems to be working. Even though the plays are set in a fantastic world of the future, the audience realizes I'm talking directly to and about them. I'm talking about present condition carried to the reductio ad absurdum of tomorrow morning.

Let us say that you were universally acclaimed and had received every prize and every recognition a writer could hope for. Would you still write?
Oh yes. The early problems of a writer are nothing compared to the later problems. It's not so much accepting rejection, getting rejection slips, but the big problem is rejecting acceptance. In the last seven years I've turned down 15 TV series offers I could have had on my own. I choose to stay free and float easily and keep an eye on myself. A writer must have the firm, hard ability to turn his eye inward upon himself. You write because it's an adventure to watch it come out of your hands. The publicity is pleasant, but it never belongs to you. You're never quite convinced the name on that printed page is you. Again you're tuned back on your hidden self, aren't you? That's all you'll ever have. One's own thoughts, these are the most important things. Not the thoughts of others, because you'll never understand them. You'll never understand another writer. You'll never understand your wife or your children or your best friends. You may try to but you can only understand them through yourself. You see a lot of people around who are trying to understand other

people, to find out what makes them tick. But they are looking away from the true object in their creativity. They should ask, "What makes me tick?" They, not others, are the true object.

Is that why you write? To understand yourself?
I know this now. I didn't know then.

Do you think a writer's object changes as he goes along? He starts out writing for one reason and continues for others?
I think he starts out with mistaken concepts and then he falls into the prime causes as he writes. He digs those out of the subconscious. He nails himself to the cross of his typewriter. He must crucify himself in order to discover himself.

This is a tough one, but when the tumult and the shouting die, what would you like for your epitaph?
I would like it to read, and it's going to take a lot of chiselling, it's going to take a big stone, but it should read: Here lies a teller of tales. If he had lived ten centuries ago, you would have walked down a street in old Baghdad or in some Middle Eastern city and there among the menders of copper and the shapers of clay turned into a Street of the Story Tellers and found him seated there among the tellers of tales who have existed since men came out of the caves. This is a proud heritage. This was his.

BY JOHN KERN

ERICA JONG

*My generation of young female writers discovered that
we could dictate the form and content of our own fiction.*

Erica Jong burst upon the literary scene during the early seventies, a period of political and social fragmentation. Her first novel, *Fear of Flying*, was immediately embraced as the bible of the burgeoning women's movement. A satirical, sexually explicit work, it electrified the public, polarized the critics and garnered some impressive praise. John Updike, writing in *The New Yorker*, spoke of the novel's "sexual frankness that belongs to, and hilariously extends, the tradition of *The Catcher in the Rye* and *Portnoy's Complaint*. It has class and sass, brightness and bite." Nora Sayre added: "A magnificent novel. Erica Jong has written about women in a completely new way."

The overwhelming success of *Fear of Flying*, however, turned out to be a mixed blessing. Although it gave Jong financial security, it also produced a backlash against her next novel, *How to Save Your Own Life*. The confessional style of her first two works gave reviewers an inviting target. "I have been bedeviled by deliberately hostile critics," she stated bitterly after the publication of her second book. "My situation as a writer has never been one of sheer acceptance."

In spite of her contentious beginnings, the next few years saw Jong's life come full circle. After weathering a second divorce and a protracted lawsuit with Columbia Pictures over the film rights to *Fear of Flying*, she remarried, settled in the Connecticut suburbs and gave birth to her first child. "My work now shows a much more reflective mood," she says. "It is the product of a person who has come to terms with existence and who has reached a certain maturity."

Jong's contentment is certainly reflected in the pages of *Fanny: Being the True History of the Adventures of Fanny Hackabout-Jones*. Unlike her first two books, *Fanny* is a joyously entertaining romp through the Fieldingesque world of eighteenth-century England. Written in the form of a book of advice from a mother to her daughter, the novel chronicles Fanny's rollicking adventures as a ravished orphan, witch, highway robber, whore, loving mother, kept woman and famous pirate. "When I was younger, I couldn't even conceive of sitting still long enough to write a novel," Jong says with a chuckle. "If someone had told me when I was 22 that I would someday write a 500-page book set in eighteenth-century England, I would have thought that they were crazy. I really think *Fanny* is the best book I have ever written."

Yet, Jong didn't start her career as a novelist. Throughout the late sixties and early seventies, Jong had an uncommonly successful career as a poet, and then established the themes that would later dominate her fiction. Long before the publication of her first novel, her poetry expanded the boundaries of feminist literature and, in the words of Anthony Burgess, explored the "pains and occasional elations of the Modern American Female."

The first thing I noticed as I approached Jong's home in Weston, Connecticut, was a brown Mercedes coupe in the driveway with a license plate that read *WING-IT*. Apart from this reference to Isadora Wing, the heroine of Jong's first two novels, nothing about the staid

After the smoke of the seventies had cleared, Erica Jong's startling first novel had sold more than 6 million copies in 20 countries, and given voice to a whole generation of women. In some ways, Jong has never been able to leave Fear of Flying *behind. Questions about that novel haunt all her interviews. In this 1981 interview, the 39-year-old author had just completed* Fanny, *(which would be followed a year later by the book mentioned as being in-progress,* Witches*), and was beginning to settle back into a comfortably distanced perspective on how* Flying *had affected both the public and her life.*

environs indicates that it is the residence of a famous writer. Though perched on the side of an isolated cliff overlooking the Saugatuck river valley, the inside of Jong's home is the epitome of domestic tranquillity. Her daughter's toys and yellow canvas playhouse dominate one corner of the high-ceilinged living room. At any given moment, her husband, writer Jonathan Fast, would stop by from his office above the garage to discuss babysitting schedules and other household arrangements.

Fast is the son of author Howard Fast, and his books include *The Inner Circle* and *Mortal Gods*. Both Fast and Jong were born and raised in New York City, but came to Connecticut because of their fondness for country living, which they developed while living in California for a time. Their mutual profession gave them the ability to live wherever they wanted, so they looked for houses across the country—from Lake Tahoe to Key West—until a friend introduced them to their western-style house.

Amidst this well-ordered backdrop, Jong curled up on her couch with a glass of white wine and talked in calm, almost blissful tones. Considering her reputation as a novelist, both the familial setting and her serene manner came as something of a surprise. So it is appropriate that our first topic of discussion was surprises.

Were you surprised that Fear of Flying *turned into such a* cause célèbre?
Totally. Before the book was published, everyone kept telling me that first novels never sell. They further discouraged me by saying that a literary novel about a Barnard girl would never make it. I had to fight to convince my publishers that it was commercial. Sometime later, after it had sold 6 million copies, everyone then accused me of adding the sex to make it sell. It was a very sobering experience to go through and it made me very philosophical about the nature of success.

What is your philosophy of success? Do you consider yourself successful?
Well, I know that the outside world considers me a successful person. I would say that a successful person is someone who is completely happy with both work and personal life. But I don't think anyone fits that definition. I mean nobody except an idiot is completely happy with all their personal relationships and work.

I have no regrets about what I've done with my life. I don't regard writing as just a trade, but really as a calling. I feel that I was to be a writer, and I consider myself a success in having found the thing that I was put on this earth to do. But I would be a fool if I thought that I had succeeded in every area of my life.

How have you changed in the past ten years? Has success changed you?
I'm much less neurotic and my life is much more together. In fact, at the risk of sounding terribly arrogant, I will say that I am one of the few people I know who hasn't been ruined by success. I will admit that I was caught up in the confusion created by my own celebrity for about a year or so after *Fear of Flying*. But the question is, How do you handle it when that intensive period of celebrity is finished? I think that you have to rededicate yourself to your writing and work more fervently than ever before.

The fact that the book sold 6 million copies must have eliminated any fears you may have had about being able to reach an audience. After a success of that magnitude, what fears remain?
A success like *Fear of Flying* creates a marvelous sense of freedom, and there is always a great joy in making money for your work. But it is also very frustrating because a lot of people who tell me that they love the book have never heard of my poetry. The reputation of a notorious novel tends to dwarf everything else. Most people think of me only as the author of *Fear of Flying*, but I hope that will change with my latest novel. It's awful to feel that a book you wrote when you were 28 is the one with which you'll be buried.

Henry Miller once said that Fear of Flying *was the female counterpart to his* Tropic of Cancer. *Do you think that is true?*
The New York Times obituary described Henry as an "artesian" writer, which I thought was a very felicitous phrase. In that respect, I think that the statement is true. I consider myself to be a natural writer in the sense that everything surfaces from the unconscious. Henry was right in comparing *Fear of Flying* to *Tropic of Cancer* in that both books throw away literary inhibitions. I was writing from the gut about female fantasies in the same way that he was writing about male fantasies.

You must remember that I grew up in a time when most important American novels were written by men. Most distinguished women writers tended to write in male-dominated prose. They did not write books that only a woman could have written. My generation of young female writers discovered its own character and found that we could dictate the form and content of our own fiction. It was given to my generation to come along and show that we had sexual feelings. It was given to my generation to assert that territory of honesty which had long ago been established by men.

When you were working on the book, were you ever worried that it might be dismissed as pornographic?
No. When I was writing *Fear of Flying*, I was aware that I was working in a literary tradition. I have a good education and nearly did a Ph.D. in English literature. I knew that what I was writing was not any more sexual than what D.H. Lawrence did in *Lady Chatterly's Lover* or Philip Roth did in *Portnoy's Complaint*. I did not think

of sex in my book as dirty. I sensed that people might be shocked because it was written by a woman. But I had no idea what an enormous double standard they had—that what was pornographic for a woman writer was literature for a man. I was quite astonished when I saw what Middle America thought of *Fear of Flying*. I really didn't think the world was that reactionary.

You must have received some interesting mail after Fear of Flying *was published.*
Oh God, I could publish a book of the mail alone. I received all kinds of grateful letters from women who said that I had freed their sexuality and made them feel less lonely. Many men even wrote that I had helped them to better understand women. However, I also got the other type of mail. I would get requests for soiled underwear and liaisons at the local motel. A number of the letters I received were full of kinky sex and anti-Semitism. But I think that women who write about sex get a different type of response than men. There is a tendency on the part of a certain type of naive reader to assume that an author who has written this type of book is available for one-night stands.

Your second novel, How to Save Your Own Life, *was subject to some pretty savage notices. It almost appeared as if the critics were reviewing you instead of your book. Was it a great disappointment?*
When you have a first novel that sells 6 million copies, anything you do after it has to be a disappointment. You set a standard that you cannot compete with, and the pressure it puts on you is almost unreal. So, if your next book "only" sells 2 million copies, everyone thinks of it as failure.

I went through a difficult period. I was coming off a notorious bestseller which wasn't just a blockbuster like *The Thorn Birds*. It was a book that signaled a switch in the female consciousness and encouraged women to change their lives. It was a book that a lot of men and reactionary women could blame for something that was happening in America that they didn't like. There was a great deal of pent-up anger about the new narcissism and women's rights, and it was all taken out on *How to Save Your Own Life*.

Despite my brassy exterior, I am a pretty vulnerable person, and it was a very painful experience. I could

scarcely believe all of the hate and personal character assassination that were in the reviews. But I lived through it, and it turned out to be very strengthening.

I think that I receive a lot of hostile notices because I have been held responsible for the emergence of women and female sexuality. Of course, it's not true. I only wish I were responsible; it would be a great honor. In any case, my work has been identified with women demanding rights in the bedroom, and I think that many men and women had a lot of mixed feelings about that and it led them to attack my work.

Our society is still very uncomfortable with the idea of successful women. Underneath all of the lip service this country gives to the women's movement, I believe that it is still very sexist. So, if a woman is conspicuous and writes about sex and makes a lot of money, both men and women tend to be very hostile toward her.

Do you have any plans to turn Isadora's adventures into a trilogy?
I'm not sure. I have in the back of my mind an idea for a book about Isadora at 40 or Isadora in Connecticut, but it seems kind of shticky. Besides, when a book becomes that famous, you tend to get very self-conscious. I think that my creativity would be inhibited. Isadora is no longer just a character in a novel, but has become a symbol of a million things. I would feel that I would have to live up not only to what I think Isadora is, but to what she has become in the public mind. In any case, I wrote *Fear of Flying* ten years ago, and my notions of a novel were very different from what they are now.

When I first began writing, it was much more instinctive. Now, my work is much more thought out. I recognize the importance of a strong storyline in a way that I didn't before. The story is the armature of the novel. You can't have a good novel without a good story. You must have that frame to build the novel around.

*You spent four years writing your latest novel—*Fanny. *After investing so much time and emotion in a book, how would you have coped with it if it had failed instead of becoming a bestseller?*
I always expect my work to fail. It's almost a protective magic that I use: expecting the worst in order to ensure success. I know how fickle the writing profession can be. I would be very disappointed, but I don't think it would

> *When a book becomes that famous you tend to get very self-conscious. Isadora is no longer just a character in a novel, but has become a symbol of a million things.*

change the direction of my life. The nature of being an artist is to have hits and flops. I could have avoided all of those risks by becoming a college professor. But I certainly would have avoided all of the wonderful things that have happened, too.

What inspired you to write a story set in eighteenth-century England?
I have always loved eighteenth-century English literature and had studied it in college. I promised myself 15 years ago that I would write a Fieldingesque novel set in that period. I knew that it would take a lot of time and research and that it would have to be done at a period in my life when I was calm and financially secure enough not to have to worry about turning out a novel every year. The idea for the book really started with the simple question, What if Tom Jones had been a woman? Given all of the problems that women faced in that era, I thought it was a delicious idea that presented limitless opportunities.

Also, I thought that *Fanny* would be a wonderful thing to try after being known for contemporary fiction. It enables you to do a historical recreation of a period and make a whole different set of satirical points. But beyond that, if you set a novel in 1740, it gives you a great opportunity to show how much has changed for women and, in turn, how little. After all, the real purpose of the historical novel is to satirize current society through the lens of the past. I have long felt that the historical novelist had missed a great opportunity to write the ultimate feminist novel.

Despite all of the carriages and petticoats, *Fanny* is the most radical book I have written. Unlike Isadora, who is always in pain and conflict, Fanny is a true heroine. She gave me an opportunity to show what women can be at their boldest, and that is something I really enjoyed.

Did you find the research difficult?
I love doing research. It was the best part of working on the book. A novel like *Fanny* could never have been written without the patience of a number of librarians. The ones in Connecticut were especially helpful to me. I went over to the Beinecke Rare Book and Manuscript Library at Yale and used every other library from the Pequot to Columbia University. I even went down to the South Street Seaport Museum in New York City and studied all of the wonderful models of the sailing ships of that period.

The book is written in the style of an eighteenth-century novel. Do you find it difficult to write in that style?

When I first started, I didn't think that I could write a whole novel in that style. But once I had completed 50 pages, I found that I could not write in any other way. I felt like I was in a trance. I started writing letters to my friends and business associates in eighteenth-century English. I even had to refuse all magazine assignments because I couldn't write in my normal style. It lasted for almost four years. I invented a voice that had the flavor of eighteenth-century England but was really contemporary. *Fanny* is a modern novel in that it moves very fast. It is not paced like Fielding's books, which were meant for a time when people had hours and hours to loll around their country homes.

> *When I sit down at my writing desk, time seems to vanish. I think it's a wonderful way to spend one's life.*

Were you apprehensive about fictionalizing historical characters like Alexander Pope and Jonathan Swift?
I was very apprehensive. But I think people understand that *Fanny* is a novel and that Pope and Swift are introduced as comical characters. You know, even biographers don't agree on what they were really like. I think that a novelist, as well as a biographer, has a right to take a position. Anyway, I think it is clear that I was being ironic with the characters. My heroine is, of course, partially a creature of wish fulfillment. She is very heroic and much braver than I am. But I think that she is a true depiction of what it was like to be a woman 250 years ago.

Still, you must admit that a character as headstrong and independent as Fanny is not your typical eighteenth-century woman.
She is a very modern wench in eighteenth-century dress. But if you read the lives of some of the women of that period, you will discover that there were many who were like her. In the afterword of my book, I write that the people we most enjoy reading about in history are the ones who transcend their own time. If you read some of the diaries of the women of that era, you will see that they did transcend their own time. Women like Mary Wortley Montagu and the pirate queen Anne Bonny were pretty amazing.

Fanny is much more lighthearted and humorous than either of your two previous books. Would you say that this is more a reflection of the material or of where you are in your life?
Well, you find me at a pretty good time in my life. I am happier than when I wrote either *Fear of Flying* or *How*

to *Save Your Own Life*, which is a very dreary book about a marriage coming apart. So, maybe that's why *Fanny* is so humorous.

I have long felt that there is too little humor in contemporary fiction. The number of women who have written funny books about the condition of women can be counted on the fingers of one hand. I feel that almost anyone can write a droopy, depressing novel, but I am one of the few women who can write a truly funny book about my own sex. I think that the humorous vision of life gives you a philosophy that the wimpy, whiney outlook doesn't permit.

You have also published four books of poetry. How do you think your poetry has changed over the years?
I think that it has become much more contemplative and philosophical. I think that I have always had that bent, but I feel that it is becoming much more apparent. I am older, and I think that in a funny way, as you age, you become much more yourself—you become the person you were meant to be. But I think that I have always had a strong philosophical bent.

The mood of your latest collection, At the Edge of the Body, *seems to be very reflective.*
Yes. I was thinking specifically of that book of poetry. But I am also thinking of the new book that I'm finishing, which is about witches. It is written partly in poetry and partly in prose. It is a beautifully illustrated art book with a short text and will be out sometime next fall.

How long does it generally take you to write a poem?
I usually compose it at one sitting, but then I may revise it. Sometimes they are written extremely fast—often as quickly as a half-hour. But then you may go on working and polishing it for months and months until you get it right.

Where do you get your inspiration for your poetry?
The inspiration can come from a conversation or something in nature or reading something in a newspaper. It's usually an inner thing that is triggered by an outer event. Sometimes you don't even know what outer event has triggered it. Sometimes it's just a feeling. Sometimes the line sort of drops down into your pen as if automatically or like a dream.

What advice would you give to someone who wanted to become a poet?
I would tell them to read it constantly, go to poetry readings, and buy new books of poetry and try to understand which ones are good and which ones are bad. I would also advise them to write all of the time and to keep a notebook with ideas and lines for poems. They should even keep a dream notebook for dreams that could turn into poems.

What are the differences in discipline between writing poetry and prose?
They are very different, and they don't conflict with each other. There is a sense that poetry comes from the intuitive part of the brain. It is much more pleasurable and euphoric than writing a novel. You feel that you are tapping the source of unconscious creativity. Nearly every poet that you talk to will tell you that it is, in a sense, an automatic process.

Writing a novel is a much more conscious thing. It's a daily job. You go to your desk at nine in the morning and work until three or four. I would say that one day out of ten you feel euphoric and the words just fly off of your fingers. The other nine days you wonder how the hell you are going to move your heroine from one place to another and what adventures will take place along the way. You find that a good part of your day is taken up inventing and devising and that most of the time you don't think it is any good.

I gather that you find the writing process laborious.
For the most part. But the thrill of writing is what emerges from the process. For instance, you suddenly realize how someone like Fanny is related to the other characters in your fable and it often shocks and surprises you. I think that the joy of writing a novel is the self-exploration that emerges and also that wonderful feeling of playing God with the characters. When I sit down at my writing desk, time seems to vanish. I think that it's a wonderful way to spend one's life.

Is it important for a writer to have a rigid work schedule?
I think the most important thing for a writer is to be locked in a study. And I am a rather serious writer. I usually write in my office on the third floor of the house. I write every day from about nine in the morning to one in the afternoon. I set myself to the task of writing ten pages a day in longhand, which comes out to about five typewritten pages. The rest of the day I spend talking on the phone with my publishers, promoting my books and answering my mail.

You recently became a mother for the first time. Have you been able to reconcile that part of your life with your writing?
Becoming a mother has really changed my life and made me much more mellow. I worked on *Fanny* straight through my pregnancy. I went back to work five days after having a Caesarean and finished it between nursing. Balancing the two was exhausting, but having a baby hardly interferes with the creative process.

Has living with another writer also changed your life?
It's great and it's terrible. What's great is that you both have a great deal of flexibility. In our case, both parents

can be involved in the child-rearing and the home. It's a lot easier for each of us to get our work done, especially when we have deadlines. What's terrible is that you tend to get very stir-crazy and house-bound since you have your home and office in the same place.

What have you and your husband been able to learn from each other as writers?
My relationship with Jon has gone through many phases. The first few months were absolutely euphoric. But I think we both have discovered that we are different people. Jon has a marvelous sense of humor that puts everything into perspective. When I'm going off the deep end, he will crack a joke that makes it absolutely clear to me that all the things I'm worried about don't really matter all that much.

We read each other's works in 50- or 100-page blocks and then offer criticisms. We both believe in a "kind but honest" approach. When Jonathan finishes something of mine that he doesn't like, he usually says, "It's not your best work." When he tells me that, I know it's just terrible.

What are you working on now?
I am working on the book about witches I mentioned, and I am working on a new novel that I don't want to talk about lest I jinx it. I always start several books between books.

How does that work?
I usually take a year of making false starts between books. I start one book and then shelve it and then start another. I am never really sure which one is the false start and which one will turn out to be the one that I will want to write. Usually the false starts end up getting absorbed in the manuscript of the real book.

Is there a common theme that runs through all of your work?
The common theme that runs through all of my work is the quest for self-knowledge. A poet friend of mine named Michael Benedikt, who used to teach my poems at Sarah Lawrence, said that what amazed him was how often I used the verbs "to learn" and "to teach." My work seems to be about using life as the learning process. In my poem "The Buddha in the Womb," I wrote, "Flesh is merely a lesson/We learn it and pass on." In a way that is my answer to those people who say that I write too much about the flesh. I think that could be my epitaph.

BY CHRISTOPHER MEEKS

LAWRENCE & LEE

Let the critics or the audience talk about the theme.
You write the play because you are possessed.

About as far from Broadway as the United States land mass permits live two of the more active playwrights the New York stages serve up: Jerome Lawrence and Robert E. Lee. For more than 43 years, they have been looking behind the paint of America and showing it for what it is. From the hilarious *Auntie Mame* and its musical version, to the provoking *The Night Thoreau Spent in Jail*, the two writers have always punctured pomposity. They have written 20 major plays, including the classic *Inherit the Wind*.

Jerome Lawrence, a solid man with a ready smile and thick, white hair, grew up in Cleveland and was graduated from Ohio State University. Robert E. Lee, a lean gentleman who never fought in the Civil War and whose face betrays a kind of Buster Keaton whimsy, was born 30 miles from Cleveland on the shores of Lake Erie.

Lawrence and Lee never met in Ohio. It was in New York, a month after Pearl Harbor. Shortly thereafter, they formed a partnership ("We really don't like the word *collaborator*. It's what they called quislings in Norway and pro-Nazis in France in World War II. It's much better to refer to writing *teams*.")

By a fluke, eight of their early works aired the same week; every major dramatic program that week presented a Lawrence and Lee radio play, and a *Variety* headline proclaimed, "Lawrence and Lee Take Over Radio."

Appointed expert consultants to the Secretary of War during World War II, the partners wrote radio plays for the armed forces. In the mid-20s, Lawrence and Lee became two of the founders of the Armed Forces Radio Service. Their work included writing and directing the broadcasts for D-Day, V-E Day and V-J Day.

After the war, they continued to concentrate on radio plays, but also began to write stage plays. Their first, *Look, Ma, I'm Dancin'!*, premiered at the Adelphi Theatre in New York City on Jan. 29, 1948. It was a success.

Their second effort had its roots in Sen. Joseph Mc-Carthy's witch hunt, which held the country in a panic. In response, they wrote *Inherit the Wind*. No one would produce it. The play lay in a drawer for a year until a scout for Margo Jones, a high-spirited Dallas theater producer, asked to see it. Jones produced the play, the Dallas critics were spellbound, and all the New York producers wanted to see the manuscript again. The play ran three years on Broadway, and has since been translated and performed in 31 languages. For the past 20 years, not a night has gone by that *Inherit the Wind* hasn't played somewhere in the world.

Lawrence and Lee have since written another 28 full-length stage plays, several short plays, nine motion picture scripts, eight television specials, hundreds of radio and TV plays, 50 magazine articles and four books. Each has produced and directed many productions—their work as well as others—and taught playwriting at several major universities. Lawrence now conducts a workshop in the Professional Writing Program at the University of Southern California; Lee is an adjunct professor at UCLA.

Their homes reflect their individual personalities.

Lee—or was it Lawrence—wondered sometime during this interview why more playwrights don't work together: "You're in a partnership with your reader—and your audience, your listener, your viewer. I can't understand why there are not more partnerships among writers. There's a fierce and often self-destructive independence about playwrights. They want to swim the Atlantic alone."

Even a quick read through this 1986 interview will reveal why there aren't more partnerships—or at least partnerships this successful: few people complement each other this well, both in the rapid-fire dialogue of ideas, guesses, jokes and asides, and in the more serious purpose of their partnership—to answer one question: "What bugs you?"

Lawrence's chalet-like house, "Walden West," hugs a mountain in Malibu and overlooks the Pacific. Inside, the high-beamed ceiling protects walls of books. On the walls without bookshelves hang original posters and Hirschfeld drawings of Lawrence and Lee plays. On the bottom floor is Lawrence's office, also studded with books; the desk is a tower of papers and paperclips. The Selectric and chair are the two free areas. "Death to Cliches" is tacked on the wall, and nearby is a headset, the thin-wire type that operators and airline pilots wear, used when Lawrence and Lee work by phone.

On the other side of the mountains, in Encino, live Robert E. Lee and his actress wife, Janet. (A frequent "voice" in cartoons, Janet is best known as the voice of Judy Jetson and as radio's Corliss Archer.) Lee's office looks out on a steep terrace of lush green ivy. His desk, almost as chaotic as his partner's, holds fewer papers. Much of his daily work is done on eight-inch floppy disks, made by his "ancient" five-year-old computer. His living room, too, is lined with books, posters and Hirschfelds. Most of the following interview was conducted there.

You once said, Bob, that you enjoyed teaching new playwrights, particularly undergraduates. Why?
LEE: I think there's a marvelous plasticity to people who are approaching writing seriously for the first time. You hear them say: "Wow! You can do this, you can do that, you can play God. You can create these characters and make them do what you want them to do."

Take them to the sun and back.
LEE: And faster. The imagination is C-squared—swifter than the speed of light.

Kurt Vonnegut once said he believes he's successful because he hasn't mastered writing yet, that he always approaches it as a beginner. It sounds like that's what you're saying.
LAWRENCE: Every play that Bob and I start to write together—or separately, which we do sometimes—we feel is really our first play and that we're starting from the beginning.

One reason that approach is good for all writers is that the so-called experienced writers don't take chances. They keep harking back to their wounds. And they say, "I did that, it was a flop, it didn't work." And that limits you.

I think Bob and I still consider ourselves young playwrights. A cop stopped me once for making a wrong turn, and he said, "Have you ever been arrested?" and I said, "Only emotionally." He didn't understand that at all. I think I froze at 18. I just feel that everything we write, every script we write, we're handing in as beginning writers.

LEE: A sudden success can paralyze a beginning writer; he may spend the rest of his life trying to figure out what he did right.

LAWRENCE: Moss Hart and Bob Anderson went to see *The Seven Year Itch*, which was an experimental comedy breaking all the rules—by George Axelrod, who in his next play called a playwright a "playwrote," and then became a playwrote himself because *The Seven Year Itch* was so successful that he never returned to the theater, he never took a chance again after his second play flopped. At *The Seven Year Itch*, Moss Hart turned to Bob Anderson and said, "They'd kill us if we wrote this play." But it was a first play by a young playwright, and the critics raved about it.

LEE: You see, a younger playwright is a *terra incognita*—a new creative landfall to be sighted. On the other hand, a known playwright wears the albatross of his own reputation around his neck. He is a *target*.

I've got to tell you a curious thing about life—and it's an observation about the flexibility of memory. My recollection is that Garson Kanin made the remark that Jerry just mentioned, to *you*, Jerry, after you both had seen David Mamet's *A Life in the Theatre*. Gar commented: "The critics would have fractured us if we'd written that play." I remember something one way, Jerry recalls it another. Neither of us is lying. It is simply the parallax of personalities. The greatest miracle of memory isn't its infallibility, but its malleability.

LAWRENCE: Every playwright must have *creative* memory. You take your past and personal history and stick to it literally, but there's no such thing as literal history. You have the obligation to be creative with personal memory and with history. Facts change depending on which part of the elephant you touch.

LEE: Now, that's not dishonest. For example, when we wrote *Inherit the Wind*, people asked why we changed the names. One of the reasons is we wanted the freedom that Jerry speaks of. When we did *The Night Thoreau Spent in Jail*, we were dealing with Thoreau, Emerson. We were dealing with people who were absolute, and we could not have that freedom. Whenever you're dealing with historically based material, just remember: Herodotus didn't have a tape recorder. No one knows *precisely* what was said (or not said). The dramatist must be granted freedom of invention.

LAWRENCE: Verisimilitude can be more truthful than truth. Verisimilitude, according to the dictionary, is the *appearance* of truth. But sometimes you want a higher truth; by boiling something down to the essence of it, you may get a higher truth and know that the essence is completely fictional. It can somehow be less of a lie than something that factually happened.

The major scene in our play is Thoreau's big showdown with Emerson. Well, there's no historical record that the meeting ever happened. But the greatest authority on

Thoreau, Walter Harding, who is head of the Thoreau Society and has written the best biography, came to see the show and told us, "I finally really understand the relationship between Emerson and Thoreau." Yet, it's something we entirely created out of what might have happened or could have happened or *should* have happened.

LEE: It was our task, as playwrights, to extrapolate what was said.

One other thing about memory—about the changing of memory—that's also very important: You forget things. You have to have *selective* memory. And there are certain things that simply do not need to be carried around.

LAWRENCE: Some of these current experimental things—Philip Glass operas like *Einstein on the Beach*—last eight hours. If you really wanted to go back and dramatize history, every play would last 30 years.

There's a line in a direction of a George S. Kaufman show: "The curtain will be lowered for 30 seconds to denote the passing of 30 years." Someday, some time, the curtain will be lowered for 30 years to denote the passing of 30 seconds, but that's another story [laughs].

You have to be creative, and you must get the essence of a work humanly on the stage in two and a half hours—or 30 to 45 minutes for a one-act play.

> *So many young playwrights take themselves so seriously they are afraid of humor. The best playwrights puncture the most serious moment with an outrageous laugh.*

LEE: But you must not lie. If you lie, the audience will know instantly. The audience will turn you off. Click.

It is only the task of the playwright to examine these things, to look back, and to try to find shape, to find reason, to find what really happened.

You once said, Jerry, that a certain play wasn't "serious enough to be a comedy."
LAWRENCE: We always say that all our serious plays are funny and all our funny plays are serious. It's more important that a comedy have something really basic to say because then you can take off and be funny about it. There are, alas, so many young playwrights who take themselves so seriously that they are afraid of humor. Wit might trivialize their profound work.

The best playwrights—Tennessee Williams, for instance—will puncture the most serious moment with an outrageous laugh. The audience delights in it. They need

the relief. They need laughter—or what Norman Cousins calls "inner jogging"—for the joy of life. The more an audience laughs, the more it feels. Shakespeare knew this—there's comedy in his most serious plays.

Not that I have a great experience in all this, but the times I've seen my two plays done, the best time I had was hearing everyone laugh.
LEE: I agree. I think it's one of the greatest feelings in the world. Sometimes I've been tired during the tryout of a play. I've gone out into the lobby and I'm lying down on a couch and I hear the bursts of laughter. You can't hear the lines, you don't know what the actors are saying. These are the "strokes" for the author.

There's one problem, however. Sometimes you can be so entertaining that people miss the point. I think that's what happened with *First Monday in October*. We were having too much fun with the relationship between Henry Fonda and Jane Alexander.

LAWRENCE: A curmudgeonly William O. Douglas character and a new, conservative woman justice. We were having such delight at it that some people missed the point.

How do you work together? What's a day with Lawrence and Lee like?
LAWRENCE: It depends on what we're working on. We try to work six days a week and, if we're lucky, get five pages down every day. When we're actively working on a play, we usually are face to face. Sometimes, when there's heavy traffic, we're on an open phone line. We dialogue together, and we talk out plots and characters together. We try to be face to face as often as possible.

LEE: On prose, books, short stories, articles, we write individually. And sometimes, when we have to write a piece we both sign, one of us drafts it and the other one punches it up. If one of us says no to an idea or some dialogue or whatever, he has the obligation to come up with something better. We work "positively."

Jerry's viewpoint is often considerably at odds with mine, but who wants a partner who just says yes to everything?

LAWRENCE: If he said yes to me all the time, I wouldn't give him 50 percent of my money [laughs]. That's an old joke.

Steering in another direction: I think there's a general belief that playwriting is like poetry—fun to tinker at but something that can't bring home the bacon. Obviously, you two have made money, but is it a profession to encourage?

LAWRENCE: It's a difficult profession, so you've got to have a concurrent occupation. You've got to have a moneymaking job at the same time you're writing plays, and then eventually playwriting will support you.

LEE: *Anything* that's hard to do is difficult to get into. Forgive me, but I think that's a foolish question. It's not analogous to poetry because there is no clear box office for poetry.

We will need plays, always. It is a standard commodity. The worse the times are, the more people will need to be relieved of reality. During the Depression, the theater flourished. Not financially so much as artistically.

LAWRENCE: Also during the war. Then, as Howard Lindsay and Russel Crouse used to tell us, Times Square was blacked out. There were no lights in the city.

LEE: The news all over the world was terrible.

LAWRENCE: Terrible. And [Lindsay and Crouse] said that at the end of *Life With Father*, which was about the Gilded Age (there was the red plush and the family and the certainties of the 1910s), nobody left the theater. After the curtain fell, they just sat. They let that glow warm them before going out into the dark night.

The theater means so many things to many people. To be a playwright, I think you've got to feel the pulse of your times and be a little bit of a prophet. And your play has got to be *about* something. If someone says, "What's your play about?" and all you can answer is, "It's about two and a half hours long," then the only answer back is, "It's two and a half hours too long." It has to have a spine, it has to have some meaning, it has to offer some illumination.

LEE: It's got to have more than a spine. It's got to have a motor.

LAWRENCE: Every scene has to have a motor in it. That's the best test. If a scene has drive, it goes somewhere.

A spine and a motor?

LEE: It's a mixed metaphor—excuse us. A motor with a spine, or a spine with a motor is bad imagery.

Is the spine "theme"?

LEE: The word *theme* is not a helpful word for a practical writer. Let the critics or the audience talk about the theme. You write the play because you are possessed. You're possessed by an idea, by a passion. You see, theme has a surgical feel to it.

LAWRENCE: *Theme* sounds like *thesis*—it's an academic word. Your play has got to have some solid structure, some *spine*. You couldn't walk around very well if you didn't have a spine. A play's a human being.

LEE: When Bob said each scene has a motor, it means you don't start and finish each scene in the same place. It has to have some thrust, some drive. It has to go someplace. It can't stand still. Stasis is dullness in the theater.

Now we go beyond that to a spine, which means every scene in a play, and every play itself, must stand up. I think *spine* is a very good word.

Spine and *theme* are fancy Christmas-ball words. There's got to be that purring, driving brrrrrrrrrrrrrr.

LAWRENCE: The breath of life.

LEE: Yes! The élan that makes a play. Without it, we couldn't write *Simulation*, a TV movie we just finished about ten students at Stanford University who are studying arms control. Up at Stanford, they insisted, "Come up here, you've got to see these students at work." All of a sudden, we were *thrust* into the midst of their situation, and we realized we could hear the motor running.

LAWRENCE: There was passion there, there was commitment there, there was reason for their going to that class every day. We could hear every one of their motors running, which meant their brains were running, their hearts were ticking, their blood was flowing through their veins. You know, that's what we're trying to say in perhaps many wild, unrelated metaphors.

How do you find a motor?

LEE: The people. The people in the play rev it up. What happens when Jerry and I are writing is all of a sudden the people begin to move, they begin to demand things.

LAWRENCE: Let the reins a little loose and let your horse go up different roads.

> *The prime definition of a play is "Something that bugs you."*

LEE: That's an old Emerson point. He says, "When a man is lost in the woods on horseback, what he should do is let the horse go home." For *Simulation*, we met those students who simulate arms talks, crisis management meetings. We met them and observed. We consolidated their characters and invented our own. And as we sat down to write them, we started to get more acquainted with them, to fall in love with the girls and feel the guys were like our college roommates. They really helped us write it, and when Jonathan fell in love with Susan, *they* did it! We didn't make them fall in love. They did it in the script because the characters were alive.

You're saying to write a good play or a good anything you find good characters and they'll write the piece for you?
LEE: It's not *all* character. You need to have something to write about.

LAWRENCE: You've got to have a purpose and a situation that contains an issue, the seeds of disagreement. We don't make it easy for our students in *Simulation*. No one lets them do anything. Yet the students remain adamant to accomplish something. It's the life of the world, the life of all of us, at stake.

So you have purpose, and then you find your characters, and the characters have their purposes, and there are two sides.
LEE: This is the best description of a thrust, the way the energy wave moves through a play.

LAWRENCE: The way to get that motor running.

I've been in classes, seen people in classes who are eager to write, and they have talent, but they don't know what to write about. How do you get them to find a purpose?
LEE: Ask one question.

What's that?
LEE: What makes you mad?

LAWRENCE: What gives you goosebumps?

LEE: What bugs you?

LAWRENCE: Reveal something. Dig out something about yourself that you haven't even revealed to yourself. Dig out something in history. Dig out something in your parents, in your government, in your church, in your friends, but especially in yourself.

LEE: Write with a spade. Go back to *Inherit the Wind*. We were bugged by the McCarthy era. We tried to write *Inherit the Wind* as a parable to show the disastrous

things that can happen if you try to legislate thought.

We were bugged by the Vietnam war, so we wrote *The Night Thoreau Spent in Jail*.

LAWRENCE: We were bugged by censorship. *First Monday in October* is not about the Supreme Court as much as it is about a battle against censorship and a battle against the control of all our lives by the multinationals, by this cabal of unseen men who can suppress inventions, who can do all sorts of things that can diminish our lives.

LEE: This bugs me. And if nothing bugs you, I don't think you should write.

LAWRENCE: It's very difficult. It's difficult because revelation is the subtext of a script and the subtext of a life and very difficult to get onto paper.

So how do you get that? How do you encourage others to get that?
LAWRENCE: In teaching, I ask students to write biographies of themselves. With that, and with questioning on my part, I hope to dig out something that I (and all the rest of us in the workshop) can see. I try to find the gold inside that each student doesn't know is there. There are an infinite number of plays in everybody, if he or she only knows how to get to them.

Many people are bugged by something, and five years later they are still bugged by the same things. I get the idea they'd be writing the same play over again in different settings.
LAWRENCE: Most playwrights do. We drive the critics crazy; they can't pigeonhole us. They can't say, "That's a Lawrence and Lee play." They can say, "That's a Neil Simon play," or "That's a Tennessee Williams play." No one's pigeonholed us because we try to make all our plays seem different.

You have the serious Inherit the Wind *and then you have the humorous* Auntie Mame.
LAWRENCE: Quite frankly, *Inherit the Wind* and *Auntie Mame* are about the same thing: the dignity of the individual human mind. About not putting on horse blinders.

LEE: And "Be a little crazy." One thing that bugs me is restraints. Sometimes what bugs you isn't in terms of being angry, but something simply bugs you because you say, "How the hell did that happen? Why does it happen *that* way? It's simply curiosity. Spading into that, digging into that, you say, "Look down there." Sometimes you're an archaeologist.

LAWRENCE: When a student or someone asks me, "What should I write about?", I say "What turns your stomach? What gives you chills? What makes your hair stand on end? What makes you angry? What makes you cry? Analyze that, and that's something to write about.

LEE: But if one word, one phrase is false, the whole bridge collapses. The entire play fails. Every character must be consistent. Characters have to be real right down to the grit under their fingernails.

For example, if Thornton Wilder at any point in *Our Town* had said, "I'm only kidding," the whole play would have fallen apart. Or the whole scheme can be whirled 180 degrees: *The Skin of Our Teeth* is absolutely outrageous, but consistently outrageous.

LAWRENCE: Sure. Sabina comes right down to the footlights and says, "I don't understand a bloody word of this play."

LEE: But the playwright is playing in his own ballpark. You can make up your own rules. Crazy or cruel. Audiences will believe almost anything—unless you cheat.

LAWRENCE: In theater, anything is possible. Anything. But this is quintessential: The play must believe itself.

LEE: The play must unfailingly project the author's belief. But the author should be invisible. If you can see the strings, the actors turn into mere puppets. Authors must be totally concealed within the performances of their actors.

LAWRENCE: And once the authors vanish, the play is free to live.

You mentioned earlier that you've each written plays without the other. Why?
LAWRENCE: [laughs] Bob wrote a wonderful play called *Sounding Brass* by himself. My play's called *Live Spelled Backwards*. We had to do these individually. I didn't think much of St. Paul, and he's no fan of camel dung. I call mine a moral immorality play.

LEE: Whereas mine is more of an immoral morality play.

LAWRENCE: My play is about a bunch of people, including a Tennessee Williams character, who are all being turned on by a variety of things, supposedly peyote, LSD, hashish, mescaline. And it turns out in the end that they were all fake. In effect, they turn *themselves* on. The whole point of the play is that you don't need drugs or booze or tobacco or artificial stimulants to turn on. The things that really give me a high are sunsets and music and people—people especially. And travel and seeing the world and the Pacific Ocean. What turns me on is when Bob and I are working together and we get a line that gives us both goosebumps. *That* turns me on.

LEE: I'm going to say something negative. As you were describing *Live Spelled Backwards*, I know why it doesn't appeal to me as much as I wish it did. The reason is that it's not about something that really bugs you. It's a marvelous comment.

LAWRENCE: That's right, it's not a bugging play.

LEE: It's a comment play. On the other hand, if you excuse my saying so, *Sounding Brass* is a play about St. Paul, who's an enormously troubled man. It's full of things that bug me. And I think it's necessary to deal with those things, not to merely comment.

LAWRENCE: They're different plays.

LEE: Totally different. Except—Jerry, I don't mean to pick on you—but the prime definition of a play is "something that bugs you," and I think that's what your play *somewhat* lacks. . . . You see, Jerry and I disagree occasionally.

LAWRENCE: Often, we get very mad at each other. I get very mad at the word processor.

LEE: Jerry has better manners than I do. Jerry has much better discipline than I do. I'm often very dilatory.

LAWRENCE: Keep writing, write every day, keep at it, keep going, keep doing some new works, new plays of size and meaning.

LEE: With motors.

LAWRENCE: Motors in every scene.

What about subplots?
LEE: Don't think about plots. There is *no* such thing as a plot. There is only what interesting people do.

LAWRENCE: People are interested in people. The human animal.

LEE: You don't have to think in terms of a plot. Think of what these people do. Then all of a sudden they will weave their own plot.

I see formulas where you set up a couple groups and they sort of interweave.
LEE: Strike the word *formula*. Never use the word *formula*. There is no *tao*, no pattern, no modus from a master. Antonio Machado speaks eloquently of a traveler walking across a meadow, he is following no path, for there is no path to follow. And when he looks back, all he sees is the crushed grass where his own steps have fallen.

LAWRENCE: It's a patrol where you are your own "point man." The playwright is in a position of great danger. There is fear and beauty on what Stella Adler calls "the platform." Glory and disaster—mixed, inseparable, unpredictable.

LEE: Think how impossible it is: We're doomed. We are absolutely doomed on this planet. You, Jerry, myself. A few months, a few years, and where'll we be? Yet we are pervaded by this totally irrational optimism!

LAWRENCE: We wake up every morning. We get out of bed.

LEE: Better than that—we *dare* to wake up every morning, *dare* to get out of bed! We *dare* to put things on the stage. We *dare* to play God as playwrights. It's the greatest sport in the world.

BY JEAN CALDWELL

MADELEINE L'ENGLE

Questions are more important than answers.
I'm looking for openings, not closings.

Madeleine L'Engle throws her hands up in the gesture that says "Who knows?" when a visitor asks how many rejections she received for her award-winning book, *A Wrinkle in Time.*

"There were over 30," she says. "It almost never got published. People think it was my first book, but it was the 11th to be written. I call it my 'Cinderella book.' You name any major publisher in New York, and they rejected it."

No one really expected it to sell, she confesses, but "it really took off." It won a Newbery medal in 1963, is in its 39th printing, has been read on National Public Radio's *The Spider's Web*, and has come to be considered a children's classic.

L'Engle is sitting in The Autumn Inn in Northampton, Massachusetts. Smith College has invited her back to give her an alumna medal. It is a good month: the medal; her book, *A Ring of Endless Light*, has just been named a Newbery honor book; and at week's end she and actor-husband Hugh Franklin (who played Dr. Charles Tyler on TV's *All My Children*) are flying to Buenos Aires to hop "a small freighter" for a cruise through the Strait of Magellan.

The bad years—the time when she was writing, writing, writing and nothing sold—are behind her. Not forgotten, though. She thinks it is a mistake for people to forget the past. Today she could easily sell the six unpublished books from that time when she was in her 30s going into her 40s. But she won't. "I'm past where they are," she explains.

She wonders aloud if she could have kept on without success. She recalls Van Gogh, "who sold only one picture in his lifetime and that to his brother." She is not sure she could have managed that kind of ignominy. "It was very difficult to keep on working when nobody in the world believed in me—nobody."

Today, readers write to tell her that they seek out her books, try to read everything she has published—more than two dozen books, fiction, nonfiction, poetry, a play. She gets 50 to 75 letters a week—"a few from kids who say they have to write to an author ... a lot from kids who say they have read one of the books seven times or sometimes more. A lot of letters on the four nonfiction books. People tell me their life stories, which is very nice, very intimate." She answers all the letters.

Although most of her books are marketed for children, she says she does not write for children: "I write for myself." She wrote only one book especially for children. That was *Twenty-Four Days Before Christmas*, and she doesn't like it and says no one has heard of it.

L'Engle knew she was going to be a writer from the moment she wrote her first story. "I was five and it was called 'G-R-U-L.' " She spells the word and adds, "I didn't know how to spell *girl.*

"My father got a new typewriter when I was ten and gave me his old one. I immediately wrote my first novel." Unfortunately, she says, both the story and the novel have been lost.

The rejection saga of Madeleine L'Engle's A Wrinkle in Time *has become a morality tale in literary legend. What most readers don't realize is that* Wrinkle *was merely L'Engle's comeback: she had established a solid, if not spectacular, career with books such as* Camilla Dickinson *in the forties and fifties before child-rearing cut sharply into her writing time. (The several-year interruption seems oddly appropriate, since L'Engle's best works deal mainly with family love and responsibility.)*

In this 1982 interview, with two Newberys and an American Book Award behind her, L'Engle talks about that family love and tells how—by working hard at play—other writers can tap their success.

Writing, to L'Engle, is "like eating or sleeping. I'm not fully human unless I'm writing." When her three children were small and she could find time to write only after they were tucked into bed, "I often fell asleep with my head on the typewriter." Now her children joke that she will die at the typewriter. "That is just the way I would like it," she says.

She reminisces about the long ago days of her childhood. Its halcyon days and its dark ones alike prepared her for her career.

She was an only child, born well along in her parents' marriage. Her father, Charles Wadsworth Camp, was a writer. Her voice glows with pride when she talks about him. He was a good writer—a foreign correspondent first and then a New York music and arts critic. Her mother was a pianist. It was a household that took books and writing and music and art for granted. Her mother (central figure in the poignant, autobiographical *The Summer of the Great-Grandmother*) read musical scores "the way most people read novels." Sundays the house would be filled with opera people, and while L'Engle's mother played the piano, everyone gathered around and sang *Gotterdammerung* or *Madame Butterfly*.

All this came to a sudden end when she was 12. Her father had been gassed in World War I. "It was mustard gas," she says. "It just keeps eating away at the lungs." The family fled to the Alps both because living in Europe was cheaper (a necessity because Camp was having trouble selling his work) and because the air was pure. Young Madeleine was shipped off to a Swiss boarding school.

She hated it, but "I learned to concentrate in the midst of sound and fury. I can write no matter what is going on as long as I don't have the responsibility for it. The only time I have not been able to write is when I've had crawling babies to tend. I write a great deal in airports, on planes. What I learned to do at that school, which is very good, is that if I'm working on a manuscript and someone comes in or the phone rings, I turn it off, tend to the business at hand and then turn it back on. That is an aptitude you must acquire young."

L'Engle attended Smith College after leaving boarding school. After graduating from Smith, she moved to New York City to earn money while waiting for her writing to bring in enough income for her to live on. "With less naivete than it might seem, I earned my living in the theater. I'm very tall. I'm very clumsy. I was no threat to any star."

During this time she kept shipping short pieces she had written in college to "little magazines"—literary magazines, university quarterlies.

"Editors read these, looking for talent. They still do. I got letters from several people suggesting I do a longer piece. I was working on a novel. I sent it to the first one who had written. I was very fortunate that he was a young editor—Bernard Perry—who was able to make me see what I needed to do to take this very shapeless bundle of material and turn it into a book." The book—*The Small Rain*—"did extremely well."

But by the time her second book was ready, Perry had gone off to start the University of Indiana Press. The publisher printed the book as she had submitted it, "printed the draft," she says. The book got good reviews but didn't sell. "I need an editor," she explains.

Fiction, she says, "is not so much written as rewritten. I do a tremendous amount of revising before sending a book off, but a good editor helps me see where a scene needs sharpening or where a transition is not clear."

Critics have praised her books for their intricate plots, their blend of science and mysticism. The *Wrinkle Trilogy* (*A Wrinkle in Time*, *A Wind in the Door* and *A Swiftly Tilting Planet*) sends the central characters through time and space and even into a blood cell in classic battles of good against evil where the fate of the world hinges on the courage and wit of a small child.

Where does she get all the ideas? She laughs and tells a story about Johann Sebastian Bach. A child once asked him, "Poppa Bach, where do you get all the ideas for your pieces?" Bach replied, "Ach, child, when I get up in the morning it is all I can do to keep from tripping on them."

"It is the same with stories," L'Engle says. "Everyone you meet has a story."

As if to prove her point, her attention suddenly shifts to the photographer who has been moving noiselessly about the room for some 20 minutes snapping picture after picture of her. The few sentences they had exchanged upon being introduced had been enough to establish him as French.

"Why are *you* here?" she demands. She clearly means, why is he in the United States?

He blushes. His role was to take pictures, not to be interviewed by the interviewee. He mumbles a little about meeting an American girl and getting married.

"The mere outline," she says with a smile when he stops.

She says she needs someone who knows the "current swear words" in French. She left the heroine of her first book at the age of 17 embarking on a career as a pianist and living in France. Now she is picking up Katherine's life when she is 80, but she says her own vocabulary "is that of a 14-year-old."

The photographer confesses he doesn't know the trendy words. He left Paris five years earlier. No matter, she replies. A heroine of 80 would use classic words. They discuss the merits of various earthy phrases, then she is back to explaining how she goes about writing her books. She says, "I have it worked out, but it still almost invariably goes someplace else. I have to go where the book wants to. To start, you need a structure, something to hang it on, but if it wants to change, you have to listen and let it change.

"It's a very important process, getting out of the way and listening. You have to have time for 'finger exercises.' You can't sit and wait for an inspiration. The inspiration comes while you're working, during the time at the typewriter."

Years back she wrote in a small bedroom. It was not satisfactory. There was the phone—"a beetle-browed black monster that just screeches. It just rings all the time." And there was the impossible juxtaposition of work and household chores. "I would be cooking dinner and go to the typewriter to write just one sentence. Fifteen minutes later dinner would be burned and the pot would be gone."

She thought about the enormous, beautiful, little-used oak-panelled library at the Cathedral of St. John the Divine not far from her home in New York City. She asked if she could work there. Of course, they said. When the librarian left a short time later, L'Engle offered to take on the task of librarian as a volunteer if she could use the electric typewriter.

That was some ten years ago. Now she walks the mile from her apartment to the Cathedral each morning, writes all day with Timothy, her Irish Setter, lying under her desk and leaves her work when she goes home.

She dedicated *The Young Unicorns* to "all my friends at the Cathedral of St. John the Divine who are as the stars of heaven for multitude and brightness."

A cathedral, in many ways, is a fitting place for L'Engle to work, since her books are filled with the kind of questioning that theologians might describe as a search for God. She says the books are "looking for questions. The questions are more important than the answers. We get so hung up on answers. I'm looking for openings, not closings."

Modern science fascinates her. "Post-Newtonian science is very exciting," she says. "Higher math is my theology. Cellular biology and astrophysics deal with the nature of being—that's modern mysticism."

Having said that, she smiles, remembering her days at Smith College when she did all in her power to avoid any science class at all.

Years later, when her characters in *A Wind in the Door* had to journey into a mitochondrion—a bit of a cell—she devoured books on cellular biology and was delighted when the very information she needed seemed to

Watch children at play. They are terribly serious. The same is true with writing: you get caught up in the rhythm. That's when it really gets to be complete play.

spring at her from the page.

When the book was finished, she shipped it off to her godson, who was working on a Master's in immunology, to be sure her science was accurate.

There is a knock at the door, and two Smith College students are there. One is writing about L'Engle for the student paper, the other is to take her picture. They say their generation grew up on L'Engle books and note that when she spoke to the Student Service Organizations the evening before, the theater was "packed."

They have heard her say before that her work is play, and they wonder how much of it really is play.

"Watch children at play," L'Engle replies. "They are terribly serious about it—even running into a jump rope. You're very serious as you get in, to be sure the rhythm is there; as you're jumping, it gets less serious and more play. The same thing is true with writing. The first 15 to 20 minutes, half-hour, is getting into that rhythm. Then once you're in it, you get caught up in the rhythm. That's when it really gets to be complete play."

She has not stopped writing because of this trip to Smith. A sturdy red box with the latest typed manuscript lies on the bed, next to a case of pens and pencils, her glasses, and her journal. The latter is a hard-covered, brown-and-yellow notebook such as a college student might use. She says she got it in Russia and that because it is a small notebook, she hopes to finish before Saturday when she leaves for vacation. Then she will begin a new and larger journal. To L'Engle, vacation means time to write without interruption.

She tells the students that the journals, which she writes in at least three or four times a week, are "a memory-setting device."

The students ask how writing and child-rearing mix. "They are a conflict," she says. "An unadulterated conflict. But if I had to go back I would make the same choices. I like my children. They are wonderful grownups. I enjoy them. It was my kid that made it possible for my mother to die at home. She died at home in my son's arms. A good and unusual thing in these days."

"I also think the stresses and strains of family life were important in developing me as a writer. I would mutter to myself, 'Emily Bronte didn't have to make the beds, or do the cooking.' I made sure as soon as my children could stand, they made their own beds. They would say, 'Mother, if you didn't teach us anything else, you taught us to make our beds as soon as we got up in the morning.' "

She admits she wanted to be read but she never expected the soaring sales or the honors, which have included the Hans Christian Andersen International Award, the Lewis Carroll Shelf Award and the Austrian State Literary Award. She sums up her reaction to the adulation: "I like it."

There is another knock, this time from students coming to take her to lunch. One of them holds the latest tribute to L'Engle—a small bunch of white flowers.

BY LOIS ROSENTHAL

NIKKI GIOVANNI

I've mellowed, but I'm not burned out. I'm still an idealist.

Nikki Giovanni is one of America's most widely read living poets, and one of the most outspoken. From the sixties, when she gained notoriety as one of the prime forces in the civil rights movement to the present, when she travels all over the world to teach and to give scores of poetry readings and lectures each year, she speaks out on whatever issues she believes are crucial. Her awards, both literary and for being an outstanding woman of achievement, are legion. Giovanni is celebrating her twentieth year as a poet, during which time she has written 16 books.

Says Giovanni: "I use poetry as an outlet for my mind. It's my justification for living. But speaking my mind is an important part of my life as well, even when it's not a popular view. Everyone has a right to the dictates of her own heart. The one thing you cannot take away from people is their own sense of integrity. I don't want my integrity impinged upon nor will I impinge on the integrity of someone else.

"Though you cannot live your life to be intimidated by lesser people under any circumstances, I don't think you should shout people down if you disagree with them—which is what people are doing in the eighties. I dealt with this subject in my recently published book of essays, *Sacred Cows and Other Edibles*.

"For instance, I don't agree with those who would attend a speech given by Jeane Kirkpatrick in order to disrupt it. I think you should find out why she has the views she does and debate with her. You don't have to agree with her, but you can't solve a problem by shutting a person up. The integrity of the individual is everything."

Does that mean the sixties fire that fueled marches, sit-ins and sometimes violent poems that reflected her fury has dimmed with age?

"Yes, I've mellowed since then," says Giovanni, "but I'm not burned out. I'm still an idealist, and if I saw something as public as a sign that said I could not sit in this hotel, I'd be compelled to sit there. I would be arrested and that would be that. But if you don't want to sell your property to me because I'm black, I'd fight in a legal way. You must fight whichever is the most effective way for what you want to accomplish. Just remember you can't use yesterday's methods to solve today's problems, and you must never give up just because everything didn't work out like you thought it would.

"I read recently about a car dealer in Detroit who gave a 1988 Buick to Rosa Parks [the mother of the civil rights movement] because he heard that she totaled her car. He said that if it weren't for Mrs. Parks, he probably wouldn't ever have a dealership, so by his gesture, he is solving today's problem. He appreciates what Mrs. Parks did for blacks. Mrs. Parks needs a car. He has a car to give.

"Some people might say that's not a big deal, but I really appreciate it. I don't have a car to give Mrs. Parks. So I wrote a poem about her. You try to do what you can to make life a little better.

"If you feel you must feed and clothe the hungry, start with someone next door who may need a sweater. Don't consider that unimportant. If you feel like you must tackle the problems of the world, begin by looking at what's next to you."

In her poem "Harvest (for Rosa Parks)," Giovanni writes about Parks' arrest in the sixties for sitting in the front of a bus and refusing to move. And Giovanni writes of the aftermath:

Nikki Giovanni lives poetry ("It's my justification for living"), and breathes it, too ("you should write the way you breathe"). In this 1989 profile, one of our age's most fearless and influential poets (she's earned the nickname "priestess of black poetry") talks about how she and her poetry have matured, tells why poets can write only about things they care deeply about, and offers a checklist to ensure a poem expresses those cares.

... you want to say things ... are better ... somehow ... they are ... not in many ways ... People ... older people ... are afraid ... younger people ... are too ... I really don't know ... where it will end ... Our people ... can break ... your heart ... so can other ... people ... I just think ... it makes a difference ... what one person does ... young people forget that ... what one person does ... makes a difference ...

And, later in the poem:

... Something needs to be said ... about Rosa Parks ... other than her feet ... were tired ... Lots of people ... on that bus ... and many before ... and since ... had tired feet ... lots of people ... still do ... they just don't know ... where to plant them ...

Giovanni's caring but no-holds-barred approach to life extends to her poetry, and to her way of teaching poetry to her students. When poems are read, critical comments can be honest but they must also be kind. She forbids vicious attacks on anyone's work—the work must not be "shouted down."

"We drink a lot of liquids. I smoke. The more you can relax with your things around you, the easier it is to establish 'the-whole-universe-loves-you' sort of attitude students need to realize their feelings are valid," says Giovanni. "From there, I begin asking them what they are trying to say in each particular poem. What started it? They are required to take their thought to the furthermost point, to push themselves a little bit beyond what makes sense to them. By the time their explanation is finished, they often wind up with a very different poem.

"If one writes that he is in love with a red-headed girl, I want to know if her mother and her sister are redheads. I want information about the girl's background. How did he meet her? How will this affair end? What is he envisioning?

"I'm trying to teach students to see the whole scene and bring all the information to bear on this love poem. Then we might have something, because it's insufficient to just write that you are in love. Nobody cares. We care about what's around it, what triggered the poem."

"If you are working on your own—not as part of a workshop—and if, for instance, you are writing about raindrops, have this conversation with yourself:

Question: Where does the rain go?

Answer: It falls to the ground.

Question: Then what?

Answer: The rain comes back as a bud.

Question: What does the bud do?

Answer: The bud gives off oxygen and oxygen goes back up into space.

"Follow your image as far as you can no matter how useless you think it is. Push yourself. Always ask, 'What else can I do with this image?', because you have images before you have poems. Words are illustrations of thoughts. You must think this way."

Giovanni suggests you make a checklist of questions for yourself. For instance, when you finish a poem ask:

1. Did you say all you needed to?

2. Did you say more than you should have? (More is better than less because it's easier to subtract than add.)

3. Is this a poem you actually like reading?

4. If you didn't write it, would it still make sense to you?

5. Is it boring? "Most writers know when they're being boring because that's the first question they ask. My answer—'Yes, dear, it is.' "

"Learn to listen when you're talking to people. So many people listen poorly. Listen to how people say things, to what they really mean because people frequently say one thing and mean another. Learn to separate the wheat from the chaff and look at your own poetry in the same way.

"You must have a built-in shit detector. For example, if you've meant to be ironic or sarcastic, make sure you're not being just plain silly. Without becoming too down on yourself, learn to be your own worst critic."

Listen to your *poetry* as well. "I'm very conscious of the rhythm in my poems, which is why I consider myself a lyricist—I write lyrical poetry. You should be able to tap your foot when you read most of my work.

"James Joyce teaches us that you must write on the human breath. This is the reason people get confused when they read *Ulysses* or *Finnegan's Wake*. There are no breaks, so people don't understand how to read them. But Joyce wrote as he breathed. And you should write the way you breathe."

The preface of Giovanni's latest book of poetry, *Those Who Ride the Night Winds*, takes the form of a poem that uses ellipses to indicate pauses, and is a good illustration of this style (as is "Harvest," which appears in *Night Winds*). The following stanza also gives us insight

> *Follow your image as far as you can no matter how useless you think it is. Push yourself.*

into the poet's feelings about her craft.

In the written arts . . . language has opened . . . becoming more accessible . . . more responsive . . . to what people really think . . . and say . . . We are now free . . . to use any profane word . . . or express any profound thought . . . we may wish . . . Sexuality . . . once a great taboo in language . . . and act . . . is fully explored . . . through fiction . . . and nonfiction . . . through poetry . . . and plays . . . Different and same gender . . . different and same age . . . different and same race . . . religion . . . or creed . . . all take their places . . . on the bookshelves . . . Ideas that once allowed the Church to force Copernicus to recant . . . Ideas that once encouraged McCarthy to destroy the lives of men and women . . . are now as acceptable as a stop-and-go light . . . or at least as well understood . . . as fluoride . . . While there is surely much . . . to be done . . . some change has rent . . . its ways . . . I changed . . . I chart the night winds . . . glide with me . . . I am the walrus . . . the time has come . . . to speak of many things . . .

In fact, Giovanni recommends that you read your poetry aloud so you can hear how your poem actually sounds, because what you hear in your head is not what you hear outside. Your poem should sound smooth. It should make sense. It should be readable. It should sound honest. Never use words you can't actually pronounce.

"Write like you talk as long as it is good English," says Giovanni. "Poor English is not acceptable. You can use dialect if you know what you are doing, but you cannot split a verb because you didn't know any better. You must write in standard English—I know that's not a popular stance, but I believe in it firmly. If you don't learn the language, you are not going to be able to pursue writing. It's just that basic. Before you take liberties with the language, you better know what liberties you are taking."

Giovanni says it's important to study classical poetry, to master the rules before attempting to break them. "I don't play the piano right now because I never learned to play the scales. I didn't like practicing them and I'm sorry about it now. Rules are there to help you understand how things work—if you do A, then B will follow. At the same time, rules should never be overbearing and should not be slavishly adhered to.

"So poetry students should study Keats, T.S. Eliot, Milton, and Shakespeare. My favorites are T.S. Eliot and Anne Sexton. But students should remember that Milton and T.S. Eliot already wrote their own poetry better than anyone else can possibly hope to. Shakespeare already wrote his sonnets. These works should be studied, but not imitated. Our job is to find a voice for our own age, which is why I am not flattered when students who take my classes try to write poems that sound like mine. *I* already sound like me. I want my students to hear their own voices, to put their own inner thoughts and what's real to them on paper, not use archaic forms because they are overwhelmed by the writing that has preceded them. I feel that as writers grow in confidence they will use their own experiences, or their interpretation of these experiences to create poetry."

Giovanni's own poetry is an example of that kind of confidence. Her love poem, "Master Charge Blues"—one of her favorites—goes to the core of any woman whose romance has gone sour, for she writes of mall therapy, as shopping binges to comfort the soul are often called. It's a blues song of a love poem and shows off Giovanni's rhythmic lyrics and style. You'll find no *thees* and *thous* and fluttering hearts in the following lines.

its Wednesday night baby
and i'm all alone
sitting with myself
waiting for the telephone

wanted you baby
but you said you had to go
wanted you yeah
but you said you had to go
called your best friend
but he can't come 'cross no more

did you ever go to bed
at the end of a busy day
look over and see the smooth
where your hump usta lay
feminine odor and no reason why
i said feminine odor and no reason why

asked the lord to help me
he shook his head "not I"
but i'm a modern woman baby
ain't gonna let this get me down
i'm a modern woman
ain't gonna let this get me down
gonna take my master charge
and get everything in town.

"I shoot the moment, capture feelings with my poems," Giovanni says. "I use poetry as a medium for what I have to say, which makes me a poet of information, of content, rather than a strict adherent to structure. I like the story and I care more about *what* is being said than *how* it is said, which is quite different from poets to whom structure means everything."

To teach her students to be unafraid of exposing their own feelings, Giovanni continually reminds them of two important ideas. "The first is that no one really knows you and the poems you've written. Your poems are what you were; they are about the moments you felt when you wrote them and those moments have already passed.

That is why you should always be ahead of your poetry.

"The second point is that readers care more about how your poems affect *them* than where those poems came from. There are a few people who will try to make a statement about you based on what you wrote, who will use your life against you, but you must overcome that. You must be unintimidated by your own thoughts because if you write with someone looking over your shoulder, you'll never write."

Giovanni says the world needs poets. "This is a great profession. If everybody became a poet, the world would be so much better. We would all read to each other. It would be an enhancing situation. This is not a restricted profession. There's a living out there; you just have to find it.

"People say poets can't make a living. I tell them to lower their expectations to match their income. Any young artist should stay out of debt so that, for instance, if an opportunity arises in another part of the country, she won't say, 'I can't go because I have a lease on this apartment or car payments to make.' You must be free."

Giovanni feels earning a living as a poet depends on how serious you are about it. She advises staying close to the writing profession—all facets of it. Learn to write magazine articles, book reviews. Give poetry readings in churches, restaurants, for civic organizations, any place that agrees to have them—for free if you have to. And Giovanni recommends doing every job as if it were the most important one you'll ever have. Just because it may not be the audience you dream of, don't think you can let up on the energy you put into your work.

What about all the people who want to be poets but can never hope to reach Giovanni's heights? She has a ready answer. "Most of them won't try. They won't risk what I did. I had a son, and an apartment, and I decided I was going to try to be a poet and do it as well as I could. If it didn't work out, I'd have still given it my best shot. Most people won't do that.

"If I had a 36-inch bust, a 24-inch waist, 38-inch hips, and I lived in Stillwater, Oklahoma, and I decided to become a ballerina, I'd try. I would never say, 'My chest is too big and my behind sticks out, and my measurements are all wrong for a ballerina.' I would get on my toes. Someone would have to stop me because I will not stop myself.

"Whatever I do in life, I want to do it to the absolute maximum. I want to be the best that I can be. I encourage every one of my students to do that. Give yourself the chance to fully realize whatever your dreams are."

BY JOHN HAYES

JAMES MICHENER

Contrary to what people think, I slave over my books.

Upon entering James Michener's large, sprawling house in Bucks County, Pennsylvania, a visitor is not afraid to plop down in a chair and relax. The house was built in 1949, so it's not new or fancy, but well lived in. The living room has high ceilings, a fireplace, and one wall is lined with books and paintings. Michener's living habits match his dress habits; they're both simple. His den is large, cluttered with desk, files, typewriter and sofa, and one wall is lined with books and record albums. Upon entering the den, it's obvious Michener is always at work. His bedrooms are also filled with books and he has a TV, which he watches in the evenings, in his bedroom. Michener is 65 years old, partially bald, with short gray hair. He wears dark-framed glasses on a full face, which is marked only by the wrinkles expected of a man who has been through two wars, in several plane crashes, is in his third marriage, and has been read, applauded and criticized worldwide.

I understand you were an orphan and that an impoverished Quaker family adopted you. How did you manage to attend 12 schools and colleges, travel the world, and become one of the most widely read authors?

I was born in New York in 1907. I think it was in Mount Vernon. I'm not sure, but I read something like that. I don't know what happened to my parents. Three women by the name of Michener adopted me, and we lived not far from here, in Doylestown. My childhood was twofold. I was raised with love and affection, never wanted for that; but there was economic hardship, and it was rather distressing. I suppose of the two it is better to be deprived economically than emotionally. But I have never felt I suffered from the latter. I had always done well in high school, was a good athlete in basketball, baseball and tennis, and I had done a lot in student government. I was pretty active and did extremely well in academic testing.

Upon graduation, I received a four-year, complete scholarship to Swarthmore. The college had some very good scholarships in those days called "open" scholarships, and I was fortunate to get one. But before college, I traveled a great deal. I traveled even while I was in high school during the summers and other vacations. As a high school boy, I had pretty well traveled across the country, and by age 18 the only states I had not seen were the Dakotas, Oregon and Washington. I got around by hitchhiking and loved it. Families took me in to live with them, so I didn't need much money. I have several times come pretty well across the country on a couple of dollars, and it never bothered me a bit.

What about your college life?

I was bounced twice from Swarthmore for infractions of one kind or another, and I was considered a troublemaker. I was, perhaps, ahead of my time in my attitude toward education. A liberal professor got me back into school saying that the college needed a student who could write his term papers in Elizabethan blank verse. Swarthmore deserves a tremendous amount of credit for having not

---

Contemplating the bulk of paper needed to produce James Michener's collective work boggles the mind— and not only in sheer numbers (more than 34 books produced since Tales of the South Pacific *won the 1948 Pulitzer Prize)—but also in the size of the books:* Poland, *556 pages . . .* Texas, *943 pages . . .* Alaska, *a frontier-sized 1,100 pages . . the list goes on. And on.*

How can one writer—dubbed the literary world's Cecil B. DeMille by Newsweek—*produce such tonnage after not even starting to write until age 40? In this April 1972 interview, a 65-year-old Michener talks with John Hayes—who would later write a biography of Michener—about the art of making each book "a world," teeming with research (and readers) and of making a living as a full-time writer.*

taken away my scholarship. They would have been entitled to do so, but I always did well in class. It was easy, perhaps, for them to make this concession.

While in college, I edited the school paper and was active in dramatics and sports. I kept a fairly good cross-section of activity.

After my graduation from Swarthmore, I taught history at a private boys school in Pottstown for a year before traveling in Europe on a fellowship I had earned. I attended a group of colleges there. Then I came back to the states and studied at Harvard and a few other universities. I still wish I could take time out for a course in economics or the geography of Africa. But in effect, since my college days, what I do in my life is more or less give myself a seminar in advanced studies when I work. So my education has really taken place after college.

Have you always wanted to be a writer?
I'm a very lucky man. I think it's remarkable that I've been able to do what I want to do, so far, and make a living at it. Shortly after I wrote *Tales of the South Pacific*, I made the decision that I wanted to be a writer. And now I'm one of the very few writers who has always been completely self-employed. I've never had any guarantees, never a salary, and there just aren't very many people who can do this. Even some of our greatest writers had jobs teaching school and working at other things to supplement their incomes. It was difficult for me, though. I made my living in the first years by public speaking, which is the hardest way in the world to make a buck. I have scars all over me from long hours, bad food, poor railroad connections, murderous drives, but I recommend it for the young artist when he's getting started. It's not easy and likeable, but it is honest. It's the hardest work I've ever done.

Did you begin writing for publication at an early age, while you were in high school or college?
No, I started writing very late in life. I was 40 before I published *Tales of the South Pacific*, and that was the first piece of writing I had done except for the usual writings one would do as a history teacher. I taught history in the United States and Europe for about eight years, and I had been editor of a history journal before I was offered an editor's job by Macmillan Publishing. They didn't need me, but they needed a man about 35 years old to fill a gap in their chain of command. Their looking at me was logical in that I had learned what editing was and had a

good use of words. They circulated a questionnaire, and my name surfaced. I went into the war after my job with Macmillan, and that is when I wrote *Tales of the South Pacific*. I was stationed on a little island during the war, and I wrote the book while I was there. I knew that when the war was over people would want to recall what had happened and so I wrote the book. I suppose I was there about three years, 1944 through 1946.

Let's talk about your novel The Drifters. *It was written before* Kent State: What Happened and Why, *but published after. Usually you leave a gap of two years between the publication of your books. Is there a reason these two came out so close together?*
It was a publisher's convenience. It was unwise, I suppose, to have the books come out so close together, but it didn't do any damage. *The Drifters* was on the bestseller list for about six months. Contrary to what people think, I slave over my books and work rather slowly. I work very painfully. I stop a lot of what I start and retype everything four, five, six times. The critical passages more, and everything at least three times. It takes me a while, a couple of years, to write a book.

> *I work very painfully. I stop a lot of what I write and retype everything four, five, six times.*

You've said that The Bridges at Toko-ri *is your favorite book and an example of your purest writing. How does* The Drifters *compare to that book?*
Toko-ri is my favorite book because I came closer to doing what I had in mind there than I've come in anything else. It's my purest writing because it's well told and a well-controlled story. *Toko-ri* is a small, compressed, artistic and intellectual problem: The problem of a democracy's endeavoring to wage war without declaring it; of its trying to impose military service on some while allowing others to avoid any kind of responsibility, and of calling back into military service men of middle age who have already served once. Just as it is easier to write a sonnet sometimes, than an epic, it was easier to write *Toko-ri*. As far as the intellectual content, I think *The Drifters* is way ahead of *Toko-ri* and a great deal of people writing to me say the same thing.

Do you set up a daily quota for the amount of writing you must do?
I set up objectives, and if I fell behind I would be worried. But no, I don't set up a quota. If I miss a day through nonproduction it doesn't bother me, it irritates me.

Can you explain your process for book writing?

I begin four or five years in advance. I keep thinking about things, what I would like to do, I make little outlines, and then I come to the moment of decision and I dig in. So we're talking now about when the moment of decision has been reached. I get up at 7:30 a.m., and work very diligently all morning. I quit about noon. I never work in the afternoons, almost never, and I do this seven days a week, month in and month out until the book is written.

Do you just sit and think during those four or five years before the moment of decision?
Sure, but mostly, however, I think when I'm walking. I do a great deal of walking. I think of the problems in the germinating period and then once I start writing I think about the next day's writing, hours at a time.

Why do you work in the mornings?
Well, I think that people are divided between day people and night people. John O'Hara, who was my neighbor to the east, did all his writing from after midnight to dawn for obvious reason—no telephone calls, he was quiet. He simply said he thought better at night. He was cleansed of irritation, his mind was cleansed of the passions that activated him at other times. I've known maybe more people who don't work in the mornings than do. But I happen to be a morning worker, at least since *Tales of the South Pacific*. In the mornings I can be quite disciplined if I want to be. If I don't want to be bothered, my wife is good at handling things. She handles the interruptions and knows just about what state I'm in and decides who will see me, where I will go, etc.

Do you travel while you're working or take any time off?
I frequently work six months without a single break, and if you do that, you get a lot of work done. I have written when I was overseas, but usually I don't mix the two.

Do you think this approach to book writing has changed with the years?
No, I would think that I have remained fairly consistent. What has changed is the rather wide variety of books I've done. I would think that has been the escape in my case; rather than shifting wildly in style and form, I've been consistent in that. But I do hold a very wide scatter of interest in types of books. There are two aspects of my writing that few people know. My book on politics, the *Presidential Lottery*, will be pretty important next year, four years late. Also, my books on oriental art are not well known, and I've often thought that if I died tomorrow, 50 years from now I would be more likely to be remembered for these books. They are trailblazers, they really did a job.

What book gave you the most difficulty in writing?

Of the books I've published, there would be no answer, but I've written a lot that I haven't published.

Are these books?
Yes, they are in various stages, and I'll probably never go back to them.

Why did you give up?
Well, you see, if I start to work it's a two-, three- or four-year responsibility, and the idea better be good if I'm going to work that long. Sometimes the ideas are not as good in writing as I thought, and so I knock them in the head.

How much research do you do for a book?
I've always done a wide degree of reading in my research. When I feel something coming on, I may get as many as 150 to 200 books on the subject, browse through them, check things, etc.

When do you know you have enough to start writing?
That's a good problem, and I've never handled it well. As I write, I sometimes move ahead in the evenings doing research. But I often may be delayed by putting a certain thing aside knowing I will come back to it in about three months, after I do more research.

Do you often find that your research leads you to other ideas and angles?
No, not in subject matter, but often it is a digressive factor in the working out of a particular outline. I make changes, yes, but if I'm researching Jews in Russia and I find something interesting about Czar Alexander, I might file it as interesting material.

How do you file material?
Well, I don't keep files exactly, and I don't take many notes. I keep it in my head. I make page references in the backs of books for pages that I might want to later consult, but I keep the rest in my mind.

Do you develop characters that you can identify with, for example, David Harper, the orphan in The Fires of Spring?
That's a very difficult question to answer. By and large, no. I want my characters to be bigger, more free and flexible than the man in life, but you obviously have to start with someone—some known experience of some known human being, and I do, but I don't stick close to it. I intended the theory in my writings of having the central character more bland than peripheral characters; I've been severely criticized for this, and I think justly so. But still, I like the device, I use it, and if I were doing it again, I would still use it. I like the weak central character and strong peripheral characters. I don't know why. I'm not good at plotting, it doesn't interest me at all, and I'm not

good at writing the well-rounded English novel. I don't care about that. Both of these things represent a deficiency in my dramatic structure. But the fact that my books have been read so very widely proves that in at least certain respects I wasn't wrong. But I wouldn't recommend what I do to any other writers. I think it would be better to have the strong central character.

Do you often add characters in the middle of writing a book?
Yes, but more often however, incidents. I usually know who I need in the book, I've been thinking about it for such a long time. But ideas run away with every writer, and it's amazing how you can start out with something and find yourself grappling with a minor character and you never intended to do so.

When do you rewrite?
I tend to work in big blocks. I will do 50 to 100 pages because I want to get it lined out, and I won't go back for rewriting until I'm finished. If I were writing a short novel of 60,000 words, a really short novel, I'd write the whole thing and then I'd rewrite. I do a great deal of rewriting, and I do it sometimes in the evenings but mostly in the mornings.

When do you decide a title for your book?
I am very bad at that, and I have usually allowed the publisher to title my books. I submit to him a group of titles that I like and ask him to recommend one. He has usually not liked any of them and has often come up with suggestions of his own, which I haven't liked. It's tedious, I'm not good at it, I don't think about it, and I don't even write titles for my magazine articles. Titles are very important, and I wish I were better at it. I think a title like *A Streetcar Named Desire* is so brilliant that it really baffles me. But titles don't interest me. There's an awful lot in the world that doesn't interest me, and titles are part of it.

In your opinion, what makes a good novel?
I think of this a great deal. I love the form and am impressed with good examples of it. For me, the criterion is that the author has created a total world in which his people move credibly. And the books that do this I prize. *The Idiot*, for example, and Thackeray's *Vanity Fair*, Twain's *Huck Finn*, which I like very much, these are fine examples. The novel is just a little cosmos, and we're prepared to accept it; it's just a real world. This is a great accomplishment.

> *If I were a young man, I would not hesitate at writing anything to get into print, except pornography.*

You said you're not good at plotting, but how do you get around it?
I get around it by spending so much time creating that world that I get thousands of letters from people who say how totally immersed they were in the world and how sorry they were to have it end. That works for me.

What do you think the chances are of a beginning writer achieving your kind of financial independence?
The average author doesn't make a great deal of money from the books he writes. He gets wonderful rewards collaterally in promotions and advanced salary within his own profession, memberships in learned societies, but the rewards come primarily in reputation and entry into a lot of different things. A writer like Truman Capote or Saul Bellow, I would think, is the exception. They make real money, and I think they deserve it. Twenty years ago, you could count on a big movie sale, and that made a difference financially. A lot of people who wrote books and just got by made livings in the bonanza of movie sales. But that's all gone. Let me say that the young writer who is good and is well reviewed and maybe has a Book-of-the-Month Club every five years and is picked up by the *Reader's Digest* Book Club would live quite well. It can be done. It's a marvelous living and one you're entitled to aspire to. And I think it can be done by piecing it together. But the easy money of 50 years ago, movie sales and publication in magazines, is all gone.

You said earlier you've been constantly self-employed; you've never been on even a newspaper staff?
No, I never worked for anyone in the field of writing. I've been on assignment for the *New York Herald Tribune* and *The New York Times*, but these have been flexible assignments which didn't mean a great deal. I've always been a freelancer.

Did you follow anyone's technique?
Journalists, no, but I've been deeply influenced by the writings of the European novelists that I studied as a young man, and I responded remarkably to Balzac, Thackeray, Goncharov the Russian writer, and Nexo, the Danish writer. I feel great debt to these men.

Is it more difficult, in your opinion, to break into freelancing today than it was when you began writing?

It's becoming so difficult I couldn't recommend the business to anyone. It may be we're in a dark age right now, and maybe television will take over and there will be an equal number of jobs that used to be available on newspaper and magazine staffs. That's all very well for the nonfiction writer, but where's the fiction writer to get his hearing?

This last week I had a seminar with a group of students, and I advocated that they publish in little journals at universities. But since I made that statement I've seen reports that some 30 or 40 of these are going out of business. So where the young man is going to get the chance to prove his writing ability I don't know. I suspect through the university, off-Broadway drama, underground movies and publications I never knew about when I was young.

This country is going to be in perilous shape if it does not keep producing a group of writers. We're going to be in tough shape, and we will have to provide some way for our writers to learn their skills. This has not ever happened before, to my knowledge. It seems we're going back to the days of Sam Johnson in the late eighteenth century when you had to grab onto somebody, and maybe the young writer today will have to grab on to a corporation and ride with it. He'll keep alive that way. I don't rule out the possibility that writers of prose will pretty soon become like writers of poetry and operate through universities.

What about commercial markets such as confession magazines—do you think young writers should support themselves that way?
When I was a young man, I knew very well one of the men who was editor of a confession magazine. I never wrote for him because I didn't have the skill. He wanted me to, but I couldn't. But I learned a lot about the market and think it would be a completely legitimate training ground for a young writer. If I were young, I said a week ago, I'd hammer the little magazines with sophisticated, erudite writing, if I could do that. Maybe the young writer will have to write confession material and then get into paperback, and get into the trade that way. Then after eight or ten of these, the young writer can do a book that catches the eye of the general public. I would say, without qualification, if I were a young man with my attitudes and principles, I would not hesitate at writing anything to get into print, except hardcore pornography. I'd be happy if as a young man I'd written *Candy*, but that's not my style and I wouldn't write it now. It's a little beyond me. But if I were the age of the fellows who did write it, I'd be proud. I have a wide limit of what I would write—advertising copy—for example, and I'd run the gamut, but I'd write and get published.

Should young writers also be willing to supplement their incomes with other employment?
Look at the books of writers who have made it, whatever that means. You'll find that their first books were written like mine, at four o'clock in the morning while they had a full-time job. I wrote my first three that way, putting in a full day at the office, working in the early hours, but I was young then and had a lot of energy. I couldn't do it now, but that's what you have to do. Many writers can get jobs in public relations or elsewhere to supplement their incomes, and with the understanding of your spouse, you can organize your life so there is time to plug away at what you want to do. I believe in this thoroughly.

Any last advice for young writers?
Young writers ought to find two or three authors in the last century who make them feel they knew what it was all about. And then try to figure out how they did it. Where style is concerned, I would go to as many movies and plays as I could, and read the words of people who are experimenting. Don't bother with Bellow, Michener or Roth; these are the old-timers.

Look at the new people to figure out what they are into, and then decide virtues of your own and go to work. But I would certainly look at revolutionary and experimental forms in all fields: poetry, drama, painting, architecture, and then I'd move into the twenty-first century 20 years early.

BY LARRY LEONARD

JEAN AUEL

I had half a million words, but it wasn't a story.

For all of her life, Jean M. Auel had been a working mother of five. Oh, she dabbled in writing. Letters to the editor, some poetry. But, she never sold a short story. She never even *wrote* one.

Yet, at the age of 40, she began a story at her kitchen table. Maybe it would be a short thing, maybe more. She didn't know. She didn't intend to try to sell anything, anyway. This was just a way of killing time.

The more she worked on it, the more it grew. The more it grew, the more she felt *involved* with it. Pretty soon it was taking up all her nights. Pretty soon, it was her obsession.

What began that night at a kitchen table has blossomed into a projected six-volume series about ancient, strange cultures. The first books of the series, *The Clan of the Cave Bear* and *The Valley of Horses*, became critically praised bestsellers.

In her new 4,000-square-foot cliff home overlooking the Pacific near Oregon's artistic community of Cannon Beach, Auel admits to being dazzled by it all herself.

She looks bookish. Her name, Auel, is pronounced "owl." Her huge, round glasses add to the owlish, literary mien. Her eyes are a fine blue. They are intelligent (she's a MENSA member, with an IQ in the 150-170 range), and quick to crinkle with delight. She's a diminutive woman, now 47, who favors a form of at-home dress similar to Dustin Hoffman's. Whoever's shirt is handy is what she wears.

Her home rises from the beach in a series of levels, decks and staircases. It features a sauna, hot tub, wine cellar, library, writing loft, exercise room and no fewer than *four* powder rooms. "For 20 years," Auel explains, "I lived in an unfinished house with five kids and one bathroom. Now, I live in a finished house with no kids and four bathrooms. And I use 'em all."

One of the living room walls is half-covered by a glass enclosure that contains all the versions of her two books: French, Swedish, Japanese and other translations. Elsewhere are cave art reproductions, primitive carvings and Northwest Indian artifacts. She has a fine collection of atlatls, the spear throwing devices that appeared in *Valley*.

The house is organized almost to a fault. Even so, it manages to avoid the forbidding quality that often goes with such organization. In fact, the compulsion for organization is a good clue to the reasons behind her success.

Jean Auel grew up in the Midwest. A precocious woman of pure Finnish extract, she married her high school sweetheart, Ray Auel, and eventually ended up in Oregon. Along the way, she read: political satires, ponderous historical treatises, dog stories—it didn't matter to her. If it had words, it fascinated her. At 12, she discovered science fiction. She loves that genre to this day.

You could argue that this affection for science fiction has shaped her. Certainly, few other novelists produce works that link mainstream and science fiction as comfortably as she does. Perhaps her analytical side has shaped her as well. She studied science in college while working for Tektronix, one of Oregon's pioneers in high technology. She's always been at home around computers, oscilloscopes and circuit boards.

In fact, for a time, she *designed* circuit boards, a

*Jean Auel had never studied writing, had never even considered writing as a career. She wrote half a million words before she picked up her first book on writing or attended her first writing class. Yet, her first novel—*Clan of the Cave Bear*—sold at auction for a $130,000 advance and earned an American Book Award nomination.*

How did she do it? In this 1984 profile, the creator of the projected six-volume Earth's Children *series (the third and most recent,* The Mammoth Hunters, *had a 1.1 million first printing) explains it all.*

symbol manipulation process that has a certain metaphorical relationship to the weaving of a complex historical novel. But novels were off in the future during those days. Jean Auel would have laughed at anyone who suggested she had a genius for something like that. It was work, family and school for her.

She abandoned her plans for the Bachelor of Science degree when a local college offered an after-work, off-campus MBA program at Tektronix. She and Ray (who also worked there) jumped into the program and earned their advanced degrees. But, where science had fascinated Jean, business left her cold. "When I was in that school, I found business books the most boring things I'd ever read. I had to hold my eyelids open with toothpicks, practically. But, boy I *loved* doing term papers."

Ray loved the business books as much as she did the term papers. A happy coincidence; he eventually had to quit the electronics firm to manage their burgeoning financial empire.

After completing the degree program, Auel grew restless. Her 11 years at one of the top companies in Oregon seemed an investment in a dirt road to nowhere. She couldn't put her finger on the problem, but she spent a lot of time complaining about it. "They hired a new young man. I don't think he liked directing a 40-year-old lady. I focused on that. Now, he should watch out. If I saw him again, I'd kiss him for being one of the reasons I left the company."

In 1976, she began a "desultory" search for work. "It was a bad time to lose half our income. We had four kids in college and a son at home." She began fishing in the employment section of the paper. "It was like, 'Well, here's an ad. I guess I ought to apply for it.' So, I'd send off a resume. 'But, remember, be sure you don't send a cover letter. Then they won't answer you.'"

Then, one winter night, something magical happened. She was sitting at the kitchen table, sipping coffee and staring out into the dark beyond the window. Ray was in bed. Jean was alone, reflective.

A story came to her. About a time in history when there were two kinds of human beings. What if a girl from one was orphaned, and came to live with the other? She began to make some pencil notes.

She didn't realize it at the time, but this was her second effort at writing a tale. Long after *Clan* came out, Ray reminded her of it. Many years earlier, the same impulse had struck her. She had gotten two paragraphs into the story and thrown down her pencil in disgust. Writing was too hard.

But, that previous incident was forgotten this night. Before she knew it, the night was gone.

Her organized, fastidious attitude toward research took over. There was no time for sleep. She headed for the library and lost herself among the archeology and anthropology stacks. When she didn't pick up her son at school that afternoon, he headed straight for the library.

He'd seen mom on a research project before. His compensation for the desertion was two armloads of books to carry home.

For months, Auel researched and made notes all night and slept all day—which, by the way, is a pattern she maintains now. Seasons came and seasons went. Ray knew an obsession when he saw one; though he knew it was straining their financial resources, he supported her, told her the work would be a bestseller before she realized she was writing a book.

And she *didn't* realize it. This was a . . . project. Something to fill in the time until she found the perfect job. But the day that perfect job came along, she finally had to face facts.

It was a wonderful chance. A top-level position with the Bank of California. It meant financial security for the family and a fine intellectual challenge. She wrestled with her problem for a long time. Then, reluctantly, she turned the job down.

The Bank of California upped the offer.

You couldn't plot a better last-minute squeeze on the heroine. The offer was just too good to pass up. Reluctantly, Ray suggested she take the position. Auel couldn't decide. She wanted that opportunity, but the thought of putting the story aside brought her to tears.

It was wearing her to a frazzle. Ray thought she ought to get away for the weekend to think things out. They went hiking in the magnificent Columbia River Gorge. It was there, surrounded by a landscape so very like that of her future novels, that she realized she couldn't give up the story. For all it meant in loss of security to her family, she just *had* to take the long shot.

Once that hurdle had been, however fearfully, overcome, she said to herself: "All right, Jean M. Auel. Now you've gone and done it! But, it is done, and you better get serious about this business of writing." This "project" of hers, with a working title of *Earth's Children*, had to somehow be made publishable. Taking a fresh look at it, she began for the first time to analyze what she had already done.

"I had half a million words, but it wasn't a *story*. That's when I decided to find out what a story was.

"I began reading books on how to write. I had this first thing done and I knew that it wasn't good. I was beginning to get a feel for what was good, but I was worried. I had never taken any writing classes. So, I decided that one of the things I had better do was associate with other writers.

"What happened was funny. I was combing my hair and I had the radio on. Somebody made this announcement: 'Would you like to be a published author?' *What? Did they say . . . what's this?* 'Come to this meeting of Willamette Writers. . . . '

"I had a friend who had talked about the group, so I took down the number, called up and went to this meeting. I didn't know what I was doing there. I mean, these were all writers! 'All I'm doing is sitting home at my type-writer. Do I really belong here?' I had all of those kinds of feelings and fears that you get.

"Now, this club is not the sort of a group where you get together and everybody sits around and reads each other's work and tears it apart. This group brings in speakers to talk about the various aspects of writing. One of the speakers was a man named Don James. Well, Don James is one of those people who has a great love and feeling for writing, and a great, wonderful ability to inspire. He gives of himself from some deep well that people keep digging into . . . and he's always there. And, he's made his living from words all his life [29 published books].

"He started talking about fiction. 'You've got to *show*, not *tell*,' he said. And then he gave an example. 'The girl went into the room and she put her hands over the man's eyes and said, "Guess who this is." ' That's telling. 'The man's sitting at the table. He feels cool hands come over his eyes. Someone says, "Guess who this is." ' That's showing.

"He was saying things like: 'You don't have to go to school to learn to write. Because, very often if you do, you'll be taking from a teacher who's teaching from a textbook. A person who's very likely never published. So, how are you going to learn about publishable writing from someone who's never done it? All they can do is teach you what's in the books. You can read the books yourself. The way to learn to write is to write. Maybe by the time you've written a million words in your life—and that counts letters—you'll begin to discover what you need to know.'

"And I thought: 'I've got almost a half a million words. I'm getting close!' You talk about somebody giving you permission. He didn't know he was talking to me. He thought he was talking to the group. But, he was talking to *me*. Speaking directly to my worries and my concerns about what I was doing at that moment. He said: 'Read a lot. That's how you learn to write. Read novels, read fiction. . . .'

"These days, I get letters from people who want to write, and they'll say that they refuse to read any other fiction. I say to myself: 'You dummy! How do you think you learn to write? You don't [do it to] copy anybody's particular style. You do it to find out what the *tech-niques* are.'

"Anyway, that night was a release. I went home, looked at my manuscript and said, 'This is possible. I'm going to do it.' "

She dug into books on writing techniques. Her favorites came to be *Techniques of Fiction Writing: Measure and Madness*, by Leon Surmelian, and *Art of Dramatic Writing*, by Lajos Egri. She dove into them. Devoured them. Read and reread them. When a section referred to a technique employed in *Madame Bovary* or *Wuthering Heights*, *Moby Dick* or *Death of a Salesman*, she studied the passage in question, then, as often as not, read the entire work (not, as in past years, for pleasure, but to learn *how* the writer did what he or she did).

Gradually, things began to fall into place. Her half-million-word manuscript became the outline for six novels. *Earth's Children* was now the series name. She titled the first story *The Clan of the Cave Bear*.

Then, a "lucky accident" occurred.

At a writer's seminar at Cannon Beach, she heard Jean Naggar, a New York agent, speak. With the fearlessness of the uninformed, she told Naggar afterwards that she was writing a book about ancient peoples. Naggar gave Auel her card and said, "Write me about it when you finish."

When *Clan* was done, Jean Auel had second thoughts. Why should she share her income with an agent? She began sending the novel out cold. Five major publishers turned it down flat. Auel decided that 90 percent of something was better than 100 percent of nothing, and sent the story to Naggar.

The agent loved it. So much, in fact, that she did something unusual with it. She put a first book up for auction. By the time the bidding was done, Jean Auel had an advance check for $130,000 and a new respect for the value of literary agents.

More checks came in when Bantam brought out *Clan* in paperback. Yet more checks rolled in when Auel's second book, *The Valley of Horses*, was released in hardcover. *Valley* recently came out in paperback with a run of 1.5 million copies, and Universal has secured an option on the first two books.

Auel is writing her third book, *The Mammoth Hunters*, on a word processor. She wrote the first two on a matched pair of Smith-Corona Coronet Super Twelves. (Because she writes at night, and in marathon sessions, she bought a backup with the same typeface. Thus, a wee-hours malfunction couldn't shut her down.)

About the much-discussed problem of "creating" on a word processor, Auel says: "My biggest problem was go-

> *I went home, looked at my manuscript and said, "This is possible. I'm going to do it."*

ing from a pencil to a typewriter. It was a decision I made very early on. I had always written my poetry on lined paper. I still have to. And, I did the first ten pages of my novel [what became the series outline] by hand. But, I realized that I have crummy handwriting. I can't read what I wrote a couple of weeks later. So, I said: 'This is silly. I know how to type.' But it took me a certain amount of effort to learn how to be creative at the typewriter. Once I had that, the transition from typewriter to word processor wasn't a problem."

She did, however, put in some time learning the mechanics of her word processor. "I had had friends who used word processors. And, at Tektronix, some of my dictation was handled that way. But I hadn't worked on one myself. When I found the one I wanted, I took four days of classes and then laid off for about three weeks. Cleaned out my closet and drawers. Then I went back to it. I took the manual and sat down in front of it, and for a solid week of eight-, ten-hour days I went from page one to the end. Now, I'm comfortable with it. I can make it do whatever it needs to do."

Her method of getting comfortable—of making her manipulations of the computer second nature—is typically Jean Auel. The techniques of craftsmanship came together via exhaustive reading and step-by-step assimilation, too. Yet, her writing these days is anything but mechanical. She *realizes* her narratives far more than she *machinates* them.

"There are two kinds of writers in the world: the organized ones and the organic ones. When you're organized, you do an outline, you do character studies, you do all of this and all of that *before* you write. The other approach is the organic one. You know where you're going and you kind of just let it take you there. The outline [for all her books in the *Earth's Children* series] I'm working from now happens to be my first draft.

"And, it turns out, I don't mind rewriting. I like it. I love that first flush, that first draft, when things are happening. That's the hardest part, too. But, I also like the rewriting because that's where I get a handle. That's where I'm fine-tuning." Auel "fine-tuned" the first page of *Clan* some 40 times.

Rewriting to her is polishing a fine gem from a rough stone. It is taking out the stupid and contrived. "In the first book, Ayla [the central character] is in trouble. She's gotten herself in trouble. She runs away with her baby. In my first thought, I had her coming back after seven days. After the time when [according to Clan law] the baby could be killed. In rewrite, suddenly I've got Creb [the

Clan shaman] and Iza [the Clan medicine woman] talking. Creb is discovering Ayla's run away—and suddenly Creb says: 'Brun won't let her get away with that. He'll lose face.' And, I thought: 'He's right! That's in character for Brun [the Clan Chief]. He would never let her get away with that. He'd accept the baby and he'd have her out of there the next second—name it and put a death curse on Ayla right away.'

"There was no way he could maintain face and save Ayla. Now, how was I going to get her out of this? So, I thought about it and decided Ayla had to come back sooner. How would I manage that? It was then that I saw the scene where Creb [who is deformed] pleads with his brother [Brun]. Where he stands up and says: 'She doesn't want to kill that baby. And, maybe that baby's deformed and shouldn't be allowed to live, but look at me. Should I have been allowed to live?'

"When I wrote that scene, I had *tears* coming out of my eyes. And it was the characters that got me there. Because once I let those characters come alive, they *couldn't* act out of character. That made a more interesting story out of it. It would have been duller if she'd just come back on naming day."

The scene involving Creb and Brun also demonstrates other principles. For instance, suspense: "Lajos Egri, in his *Art of Dramatic Writing*, taught me how to create a scene. How to go from one scene to another. He's very good at describing how a play [is constructed]. Before you finish a scene, you have to lead to the next scene. What you are doing is maybe not a linear, upward suspense. A sustained sort of thing. It's in incremental jumps.

"In terms of *Clan of the Cave Bear*, I thought of it as a sequential thing. The first sequence is Ayla's loss [being orphaned by an earthquake]. The second sequence is the Clan finding her, they find the cave and she gets adopted. The next sequence is Ayla learning to use a sling. We have a whole Ayla-becomes-a-hunter sequence in there.

"She's at risk because she's lost her family. She's at risk next because the Clan hasn't accepted her, yet. And she's at risk in the last case because she's doing something she's not supposed to do. I don't know that I ever specifically thought about it as suspense. I see it as a question: 'Why do you want to find out about that character?'

"In the second book, we've got Ayla and Jondalar. Well, they're not at risk in that sense. But, there's a tremendous suspense factor there because you know from the first line in the second chapter that Ayla and that

> *I had tears coming out of my eyes. And it was the characters that got me there.*

man are going to meet. [The suspense isn't rooted in] *if*, it's *how* and *when*."

Another important principle is dialogue. "Dialogue for me is something I see because I visualize what I'm writing. I visualize description, I visualize my characters there, happening. I've got my eyes shut and I'm thinking about what they're doing. I don't really try to write dialogue to be cute or clever. That's not the kind of books I'm writing. I had to make some decisions about what level of dialogue I needed. I thought because I'm writing about prehistory, maybe I ought to invent some kind of a primitive, phony-sounding language. And then I thought: Number one, that's going to be awful hard for a reader. But even equal to that, scientifically it's not as accurate. People don't talk to each other in phony, archaic constructs. They wouldn't have then. They would have talked to each other with as much ease and facility as you and I.

"I decided that the best way to write the dialogue was to use normal, human English. I tried to think of it in terms of translation. What does a translator do? He not only [interchanges] word for word, but he also tries to capture nuance and idiom.

"Like with the two brothers [in *Valley*]. What I really wanted to do was show that these were people who could have been alive today. They could be your brother, your college friend, your neighbor's son. That was the point I wanted to get across. That these people were as modern as we are today, *but* they lived in a totally different culture.

"Now, how does culture affect character? How does culture affect action? How does culture affect speech patterns? I had some fun inventing sayings that might have existed then and tying them to story action. You know how we say, when somebody gets married, that they're tying the knot? I thought, Well, why not? I had them actually do it as part of the ceremony.

"You identify and separate characters with dialogue. For example, Creb is a more intelligent speaker than Broud [the Clan Chief's son]. Broud is egotistic. That comes out in his dialogue.

"[In *Valley*] I tried to separate Jondalar and Thonolan with Jondalar being much more serious and Thonolan the one who usually makes the sometimes broad, corny humor—though he thinks he's funny."

This scene from *The Valley of Horses* demonstrates (Jondalar is speaking):

"Little Brother, what makes you think you're the only one in this family with an urge to travel? You didn't think I was going to let you go off by yourself, did you? Then come home and brag about your long Journey? Someone has to go along to keep your stories straight, and keep you out of trouble," the tall blond man replied, then stooped to enter the tent. . . .

"Keep me out of trouble!" Thonolan said. "I'm going to have to grow eyes in the back of my head to watch your rear! Wait until Marona finds out you're

not with Dalanar and the Lanzadonii when they get to the Meeting. She might decide to turn herself into a donii and come flying over that glacier we just crossed to get you, Jondalar. They started folding up the tent between them. "That one has had her eye on you for a long time, and just when she thought she had you, you decide it's time to make a Journey. I think you just don't want to slip your hand in that thong and let Zelandoni tie the knot. I think my big brother is mating-shy." They put the tent beside the backframes.

"Most men your age already have a little one, or two, at their hearths," Thonolan added, ducking a mock punch from his older brother; the laughter had now reached his gray eyes.

"Most men my age! I'm only three years older than you," Jondalar said, feigning anger. Then he laughed, a big hearty laugh, its uninhibited exuberance all the more surprising because it was unexpected.

The serious Jondalar is not speaking out of character here. The banter with his brother is the only time he demonstrates a humorously lighter side, an acceptable way of communicating affection. Yet, even within this break of character, Thonolan, with his references to magic and Jondalar's supposedly steamy romance, still comes off as the brassier of the two.

Changing moods require, of course, more than altered speech patterns within character. There's the matter of pace. "Pace to me is a great deal more than just turning the pages fast. Sometimes the pace needs to be slowed down. Sometimes you want that change in texture. I'm conscious of pace. It's a thing that I think about when I write.

"There are times, for example, in *Valley* where Ayla is getting so tired, so exhausted. Giving up hope. I want the reader to feel this agonizing slowness, the time it is taking her to get someplace. And, there are times, when you're going to have, for example, a hunt scene. Those are the times you're going to use those quick, incisive sentences," as in this scene from *The Valley of Horses*:

The rhino came to a stop; he seemed unaware that the rest of his troupe were rapidly moving ahead. Then he started out at a rather slow run, veering toward the hood fluttering in the wind. Jondalar moved in closer to Jetamio, and he noticed Dolando doing the same.

Then a young man, whom Jondalar recognized as one who stayed on the boat, waved his hood and rushed in front of them toward the animal. The confused rhino stalled his headlong run toward the woman and, changing his direction, started after the man. The larger moving target was easier to follow even with limited sight; the presence of so many hunters misled his acute sense of smell. Just as he was get-

*ting close, another running figure darted between him
and the young man. The woolly rhino stalled again,
trying to decide which moving target to follow.*

*He changed direction and charged after the sec-
ond who was so tantalizingly close. But then another
hunter interceded, flapping a large fur cloak, and,
when the young rhino neared it, still another ran past,
so close he gave the long reddish fur on his face a
yank. The rhinoceros was getting angry, murderously
angry. He snorted, pawed the ground, and, when he
saw another of those disconcerting running figures,
tore after it at top speed.*

The lengths of the sentences vary and the dimensions of
the paragraphs change to generate a feeling of increasing
activity, of urgency, in the reader's mind.

So, Jean M. Auel knows her technique ABCs. But, in a
sense, she's gone past the conscious awareness of them.
Her attitude toward plot is a good example. She doesn't
believe in plotting in the strictly mechanical sense. "I
think the plot—and every other aspect [of a story]—
really hangs on character, because what you have is, to
me, really an idea about a story. How does that story
work out? In my mind, I've got how it's going to work out,
but how it really happens is how the characters work out.

"I've come to the conclusion just from the things I've
read, the things I keep reading, and from my own experience that while plot and theme and pacing and every
other element in fiction is important . . . the really key
element in fiction is character. Because if you've got characters that have come alive—have come off the page—
they tell your story.

"I just read a review in *The New York Times* about a
new book. The reviewer said that one of the things the
author did was to make each person so *individual*. So,
we don't just have a woman lawyer who's busy. She is
busy on a case involving a man who decided to will all of
his money to the US Army. And all of his sharkskin suits
to J.C. Penney! Now, you've got a particular lawyer who is
dealing with her particular case.

"It's the little details that do it, that bring a character or a scene alive in the reader's mind. I'm a visual
writer. When I write, half the time my eyes are closed
because I'm seeing what's inside of this cave, what this
person looks like . . . what the person is seeing.

"I mean, what are they doing? Jondalar is one of

these worrywarts. You know that he's tied up about
something because his brow always furrows. He's got that
kind of, you know, frowny look. That's a characteristic of
his.

"I just got through with a sequence up there where
Ayla's standing on the edge of this group of people, looking at them. Now, I could say they're involved in various
activities. But, I said, 'That's lazy. I can't do that. I've got
to say *what* they're involved in.' So Jondalar and the
other flint knappers are in one spot. You know what
they're talking about. And, then there's a group of people
taking a hide off a frame. They're untying the strings.
And, there's another group of people digging these holes
and filling them with mammoth bones, getting ready for
the winter. These are the things that she's seeing. They
impinge upon her. They're going to have an effect on her.
When you tell the world what she sees and how she per-
ceives it, that makes her come alive.

"When you work it this way, these things [story tech-
niques] start to work themselves out. More than plot, I
keep in mind theme. Theme is harder to define. Lajos
Egri talks about it a lot in *Art of Dramatic Writing*. You
can state the theme of your work in one sentence.

"So, I decided early on I would know what my theme
is: survival. It's expressed differently each time, but it's
the same theme. You've got to have the strength to
change in order to survive.

"In the first book, I said, 'If you do not change, you
will become extinct.' In the second book, Ayla's overcom-
ing her childhood conditioning. If I keep that theme in
mind, the story and the characters will take me there.
Now, plot is what's happening. Before I ever sit down, it's
whirling around in my head—I'm thinking, 'What's going
to happen here, now?' Plot is the *tell*. The getting from
here to there.

"I'm conscious of all these things, even though my
characters are leading me by the nose. I'm making decisions about the story. On top of it. I mean, some people
have this funny idea about writing. That you just sit at
the machine and it just flows out of your body. Even if
you're an organic writer, it doesn't work that way.

"Writing is damned hard work. But, if it's done properly, it'll touch people. I don't like intellectual fiction. I do
my intellectual reading in nonfiction. Fiction and poetry
have a common goal. They should touch you, move you,
grab you."

BY JAMES W. MCLEAN

WILLIAM SAROYAN

You are what you are and it isn't much but you have to make do with it.

Some observers say that your first book The Daring Young Man on the Flying Trapeze *was a peak that you never surpassed. Do you feel that's so?*
Well, I have to be respectful of that opinion. It's been a common one for years and was certainly alive when I was in London a year ago. Everybody wants to know how I could keep steadily declining. When *The Daring Young Man* came out, I had that special good luck a writer has when he gets his audience right. That was the right time for that book. It was full of experiments because I loved the short story form. As you know, after *Story Magazine* had accepted the title story, I told them I would write a new one every day for 30 days and send them along, to illustrate the problem of the short story writer. On one of the days, I wrote *three* short stories. I wanted to demonstrate to the editors that there could be writers who wanted to write but had no place to dispose of their work. We had a very bad situation in the short story field then. We still have.

Did Story Magazine *do the whole lot?*
They turned them over to the man who was backing their venture. That was Bennett Cerf at Random House. He did them.

It was Cerf who put them together into The Daring Young Man *book?*
Yes. There were 36 and he published 26. I argued with him about that, and he said the trouble with me was I wanted everything I wrote published. I said of course I did. That's one of the reasons I left Random House after two books. Publishers have a way of being publishers.

With Story *back in business, will you be doing any writing for them?*
I'd like to. I've been invited to. But I don't think you can go back. We all move along. *Story Magazine* belonged to

that world. What you have now is a new magazine with new writers and a new audience.

You've written about 30 books and 20 plays, as well as any number of magazine stories. What's your favorite piece of work in this Niagara of production?
My Heart's in the Highlands, which happens to have been my first play. I also liked a book called *Rock Wagram.*

Yes. Wagram. *I read it about ten years ago.*
That makes two people who've read it: you and me.

The recurring theme in your writing is that love is everything. Do you practice what you preach?
It isn't quite that deliberate. I think you are what you are and your way is your way. I have to tell you that I am profoundly discontented with who I am and respectful of it. You are what you are and it isn't much but you have to make do with it.

You once said that a writer may lead a fuller and

The comparison is so easy, you hesitate to make it: William Saroyan as The Daring Young Man on the Flying Trapeze. Exuberant, reckless words reopening critical eyes to the short story form with the 1934 publication of his famous collection.

Saroyan's life was as unfettered as his style: the son of Armenian immigrants, he dropped out of school at 15, exploded into fame at the age of 26 with The Daring Young Man *collection, wrote the Pulitzer Prize-winning play* The Time of Your Life *five years later, and capped his career with the novel* The Human Comedy *and its Oscar-winning screenplay in 1943. This 1962 interview catches vintage walrus-moustached Saroyan: jokingly boastful, startlingly sincere, and confidently carefree.*

deeper life than anyone else if he is a hard and honest worker. Could you elaborate on this?

The meaning there is that, if a writer is constantly concerned with truth, grace, order and other verities, his inner life just naturally enriches in proportion to his working. Mind you, I wouldn't bet my life that this is true. A friend of mine was once talking about Joan of Arc. He said he couldn't understand people who suffer themselves to be burned at the stake for their ideas. I asked him if he wouldn't be willing to forfeit his life for his ideas. "Oh, no," he said. "I might be mistaken."

Brooks Atkinson once called you the most undisciplined of writers. Do you agree that you are undisciplined?

Well, I've never said I was, but Brooks is a friend of mine so we'll let that go. I don't feel I'm especially undisciplined. I try for an order of usage of creative energy. It can *look* undisciplined. But ten years later critics like Brooks look back and agree that the work they said at the time was loose now looks pretty good.

I used to throw things out, saying, "This isn't great." It didn't occur to me that it didn't have to be great.

Would you tell me about your work habits?

I believe in anything that works. With me it varies. When I'm seized by a chore, an assignment, a job, I need to do it quickly. This is not necessarily a virtue. It's just that I'm always afraid that if I don't do a thing right away I might never do it. I usually write a play in six days, a novel takes a month. The play I wrote for Daryll Zanuck last year, *The Paris Comedy*, took 13 days because there was so much partying going on at the time.

When you're actually working, though, do you hold to a nine-to-five routine or work until you fall asleep?

It has to do with the amount of writing I have to get done and with how I'm feeling about the quality of work I'm doing after five or six hours. Sometimes out of very great fatigue my best work can come.

How does pressure affect your work?

Sometimes, without pressure, the work doesn't get done at all. You abandon most readily those works that have no destination other than your own wishes; there is no editor or producer standing there waiting for them. I often do this, although I don't like to. I prefer a pattern of seeing a job through. In fact, not having such a pattern is what holds many young writers back. Their high standards, the demands they make of themselves, are so great

they get a novel about a third done and then give up because they think it's not good enough. I've told every young writer I know to do the job all the way through even if they think it's no good. Then he'll have the precedent of having finished a work. It isn't unlikely that he's been mistaken anyway. All writers are discontented with their work as it's being made. That's because they're aware of a potential, and believe they're not reaching it. But the reader is not aware of the potential, so it makes no difference to him.

You're suggesting you suspend your critical faculties until you finish the work at hand?

Oh, you can't suspend them. But don't pay too much attention to them or you'll quit. As a kid I used to throw things out, saying, "This isn't great." It didn't occur to me that it didn't have to be *great.* Then some of the things that I thought were useless, as the years went by, took on more and more meaning. This was because I was *not* straining for greatness. This gave them a freshness, an inevitability that had to flourish. Even when you think you're writing badly, the inevitability will flourish. And it may not be as bad as you think.

In a story called "The Sweet Singer of Omsk," you say that it isn't you that's doing the writing. It's "The Presence." I've heard William Faulkner say the same thing. Can you tell me about it?

I don't think this is limited to Mr. Faulkner and myself. It's known and recognized pretty much by all writers. After you've taken your chair and have written a while—perhaps an hour or so—it comes along, and you start to move ahead strongly. It appears to be a very deep order of energy. Psychiatrists say you're drawing on the collective memory in the Jungian sense. It's like the prizefighter who crosses himself before a fight. It isn't he who will win, it's something else *through* him. Same goes for writing.

You said recently that you're in Europe to make enough money to pay off your $60,000 back-tax debt, so you can return to America. What's the matter, don't you like this part of the world?

Oh I *do* like Europe. But one goes back to function. I've been away from the theater as a producer since the war. My wanting to return has to do with the fact that I want to produce my own plays.

Well, you've just had a play in London that flopped. Did that embitter you?
The play was so simple that I was disappointed when the critics said it confused them. I wrote a letter to the 15 critics, pointing out that they were wrong about the play and I was right.

And what was the result?
One of them wrote another column about the play. He said he had to go along with Saroyan. He said that it *isn't* the majority that decides about a work of art. Thus, one playwright is just as likely to be right as 15 critics.

How do you feel about critics in general?
I have no quarrel with them. How can you quarrel with people when at any moment they are liable to praise you? But about that London play, they'd all heard that I was writing it as we went along. During rehearsals, that is. So they claimed I was having a laugh at the expense of the public.

You mean if this play had been written by a young unknown it would have been judged by different standards?
No doubt about it. An entirely untried playwright from whom so much might not have been expected would have received another order of review. Then the spontaneous writing idea might have appealed to the critics.

What about audiences? What differences do you find in audiences in different parts of the world?
I used to be able to understand the response of an American audience and be able to tell on opening night how a play would be reviewed. But in London, I couldn't tell at all. The audience goes to the bar at intermission and praises a play, but the critics go away and write bad reviews. On the other hand, I was amazed when I went to some of the London long-running plays and found audiences so unresponsive.

Americans react more openly?
Generally. I remember going to *The Male Animal* by James Thurber on Broadway once. Everybody was laughing, and so was I. Then the usher came up and asked could I laugh a little bit quieter. Later I asked the producer how come his usher got upset because I enjoyed the play. The producer said, "Billy, you've got a real loud laugh."

So I've noticed. Speaking of New York, you had no plays there between 1943 and 1957. One reviewer said it was self-doubt and injured pride that kept you away for those 14 years. What about that?
I never permit anything anybody writes about me to be dismissed entirely as untrue. It was Henry Hewes of *The Saturday Review* who wrote that self-doubt bit, and he meant it to be really profound stuff. But my 14 years

away, as he called it, were chosen. I didn't *offer* any plays to producers, though many producers were eager to just *look* at one of my plays. I said no, I'm waiting for the time when I can produce my own plays. As Jimmy Durante once said, I can get along without Broadway, but can Broadway get along without me? The answer is, bet your life it can.

How many plays have you on hand yet to be produced?
I have 20 full-length ones. Two I wrote last year in Paris. I also have any number of shorter plays, about a third of which have been done on television. *Omnibus* has done about ten of my plays since its beginning. You don't forfeit your rights when your plays are done on television.

What are you working on now?
I want very much to make use of this new apartment, this new luxury of space, so I set myself to do a novel in a month. I'll also do another play this year, and some short stories.

Have you a name for the novel?
I don't have a name and I don't have a plot. I have the typewriter and I have white paper and I have me and that should add up to a novel.

You've said repeatedly you're one of the best writers in the world. Are you trying to convince us or yourself?
I get a kick out of saying that. It's a kind of Californian-Armenian-Saroyan bragging, for fun, a superficial remark you throw out just to let people have a laugh. And it isn't that I don't take what I say seriously. I do. At the same time, how can you take *anything* terribly seriously? The writer who today may seem to be grand, tomorrow may be trash. We write for a human race that is constantly changing. Our particular creature is becoming obsolete— he may be gone long before any bomb destroys us. I think all our values, all the points on which we judge things, are going to change. I think both love and hate will be judged differently in times to come; for instance, if we get rid of one, we get rid of the other. How the devil could you have love if you didn't have hate?

What do you hope to have accomplished by the time your writing career is over? What would you like your obit writers to say about you?
I suppose that most of all I would like them to say that I cherished mankind and wasn't too impatient with anybody. I have to remind myself that if it were not for my good luck in having the profession of writing and the compulsion to write, the human experience would be for me a very different order of thing. I could never be a worker, a slave. So if I hadn't been a writer, I'd have been a bum. This would not necessarily have been unwelcome.
I remember talking to Shaw once when he told me he'd just had a call from H.G. Wells. Wells was sick and dis-

heartened. He was sad, because he felt that all the efforts he'd made to influence the human race had failed. So I asked Shaw if he thought his own life would be an influence on the human race. He said, "Not in the least." I was touched by Wells, but I agree with Shaw. I can't imagine why we should think we can influence the enormous situation. We fancy that we're taking charge. But that's only a fancy. We're never in charge at all.

What more is there to say?
Just everything, most likely, but let's agree on no more for a moment.

BY ROY NEWQUIST

TRUMAN CAPOTE

The only obligation any artist can have is to himself.
His work means nothing, otherwise.

Other Voices, Other Rooms introduced one of the great literary talents of our time: Truman Capote. Without Voices, The Grass Harp, The Muses Are Heard, *and* Breakfast at Tiffany's—*to mention only some of his fiction and reportage—contemporary American letters would present a far slimmer file in the valuable pocket labeled "quality."*

In talking with Mr. Capote, I would like to begin by asking him the essential autobiography—where he was born, reared, and educated, and when his interest in writing developed.

I was born in New Orleans in 1924. (By the way, my name isn't Capote at all—I'll explain that later.) My father's name is Persons, and he was a salesman. My mother was only 16 years old when they were married, and she was very, very beautiful—a beauty contest-winner type of child who later on in life became an enormously sensitive and intelligent person. But she was only 16 when she married—a normal, beautiful girl, rather wild—and my father was 24.

My mother wasn't able to cope with the situation. She had a baby and she traveled with my father all around the South, and when she was 18 she decided that she wanted to go to college. So I went to college with her, all the way through, and by the time she was graduated, she and my father were divorced, so I went to live with relatives in a rather remote part of Alabama. This was a very strange household. It consisted of three elderly ladies and an elderly uncle. They were the people who had adopted my mother—her own parents had died when she was very young. I lived there until I was ten, and it was a very lonely life, and it was then that I became interested in writing. You see, I always could read. I have the illusion that I could read when I was four years old, and I actually could read before I ever went to school. In first grade, reading was the only thing I liked to do, because I had

this lonely childhood, and reading took me out of it. I began to write, and also to paint—another deep interest I had. (I was also interested in music, but for various reasons I was not allowed to take music lessons.) Anyway, I started to write when I was eight years old and wrote a book when I was nine.

I spent every summer in that town in Alabama until I was 16. In the meantime, my mother had gone to New York and had remarried. Her husband was a Cuban businessman named Capote, a name Spanish in origin. He adopted me, and my name was legally changed to Capote. I came to New York to school for three years. I went to different boarding schools around New York, and when I finally left school I was 17 and went straight to work at *The New Yorker* in the art department.

Originally I was to work for *The New Yorker* in the "Talk of the Town" department. I had been sending them stories and articles, and I went to see the people I had

---

The tragedy of most Truman Capote interviews—if you're a writer—is that the celebrity overshadows the literary: the shocking appeal of that Capote personality, those parties and appearances and controversy, take precedence in the general public mind.

The tragedy, and beauty, of this interview is its maddening tease. Given just before the publication of In Cold Blood *in 1966, the interview finds a 42-year-old Capote eager to open up about a new book, a new kind of book—a "nonfiction novel" that would become the flagship of a new era in journalism.*

But the interviewer—and probably wisely so at the time—skipped on to more relevant subjects. Imagining the interview that might have been is almost painful; the best salve is to sit back and enjoy what's here: the first-draft (the taped interview is reproduced "live," as you'll notice in the short introduction), elegant voice of a language master.

been corresponding with; they were going to give me a job. It was during the war, and they had lost all their staff. Well, I arrived, and they took one look—I was 17 and looked about ten years old—and realized they could never send this child labor case out to interview anybody, so in the end I worked in the art department and turned out ideas for "Talk of the Town" every week and suggested personalities for "Profiles."
I worked there for two years, then began writing my first novel, *Other Voices, Other Rooms*. When I really got into the novel, I went back to New Orleans to finish it, and I've never set foot in a another office. I must say that I really hate offices.

Now, Other Voices, Other Rooms created quite a stir for a first novel, and certainly established you in the front rank. What was your reaction to its success?
So many things happened that were extracurricular to the work on this book that I mostly remember being shocked. There were so many cruel things written about me at the time, and a great deal of comment about the photograph on the back of the book (which was perfectly innocent). Somehow, all the publicity I read about in the newspapers . . . well, I wasn't used to reading about myself. I was so shocked and hurt that I never got any pleasure out of it at all. Everything was different than I had always thought or hoped it would be.

Of course, the book was a literary success, and it sold quite well, but it has only been in the last six years that I could bear to think about certain things surrounding that book. I know it's a very good book, and it's coming into perspective and focus, and finally I feel no pain about anything connected with it. I just feel gratitude because, in a sense, it freed me to go on and do my own work. If I hadn't had that success, no matter what it was based on—publicity, notoriety, whatever it may have been—I would have never had the freedom to go on developing and maturing as an artist. (Perhaps I would have; I don't really know.) But I don't think it hurt me to have a success at that very young age, because it wasn't really a success in my eyes. If I had had any sense of fulfillment, or any of the things that go with that degree of success, it might have had a bad effect on me. But since I didn't get that satisfaction from it—in fact, got the exact opposite—it just sobered me up a great deal and made me realize on what paths I truly must go.

There is a later book I would like to touch upon. What was your motivation in writing The Muses Are Heard?

> *I've always had the theory that reportage is the great unexplored art form.*

This was the beginning of a long experiment. I've always had the theory that reportage is the great unexplored art form. I mean, most good writers, good literary craftsmen, seldom use this métier. For example, John Hersey is a very fine journalist and an excellent writer, but he's not an artist in the sense that I mean. Even Rebecca West at her best (and I think she's a remarkable reporter) doesn't do what I'm talking about. I've had this theory that a factual piece of work could explore whole new dimensions in writing that would have a double effect fiction does not have—the very fact of its being true, every word of it true, would add a double contribution to strength and impact. The "Porgy and Bess" piece, and one other piece I did for *The New Yorker*—a profile of Marlon Brando—were parts of this experiment. I originally did them just to see if I could do them. After I did the "Porgy and Bess" tour of Russia for *The New Yorker*, I wanted to see what I could do within the scope of something truly banal, and I thought, "What is the most banal thing in journalism?" After a time, I realized that it would be an interview with a film star, the sort of thing you would see in *Photoplay* magazine. I decided that it must follow the absolute path of these things, in that they're always done as interviews that take place at one time with a person more or less on the fly. So I put a number of names into a hat and pulled out, God knows why, Marlon Brando. He was in Japan at the same time, so I went to *The New Yorker* and asked them if they'd be interested in this, and they were. So I went to Japan and spent the prescribed time with Brando—an evening. I had actually known Marlon Brando before, so in a way I was cheating, but I didn't know him very well. I had dinner with him and talked with him and then spent a year on the piece because it had to be perfection—because my part was to take this banal thing and turn it into a work of art.

Anyway, I'm pleased with that piece. Lots of people can't understand why I wrote it, especially Marlon Brando. But it definitely had a point for me—an artistic one—and I moved slowly on this path because all the time I knew I was going to write a book, based on heaven knows what. I didn't know what the theme was going to be, but I knew it would be reportage on an immense scale.

I worked on other things, now feeling in complete control of myself within this form, becoming technically adept, just like one becomes technically adept at drawing skeletons to become a doctor. What I wanted to do, of course, was a great deal more ambitious than sketching skeletons; I was then going to fill it in, flesh it out, as it were. But it wasn't until five years ago that I knew what the subject would be.

One day I picked up a paper, and in the business section of *The New York Times*, I found this very small headline that read, "Eisenhower Appointee Murdered." The victim was a rancher in western Kansas, a wheat grower who had been an Eisenhower appointee to the Farm Credit Bureau. He, his wife, and two of their children had been murdered, and it was a complete mystery. They had no idea of who had done it or why, but the story struck me with tremendous force. I suddenly realized that perhaps a crime, after all, would be the ideal subject matter for the massive job of reportage I wanted to do. I would have a wide range of characters and, most importantly, it would be timeless. I knew it would take me five years, perhaps eight or ten years, to do this, and I couldn't work on some ephemeral, momentary thing. It had to be an event related to permanent emotions in people.

Now, there are thousands of crimes I could have picked, but I felt that this was mysteriously ordained. Why should I go to a small Kansas town? Why should I be interested in the number of a wheat grower? I don't know, but it hit me head-on. The next thing I knew, I got on a train and went to this little town in western Kansas. I was there for seven months that first time, and I've been back there many, many times since. I worked on the book for five years.

To turn briefly to a more general topic—since you, yourself, are southern-born, you might have some opinion as to why such a disproportionate number of our leading writers come from the South.

I don't think this is true any more. During the last ten years, the large percentage of the more talented American writers are urban Jewish intellectuals.

But in decades prior to this—

Oh, yes, then a large number did come from the South and Southwest. I think one reason is that there is a definite code of values, of regional values, regional speech, regional attitudes toward religion, race, society. Rightly or wrongly, a whole code of behavior. I think all this is beginning to blur considerably, but in the South, you knew where you stood and you knew where other people stood. If you lived in a southern town, you could, from the time you were seven (provided you were reasonably bright), make a social chart of the whole town—morals, religions, social status. The rest of the country has rather lost this. It presented, for the artist, the "perfect prospect," as it were. In the sense that Jane Austen had a perfect prospect from which she could view life, southern artists, regionally oriented, have this—or did have it.

I, personally, have never thought of myself as a writer regionally oriented. My first book had a southern setting because I was writing about what I knew most deeply at the time. The raw material of my work usually depends on events lived ten years beforehand (in fiction, not nonfiction). Now, of course, the South is so far behind me that it has ceased to furnish me with subject matter.

I don't think that *Other Voices, Other Rooms* can be called a southern novel. As a matter of fact, it is sort of a poem, not a novel; it was a poem about an emotional situation. Everything in it has double meanings—it could as well have been set in Timbuktu or Brooklyn, except for certain physical descriptions. Actually, the only thing I've written that depended on its southern setting was a story called "A Christmas Memory" in *Breakfast at Tiffany's*. The moment I wrote that story, I knew I would never write another word about the South. I'm not going to be haunted by it anymore, so I see no reason to deal with those people or the settings.

Another question in the realm of theory: What obligation, if any, do you feel the writer owes the subject matter he works with and the public to which he writes?

I think the only person a writer has an obligation to is himself. If what I write doesn't fulfill something in me, if I don't honestly feel it's the best I can do, then I'm miserable. In fact, I just don't publish it.

The only obligation any artist can have is to himself. His work means nothing, otherwise. It has no meaning. That's why it's so absolutely boring to write a film script. The great sense of self-obligation doesn't enter into it because too many people are involved. Thus, the thing that propels me, that makes me proud of my work, is utterly absent. I've only written two film scripts, and I must admit that in a peculiar way I enjoyed doing them, but the true gratification of writing was completely absent; the obligation was to the producers and the actors, to what I was being paid to do, and not to myself.

The only really gratifying thing is to serve yourself. To give yourself free law, as it were.

If you were to give advice to a young person intent on a literary career, what would that advice be?

People are always asking me if I believe that writing can be taught. My answer is, "No—I don't think writing can be taught." But on the other hand, if I were a young writer and convinced of my talent, I could do a lot worse than to attend a really good college workshop—for one reason only. Any writer, and especially the talented writer, needs an audience. The more immediate that audience is, the better for him because it stimulates him in his work; he gets a better view of himself and running criticism.

Young writers couldn't get this even if they were publishing stories all the time. You publish a story and there's no particular reaction. It's as though you shot an arrow into the dark. You may get letters from people who liked or didn't like it, or a lot of reviews that really don't mean anything, but if you are working in close quarters with others who are also interested in writing, and you've got an instructor with a good critical sense, there's a vast stimulation.

I've never had this happen to me, but I know it must be so. I've given various readings and lectures at universities, so I have had some firsthand observation of it, though I never attended such a workshop myself; but if I were a young writer I would. I think a college workshop would be enormously helpful and stimulating.

In looking at today's creative arts, literature in particular, what do you find that you most admire? Conversely, what do you most deplore?
I find that a very hard question to answer. I really don't deplore anything, because I like all creative actions themselves, whether I personally enjoy them or not. I can't deplore them just because I don't think they are right. Now, none of this Beat writing interests me at all. I think it's fraudulent. I think it's all evasive. Where there is no discipline there is nothing. I don't even find that the Beat writing has a surface liveliness—but that's neither here nor there because I'm sure that eventually something good will come out of it. Some extraordinary person will be encouraged by it who could never have accepted the rigid disciplines of what I consider good writing.

On the other hand, what do I most admire? Perhaps *admire* isn't the right word, but I think it's a fine thing that Katherine Anne Porter's *Ship of Fools* sold so well. Why? Because she's a remarkably good artist. And I think it's wonderful that her book was so popular and successful, whether people really read it or not.

I think it's fine that a young writer like John Updike can have a large success, because he's an exceptionally gifted young man. The attention shown to young writers in this country is greater than anywhere else (except France), and this is encouraging. I suppose Russia gives their young writers more attention than any other country, but I don't happen to admire any of the young Russian writers. I like some of the Communist film-makers, who do extraordinary work, but I don't care for the younger writers.

What do you think of American criticism and review as a whole?
I don't think the problem is as much a question of the level of American criticism as it is the outlets for it. I suppose *The New York Times*, commercially speaking, is the most influential of all book-review outlets, and it's appall-

ing. It's as middle-class and boring and badly put together as it can possibly be. I thought it was interesting that the *Herald Tribune* started "Book Week." The way "Book Week" started out, it promised to be good, but it hasn't turned out that way. However, *The New York Review of Books* is excellent. This is really a step in the right direction.

As far as the little magazines are concerned, each seems to be in the hands of a separate fleet and is at war with all the other little fleets. You can't pay too much attention to them, if you're a writer. But then, I've developed a very thick skin about criticism. I've had to. I can read the most devastating things about myself, now, and it doesn't make my pulse skip a beat. You know, the writer is inclined to be a sensitive person, and he can read 100 good reviews and one bad review and take that bad review to heart. I don't do it, not any more.

As far as your own career is concerned, could you state your own objectives? Perhaps this should be placed in the perspective you would like applied?
Well, I think I've had two careers. One was the career of precocity, the young person who published a series of books that were really quite remarkable. I can even read them now, and evaluate them favorably, as though they were the work of a stranger. In a way, they are. The person who wrote them doesn't exist anymore. My metabolism, artistically and intellectually, has changed. I'm not saying it's for the better; it's just changed. The way one's hair changes color.

My second career began—I guess it really began with *Breakfast at Tiffany's.* It involves a different point of view, a different prose style to some degree. I don't find it as evocative, in many respects, as the other, or even as original, but it is more difficult to do. But I'm nowhere near reaching what I want to do, where I want to go. Presumably this new book is as close as I'm going to get, at least stylistically. But I hope to expand from that point on in the multiplicity and range of characters I can deal with, because until recently I've been quite limited. Now I feel capable of handling all sorts of new and different characters which I couldn't approach before, and I think reportage has helped me. I think it freed many things inside of me—this opportunity to work with real people, then using real people under their own names. It has freed or unlocked something inside myself that now makes it possible for me to return to fiction with ability to use a far greater range of characters.

BY JOHN BRADY

JOSEPH WAMBAUGH

I was never a wet-eyed, passionate writer; I was always a policeman.

*M*uch of your success—and the strength of your writing—comes from translating your experiences as a cop into print. Do you ever become confused—wonder if you're a writing policeman or a policing writer?

Well, I first became aware of myself as a writer about three months ago, I think, with the completion of my third book. I always felt after the first book that it could have been a fluke; I was the first police officer to ever write a commercially successful book (that I knew of), and maybe one that was received reasonably well by the critics. I don't know if any other cop had ever done that. I assume I'm the first. And then I always felt that perhaps the second book could have been received as it was mainly because of the first book; maybe I was still a publishing freak—a cop that writes books—and maybe some people were enamored of *that* and not of the book, and bought the book because of that.

Consequently, I never really felt, even after the first two books, that I was truly a writer. I wasn't sure. But after writing this third book, I'm sure that I'm a writer. I don't know how the book is going to be received, but I know a *writer* wrote this third book. As a matter of fact, this was a nonfiction experience, and I got so emotionally involved with all the people I wrote about, and all the research I did, that I feel fiction is somewhat frivolous. I don't hope to go back to writing novels now after the experience I've just been through.

Do you sometimes wish you'd started writing earlier?

Well, no. I don't think I was ready to write earlier; it took a little aging, at least for me, to acquire experience and a reasonable amount of maturity and discipline, although I don't know how much I have even yet. I don't think I could have written earlier. I was also going to college all this time, and I don't pooh-pooh the formal training; I don't necessarily subscribe to the old cliches of the writ-

ing class when they walk in and say, "Okay, now, we can't teach you to be a writer, *but*. . . ." I think that I did learn a lot in my formal education, going to college part-time as a policeman. After reading all those people, taking seminars, and listening, I *did* learn a lot about writing, I really did. I don't think I was necessarily born with the ability to put down a hundred and forty thousand words between two hard covers. I needed the schooling, the formal education.

Your career began late, but it has been, in a few short years, a highly successful one. Was there ever, though, a moment when you wanted to just chuck it all?

No. Because I was never a wet-eyed, passionate, dedicated writer; I was always a policeman. I'm still not sure which I am mostly, a writer or a policeman. Writing was always my avocation. You don't get suicidal, I don't think, over your avocation when you fail at it as you do over your life's work, your profession, which for me was police

---

Joseph Wambaugh has often described himself as a hard-drinker disciplined enough to run two miles each morning. Hard-writer belongs somewhere in there too. As the altar-boy-turned-cop-turned-writer says in this 1973 interview, "Maybe there are more writers around who are more talented than I, but there are no writers who are more disciplined than I."

And the 52-year-old author sells himself short there: The New Centurions, The Blue Knight, The Onion Field, The Choirboys *and others have sold more than 15 million copies and gathered praise for their realism and humanity.*

Still a policeman at the time of this interview (he would retire a few months later), Wambaugh—much like Truman Capote in the previous interview—was eager to discuss his just-finished nonfiction novel, The Onion Field. *This time, the questions were asked.*

work; I always did pretty well at that. I think I was more upset over setbacks as a police officer over the years than I was over my first setbacks as a writer. So maybe that would be the reason I felt more like a cop than a writer. Today I'm not quite sure; I think I feel more like a cop than a writer even *now*, really.

Did you do any research for your first two books?
Well, I had drawers full of notes, scraps of paper, that I saved over the years with all of my ideas, thoughts, observations and so forth as a policeman. I sometimes worked in a radio car and would jot down something on a hamburger wrapper or anything and throw it in the drawer. If that's research, yes. I had years of that stacked up in the drawer, which I pulled out when I started putting the books together. So, yes, I guess that a lot of the incidents in the books are incidents I'd observed or things that had happened to my partners as well.

The research is mostly collected personal experience?
Yes, right. The third book I did true research on. I interviewed 62 people, much as you're doing now, and I read, no, I *studied* 15,000 pages of court transcript, and I collected articles and exhibits and went over the tapes that were taken during the confession period of the killers during the trials—a video tape under sodium amidol. I went to San Quentin to see one of the killers. I just interviewed anybody and everybody that I could, and it was an enormous amount of research before I ever wrote a word—not to mention getting legal releases. I had to get legal releases much as Capote did [for *In Cold Blood*]; in fact, I used his release. I expanded on it, made it a little more binding and sophisticated than his original research was; legally speaking, that is.

What you started writing at first were short stories, and your first two novels were largely episodic. Do you have any difficulty sustaining a narrative thread? Your style seems to be mostly hit and run.
Well, I thought that the second book wasn't as episodic as the first in that I selected the episodes carefully to keep driving home the point of the man's aging, and the aging-equals-death sort of thing. All of the episodes in that book either dealt with his inability to nurture personal contacts, or love, if you will, with other people; *or* they dealt with the aging process, the dying process of

> *This thing happens, where the characters take over and you almost want to look behind you to see who's writing your story.*

that man, Bumper Morgan. There are no episodes that don't deal with that one way or the other, so I don't think that it's as episodic as some people thought. Maybe the themes were disguised in some of those episodes. Perhaps because the material was entertaining and diverting, maybe people didn't really appreciate that there was some thematic material in the episodes. But *The New Centurions* was much more purely an episodic book, I think. *The Onion Field* is not episodic at all, not at all.

When you're writing fiction, do you approach the novel chronologically, or is there a lot of juggling? Do you have—
An outline? I start with one, but then I always abandon the game plan when the characters take over the story. I just let them do their thing and see what happens. Sometimes it works out—*usually* it works out. Sometimes it doesn't, but usually if I just let the characters take over, I do better than if I sit down and calculate and try to plot the thing. I just write, and it works out for me.

Can you give me an example of the characters taking over?
In *The New Centurions* I was writing about the Watts riot. In the Watts riot scenes, everything was chaotic—there was no order and the cops were bewildered and frightened. I felt that these people were acting almost like bugs in a campfire, just popping around and going this way and that; there's absolutely no thread here or any narrative drive, nothing's happened. This is just sheer utter chaos, and I started feeling uncomfortable. I thought, "I've got to make these cops do something positive for the sake of the story, the narrative. They've got to take some positive action."

So I deliberately sat there late at night and I wrote a scene wherein they surround a furniture store, and they believe that the looters inside have guns. I decided that they were going to make an arrest, actually take some positive police action. I had planned that when they put the lights on and surround the store and yell for the looters to come out, the first looter out of the store would be a militant-looking black with a natural hairdo and a black silk undershirt, with some sort of Afro necklace, with the slogan and the whole thing. And I deliberately had that planned as I sat there writing.

I don't know—this thing happens, where the characters take over and you almost want to look behind you to see who's writing your story: the first person out was a little boy. He had his hands up and he was crying. I was surprised to see that the sole of his shoe was loose and flip-flopping across the sidewalk. I could really see him as he walked into the light of the police spotlight. The next person out was not this young man I had envisioned; instead it was a woman, and she was crying. And then there was an old man, then an old woman came out and—like *that*. When the scene was finished, I showed it to my wife and explained what happened. She said, "Is that what the Watts riot was really like?" I said, "Yes, that's what it was really like, nothing like what you would *expect*." And she said, "Well, then leave it, just leave it; leave that scene."

That scene was commented on, I guess, by critics as much as anything was in the book as being a successful scene to show the pathos and the confusion of the riot; the pathos of a riot where nothing was as you would expect. The looters weren't what you'd expect them to be. Nothing was. How unsatisfying in a cops-and-robbers tale for *these* to be your looters. Right? But it worked because it was true, you see? It was true and it just happened.

I've read somewhere that your novels are generally written in about six months.
Six months. Right. Part-time. I write a thousand words a day when I'm writing. Minimum. There's no deviation from that. I write a thousand words a day, *every* day. And if an emergency would happen that I couldn't write a thousand words on Monday, then I will write 2,000 words on Tuesday.

Nothing will stop me, I mean *nothing*, until the book is finished; I will write a thousand words a day. I feel that writing is a mix of talent and discipline, and I think under talent, I don't know what to lump—maybe an ability with language, maybe an ability to handle it; I'm not sure that I have that as well as a lot of my friends who are writers. Maybe a logical mind, I think I have that; an ability to perceive truth in things, I think I have that pretty well. Maybe if you lump all those things under a heading called *talent*, maybe that's half of it. The other half is discipline. And maybe there are writers around who are more talented than I, but there are *no* writers around who are more disciplined than I. There are none that I've ever met, and I don't think there exists any because I *do* that thousand words a day, by God.

You know, if I do 15 hours of police work and I come home I cannot sleep, much as I want to, until I go in and do those thousand words. Something inside me will not let me sleep, so I'm disciplined in spite of myself—I don't want to be this. I'm a fanatic, actually, when you come right down to it. And I'm not recommending this, I'm not happy being this way, really, but I am, and there's nothing I can do about it. So the book that is 140,000 words long will be written in 140 days, more or less, because some days I write 5,000 words; there have been a few days

when I've written 10,000 words. But there will be at least a thousand words a day.

When you say a thousand words, are you talking about a rough draft?
Yes, a rough draft. They're not polished words, no. A thousand. I get them down on paper. I've read where some famous writers like Hemingway polished as they went; I don't. I get them down on paper—I just blurt it out.

And then at the end of three months or so of part-time writing, I've got a book there, I've got a big, fat book. And *now* I can go through it and polish it; it's not so painful. Getting it out is the most painful part, it seems to me, with the exception of having to go through it ten times with your editor, and that's painful. By then you don't want to see it anymore, but you have to do it again anyway.

Do you envision a particular reader or any kind of reader when you're writing?
Yes. I think I try to write for someone who's reasonably intelligent, though I don't try to write over or under anybody's head. But I think I do expect someone who's read a few books to read my stuff.

Do critics have any effect on you?
Well, of course they didn't in the first one because I didn't know anything about them. In the second one, I don't know for sure if they did or not. Now they *might* if I write another novel. But in this third book, I can hardly explain the experience of writing this true story; I didn't think about critics, I didn't think about *anything*. I just thought about telling this story that has been on my mind for years. Actually, this third book made me want to be a writer. When I *thought* about being a writer, it was to write *The Onion Field*. I didn't have the title in my mind, but *this* story. But for one reason or another, I couldn't write the story until just this year. As a matter of fact, I only got the release that I had to have last summer. I had approached this man long before that to get a release, but he wouldn't do it.

Which man?
The surviving policeman. He wanted no part of it. I wanted to write this book since 1966, when he was fired from the police department. The murder was in '63. It didn't bother me that much then. When he was fired, then I saw a real story, and that's the one I wanted to write. And when I first started writing short stories, I thought that if I ever write a *book*, it's going to be about this incident, which is so incredible that it would affect me all these years. When I started *The New Centurions*, I was fooling around, I felt, trying to get some experience to be able to write this story. After *Centurions*, I approached this man, and that was going to be my second

book and maybe my last. This is the story that I wanted to write. He wouldn't go for it, so I wrote *The Blue Knight*. Then I approached him again, and I finally persuaded him to cooperate with me and let me do it. You know, this is the story that made me want to be a writer, so I finally got it out of my system after all these years, thank God.

What did you say the third time around that convinced him?
Nothing. He had recovered emotionally to a greater extent, I think from a . . . I really can't go into it now, but from all the things that had happened to him over the years since this killing. He had recovered from it all to the extent that he was capable of dealing with it, talking about it, and letting me write about it. So we finally got it done.

When you saw Capote's In Cold Blood, *did that have any influence on you? You mentioned Capote before. . . .*
Oh sure. Definitely. I first read that book at about the same time that this police officer left the department under fire. And I did immediately make the connection and I thought, "If I could ever write something, it would be this story in the style that Truman Capote used in his book." So, yes. His book was very much on my mind all these years. As a matter of fact, I probably know more about *In Cold Blood* than anybody in the country, including Capote. I studied that book before I set about writing my book. I thought that he did better than anyone ever has at the nonfiction novel. I can't think of any book I've ever read over the years that was a true story written in the fictional style that approaches his tour de force, really. And whereas I didn't write mine as he did, I certainly learned a lot from what he did, as I think anyone can see in *The Onion Field*. I'm sure that it'll be obvious that he had an influence on me, for which I give him due credit.

Truman was very kind to me. As a matter of fact, after *New Centurions* and after my failure to get the cooperation of this ex-police officer, I was really down. I was doing *The Blue Knight*, getting it polished up, but I wanted badly to do this third book, *The Onion Field*. He had turned me down flat, and I thought it was rather hopeless, you know, and I was out at Truman Capote's home. We were on a TV show together. He's a very gracious man, especially to young writers, and he invited Dee and me to his home in Palm Springs. We had lunch with him, went swimming. I couldn't resist telling him about this story that I was never going to get to write.

I sat down with him for about two hours, I guess, and just spilled it all out, told him all about this marvelous story I'd envisioned, this story called *The Onion Field*. When I was finished, he just sat there for a second and said, "My God, that's a marvelous story. I wish I could write that." When he said that, then by God I knew I was

going to try again somehow. I was going to wait and just bide my time, be patient, and not give up, and somehow get the cooperation of this man and write this damn story—when Capote said that. And so, I just waited another year, and approached him again, and finally, thank God, he said, "Yeah, write that story and get rid of it."

But I've been carrying it around with me—I could not have written it without him; I mean it would just be impossible. For instance, to draw an analogy, how could Capote have written *In Cold Blood* without the complete cooperation and release of Perry Smith? It would have been impossible. It would never have been *In Cold Blood*. He would have written a story about a terrible crime, and that would have been it. And that's how badly I needed this guy, if not worse; I needed this guy more than he needed Perry Smith, you see.

Now, is there any sort of financial consideration that the main character, the protagonist here receives?
Not just the main character! I paid everybody! I paid lump sums to everybody. That's what Capote did, as a matter of fact.

Scaled to importance?
Yes, according to importance. Some people got a nominal payment just to make it legally binding. And some people got large amounts of money; it depended on how badly I needed them. A lot of the people in my book didn't get anything—they are just peripheral characters. Some who actually appear in the book weren't interviewed by me; I used other information I had and drew them in, but there were actually 62 people interviewed. And they were all paid something.

Did this come out of your own income?
You'd better believe it. I took a chance on this. This book's cost me a small fortune, not just in legal releases but in lawyers doing research for me. I had to retain a lawyer for most of the six months I spent writing the book. He spent that time at the law library doing various kinds of research, giving me material on the case. I mean, I had to do all sorts of things to get in to see my two killers. To get into San Quentin, I had to get the one guy's lawyer and fly him up there and go with him. And I had to get the retired detective who handled this case and is now Chief of Police in Colorado—I had to bring him out there and go over the whole crime scene and do all that. So I had an enormous amount of money invested in this, but I would've spent anything. I would've spent every cent I made on *The New Centurions* and *The Blue Knight* to get this story done.

Aside from my telling of it—I don't know whether I've done it justice as writer—this story itself, the material as it exists without Joe Wambaugh, is a very important story that somebody had to tell. I hope I've done it justice. The story itself is actually crucial, it seems to me as a policeman and someone who's interested in law and crime and justice and guilt—the story's mainly about guilt—somebody had to tell it. So I invested all of this money. I didn't know what was going to happen, but, fortunately, it was a big hit with my publisher, who bought it and gave me a huge advance. They bought it really sight-unseen, but I couldn't wait. I sent them the manuscript before they sent me the check, so they could've said, "Well, we don't like it. We've changed our minds," and I would have been stuck. But I had faith in it. After I got it written, I knew they were going to buy it. I just knew. And they did.

Columbia Pictures has just bought it, too.

Who do you read? What contemporary writers do you admire?
Oh, I don't think I really have a favorite. I'm pretty catholic in my tastes; I just read anything and everything. In the last few years I seem to, despite myself, end up reading books that are connected with police work or crime because everybody sends them to me. I get every damn book that comes down the pike on crime, police; every publisher sends them to me. The best book I've read in the last few years I *think* was *In Cold Blood,* the one that I studied. For a pure storytelling, lusty sort of adventure story, the best one I've read in recent years was *Sand Pebbles,* I think. The most stylish book and the most brilliant piece of writing that I've read in recent years was *Portnoy's Complaint.*

Do you read many detective stories?
No, I can't stand them. I can read other kinds of fantasy and enjoy it, but the minute it comes into my environment, I just can't appreciate it unless it's realistic and true to life. I've tried, God knows; I've tried reading the best detective fiction, and to the point when they say this case is solved or whatever, really it's not. I meant there's no way it could be prosecuted. In the best detective stories I've ever read, at the point when they said it's solved, really, I'd just be *beginning.* The solution usually depends on some ridiculous confession that's illegal to begin with; the whole things are so totally absurd that I just can't tolerate that kind of fantasy. It has to be fantasy aside from police work. I guess my professional training is in the way.

Does your writing affect your working relationships? Are there, for instance, guessing games about the real

I write a thousand words a day. Nothing will stop me, I mean nothing, until the book is finished. I'm disciplined in spite of myself.

identities of your characters?
Well, they're composites, but there are guessing games in the police department. Someone's always saying that he recognizes one of the characters, "Isn't it really so-and-so," you know. "I know who you *really* wrote about in that scene." That kind of thing.

Has that type of talk ever caused any conflicts?
Well, there has been in other people's, in my superiors', but never in *my* mind. I always felt I could do both jobs. I only had problems when other people were creating problems for me, telling me to be one or the other, or they didn't like my books, that sort of thing. I've gotten over all that.

This is kind of ancient history, but at first they [his superiors] didn't like the galleys of *The New Centurions* because it wasn't the Jack Webb *Dragnet* kind of story, the police propaganda image. The cops drink and falsify reports and beat people up—they do all the things that people do. I guess they didn't like that humanizing of the cop. That attitude has stayed with a lot of the administration, but I think most of the working policemen have accepted it very well, the things that I've written. All the ones who talk to me—of course, maybe I don't hear from the critics—but the ones who talk to me say things like, "Well, you just write about policemen as people. That's not so bad. If people identify with us as other people, then it will be difficult for them to throw rocks at us for no reason at all, or shoot at us for no reason at all."

I don't write my books, though, to propagandize or to get to anybody. I don't really give a damn who likes them and who doesn't. I write them because I want to tell the stories.

When you get letters from someone in Des Moines who's asking you for some advice, how do you reply?
I answer all letters, I'll tell you that. I feel an obligation. Sometimes I only send an autographed bookmark, but I send something. Everybody hears from me. Unless it's a real crazy—I get crazy letters, too, you know. Real cuckoo stuff. I try to emphasize the importance of discipline for a writer. I know a lot of writers who are so damned undisciplined—with all the talent in the world and they don't have the guts to sit down and pull it together. I've just met a million of them. I don't know writers personally, but I've met so many briefly in the last three years, I meet

them here and there and everywhere, and after five minutes' conversation, you can tell the person just doesn't have the self-control to do the terribly hard work that it is. They talk about it. And when I really question them, and I've made a point—questions, that sounds like a detective—I say, "Well, tell me about the story you're writing. When did you write? Did you write last night?"

"Well, no, uh."

"Did you write last week? When did you last write on it? What are you going to do? What's your plan for tomorrow?"

"Well, I'm going skiing tomorrow. . . . "

No, they don't have it! They don't have it. I think one writer in a thousand has it, and I think that that's the writer who succeeds.

One lone last question: Ultimately, how would you like to be remembered?
Oh, I don't put too much stock in that kind of thing. I'm pretty much antimemorial and memories and all that kind of thing. I even rebelled against donating a dollar to the police memorial they put up at the police building for fallen policemen. I thought, "What the hell do those guys care whether somebody puts up a lousy piece of stone at the police building? Let's take the money and put it in scholarships for kids in the underprivileged area of L.A. in the name of the L.A.P.D. How's that?"

So I never think in terms of being remembered and memorials. My attorney has instructions in a will, as a matter of fact, to put my remains in a Baggie or the least expensive container he can find and take it to some potter's field with no marker of any kind so that no fool ever wastes his time standing on my grave when he could be doing something constructive. Even a member of my family. So when you say "remembered" or "memorial," I think if anybody is going to remember me as a writer, and they probably won't, but if they ever do, it will probably be for certain truths in *The Onion Field*. That's about it. I don't take myself all that seriously as a writer or a policeman or as a person.

BY KIRK POLKING

IRVING STONE

*If you stay with a thing long enough you can find it,
documentation that no one else has ever found.*

*Y*ou've said in your notes that when you originated the biographical novel you didn't have any established methods to fall back on the way people now have—especially in research—and you had to dig it out yourself. Is this modus operandi pretty much still as you conceived it, or have you changed?
Well, I think I have grown, I think my perseverance has grown, my ability to stay with the problem that I cannot find material on in my first hundred tries, my ability to come up with fresh ideas and fresh approaches so that I can flush out the documents on the hundred-and-first. I have added confidence; I know that for the most part if you stay with a thing long enough you can find it, documentation that no one else has ever found.

In the case of books set in Europe, do you hire a foreign researcher to help you? How do you know where to look?
With the Freud book, this was my third trip to Vienna. After living there for six months, I had become friends with the Austro-American Institute, an institute that has existed for half a century to promote the learning of the English language in Austria and the German language in America. They bring in whole classes from schools and colleges. This is a very great group of dedicated people who work for friendship between young Americans and young Austrians. I had written to them a year in advance telling them I would need a staff of young people, and by the time I got there, they had lined up three or four university graduates trained in English.
    When I was in Italy for the Michelangelo book, my wife engaged a young woman to teach her Italian. By a young woman, I mean a young woman with her Ph.D. in Roman sculpture, a woman about 35, and then I started to look for someone to be my full-time assistant and guide, and she said, "Why can't I have this job," which she got. In Rome, friends guided us to a principessa, who again in-

troduced me to many of the great families and the customs and mores.
    You have to work. It takes time and patience and you get discouraged, and I hired a lot of wrong people.

So you don't have a historical researcher, you have teams of historical researchers.
That depends on where you are in your life. I could never have afforded a researcher on my books up to Darrow, which was what—1940, 1941? But then I engaged one girl from UCLA on a half-time basis. For *Men to Match My Mountains*, I engaged a young European Ph.D. who had to get his Ph.D. again at UCLA, on a half-time basis. One of the good things about having a success with a book is it gives you some money to go out and hire very competent researchers and take the time to train them. And also to live for long periods abroad.
    I have never had a scholarship, and I have never had anything given to me by a foundation or a fellowship or

---

Before he created the biographical novel, Irving Stone was writing confession and detective stories for $25 apiece. Tiring of that lifestyle, he wrote six stories in six days, then used the money to travel to Europe and research the life of painter Vincent van Gogh.

Three years later—in 1934—he sold Lust for Life, *and a new form was born. Since then, Stone has used his trademark technique of extensive research spun out with fictional techniques to dramatize the lives of Jack London, Mary Todd and Abraham Lincoln, Michelangelo, Sigmund Freud, Charles Darwin and others. Critics have remained divided on the merits of the form, but the genre has found steady public approval.*

In 1968, during work on the Freud book, Passions of the Mind, *the 65-year-old author took time to discuss his research methods, his detractors and the inspiration behind his innovation.*

grant, nothing. All the money that goes into researching my books and traveling the world comes out of my savings, out of what the last book earned, and if the last book didn't earn anything—in other words ended up costing me money, which two of my books have—then I'm in trouble, because I don't have the means with which to research the next book.

Which were the two you had the most trouble with?
I didn't have any trouble with them.

My novel about Eugene B. Debs, *Adversary in the House*, however—which was about the history of industrial unionism and the founding of the American Socialist party—was an unsympathetic subject at that time to the American public. I worked on it for like two-and-a-half years, with tremendous research and purchases of pamphlets and books on everything I needed for it. It has never earned back for me the tens of thousands of dollars I poured into it. I don't think it ever will.

The Clarence Darrow book was published just six weeks before Pearl Harbor. Interest in the book vanished at that point, but it returned in a year or two. I only finally earned back the money I had poured into it 11 years later. People writing straight fiction are in a very different position. Take for example, my friend, Robert Nathan. He sits down at his desk with an idea and writes a book, and if he needs a little research, he calls me for help—if he only needs a line or two, of course. But a book like Sigmund Freud will take me a minimum of five years. It has meant many trips to London, Vienna, Zurich, Germany.

At what point are you confident in your viewpoint on a historical figure? Does it come to you in different ways on different books? Can you give us an example of when you knew after years of research that you had it?
You mean when did I have him or that there *was* a biographical novel in this figure?

Well, let's discuss both.
Let's say it is a biographical novel. In order to determine whether it will make a biographical novel, I first have to determine whether or not I can understand this per-

son, grasp him, whether I can realize his values, whether I can live through his adventures, experiences, his failures, weaknesses, his faults, his errors, his collapses, as well as his successes, his ecstasies, accomplishments, realizations.

It is imperative that I identify that closely, because in my way of writing, the reader must identify with the main character by the end of page one or two, or the book is dead. I must feel that I can identify with and become that person and that this story is well worth having lived and it is meaningful; that this life accomplished something, this life went through all the drama and against all of the obstacles and the stone walls that any human being can ever face and yet climbed the wall and emerged on the other side. There has to be some kind of triumph along with the corollary defeats. Once I think that this is a biographical novel and I can handle it, then all the elements come together.

And this varies from time to time in how long you go before you feel this identity?
Yes, every story is a different one. For example, when I lived in Italy in 1926, I fell in love with Michelangelo, and the Medicis and Ghirlandaio and Donatello et al., and I knew that one day I would want to write about Michelangelo. It took me 30 years to get back to him.

With Freud, I first became interested in August, 1920, when I entered the University of California at Berkeley. I began reading Freud immediately in early August, and from that point to this, I knew that one day I would write a book about Freud. Part of the reason it has taken me so long is that for 19 years I have been communicating with the Freud family trying to get documents and cooperation. I haven't gotten much, but I have gotten enough; and in the last five or six years have gotten many volumes of letters, and very confidential materials have been published, so now I know I can get the book done.

Now that you have become established, you have deadlines preset for you by your commitments and your own compulsion as a writer. What did you do to start yourself before you had this?
My problem is not to start myself, but to stop myself. I'm a compulsive worker. I have been called a compulsive

> *I have to determine whether or not I can understand this person, whether I can realize his values, live through his experiences, his failures, weaknesses, his faults as well as his successes.*

writer; I don't think that is totally true, but I am a compulsive worker. And if I am not at my desk by 8:30 in the morning every day including Saturdays, I hear my grandmother's voice over my shoulder saying, "Irving, why aren't you at work?"

So that has never been any problem. I know it is a major problem for some writers. But let me make something clear. The fact that I go sit down at my desk doesn't mean that I begin work. Because sometimes I can go sit down and am absolutely obtuse. I'm dense, I'm confused, I feel lousy, I wish I had another job, and for a half-hour, hour and a half, while I piddle, I read a little bit out of a book, I read the morning paper, you know, just like every writer. But at least I'm there, and when my mind clears, which hopefully it does every day, I can get some work done.

You are an indefatigable researcher and sometimes spend weeks, months and years seeking some particular fact that you question, or think must exist but hasn't been found before. How do you justify that trait with the personality trait that says: I am going to take this leap of imagination to what I sense about this person?
That is a good question. Certainly I have both traits; I think that the answer is that, first of all, you can never get 100 percent documentation on what a man or woman thought and did throughout a lifetime. Even if you get everything available, and that is what I strive for, you are still a way short of a full understanding of that individual because thousands of hours of interior monologue are unrecorded—many of the days, weeks and months of worry and anxiety and frustration and taking time to think through a problem, when they finally come to a conclusion as to what has to be done—it is very difficult for the author to know what went on in that mind, step by step.

And I think this is where the imaginative leap is important. If you understand your character and identify with him thoroughly, I think you can make that leap with accuracy.

You said once that "there are many lives important and significant in their end results, which are nonetheless diffused, their contents and design antithetical to the nature of the novel." You have, then, discovered people you identify with, but whose lives were not the kind of subject matter you need?
Yes, I have found lots of very interesting people, and read about them, and decided that the material would not coalesce into a novel. They might coalesce into a biography, because the substantive portion of their work—which was some cause or science or whatever it may be—proved important and has that background of importance. But the personal life, for example, just won't come into focus—the day-by-day or year-by-year familiarity of work in the laboratory or field or whatever they happen to be in.

Can you give me any examples of that happening?
Well, I can give you one, I can give you the best example. I was just finishing a book, I think it was *Immortal Wife*, and there came to my house for dinner a friend who had worked next to Henry Ford and Edsel and Harry Bennett all of his life. He began telling me the story in my house, with all the inside material. It was an exciting story, and it interested me very much. When I was in New York the following week, I told the story to Ken McCormick and Lee Barker and Walter Bradbury, who were my trio of editors and friends there. I told it for perhaps an hour and when I got all through, Ken McCormick said to me very quietly, "You know, Irving, you have no hero."

Is there much byplay between you and your editors? Do you prefer to talk to them or not talk to them?
I haven't shown many manuscripts. Unless Ken happens to come out. For example, he came out on a visit for other purposes when I had about four big chapters in Michelangelo, and he asked me if he could read them. They were already in the seventh draft and finished. He sat a day or day-and-a-half in the living room with that manuscript on his lap, reading Michelangelo. Not with pencil, just reading.

However, on *Those Who Love*, when I got in the middle, because of the enormous abundance of political and historical material, I felt that the manuscript was probably overlong and overly burdened and that we had stripped away as much as we could at that point, so I asked Ken to come out and spend a week if he could arrange it, which he did.

In all the manuscripts prior to *The Agony and the Ecstasy*, I never showed the unfinished manuscript.

I read somewhere that your then fiancée, now wife, looked over your Lust for Life *manuscript and suggested some reductions. Were the reductions primarily in wordiness or subplots?*
No, your point of view is mistaken, that is not what the material says. The actual situation was this: We had three years and 17 rejections by the major publishers in New York, all of them saying about the same thing: "How do you expect us to sell a novel about an unknown Dutch painter in the midst of a depression?"

About the middle of 1933, I said to Jean, "Do you think you could cut this manuscript? It may be long and it may be the readers are bogging down; it may be that is our problem." She said, "I've never even seen a manuscript, let alone cut it, what do you mean?" I said, "Well, read it very carefully over and over again, and anytime we can spare a word or phrase or sentence, or anything you think I am duplicating in my own thinking, or a character statement or description—cut it—in other words, sweat out as much as you can."

So she did, working evenings and weekends for about six months. At the end of that time, I was going down to

Arkansas for my research on the bread riots, and she had finished the cutting, and I had gone over it and approved it, and asked her to take the manuscript over to the home of Maxwell Aley, the editor at Longman's whom I had met at a cocktail party. She did and Maxwell Aley accepted the manuscript while I was in Arkansas. I learned about it New Year's Day when I came back.

Jean's job with *Lust for Life* was confined to cutting only; no discussion of the manuscript, just cutting, but she has grown all the way through. She'll say, "I think you need to stop here, I think you need writing here—you have been staging drama, violent emotional scenes, and I wish you would stop for a moment. Give the readers a paragraph of writing about landscape, about the weather, about anything you'd like, just give them a breathing spell."

Or she'll say, "Look, this point must have been very important to you because you have staged four master scenes trying to prove the one point. The second time you said it is the great master scene." Or, she will say, "You don't like this woman, do you?" And I'll say, "How do you know?" and she'll say, "Any idiot could know, you're writing against her. You're not trying to help people understand her or know her or see her or receive her, you are taking sides against her, and that is not legitimate writing."

She edits my third draft and she writes notes extensively, and then she types from there.

She must be an invaluable sounding board for you to know what effects you're creating.
Oh, enormously valuable because she insists on remaining a lay reader. With the one exception of some material she researched for me up in Idaho on the Darrow book, I never let her research, and I never let her know what I'm finding or getting. There is no discussion. I'm now doing a biographical work on Sigmund Freud, but not one word of discussion of Freud goes on in this house from one month to another.

You also must be an editor as well as writer. Early in your career you threw a "straight" novel away.
That's right, yes. It was called *A Portrait of Love*, and I did a story of a couple in love, 250 pages, against no background. Perhaps the city was there unnamed, but just as *Lust for Life* is against a background of painting and Clarence Darrow is against the background of rights

and freedom, and *The Agony and the Ecstasy* is against the background of marble carving, and *Sailors on Horseback* is against a background of the formation of the Socialist Party and writing, and *Love is Eternal* is against the background of the Civil War, et al., this novel existed in a vacuum; it was actually worthless. Now I think that some of the writing was nice between the young girl and the young boy; it was a good story in that sense, but it had no background, it existed nowhere.

You've said that you learned for several reasons that the creative novel is not for you. Were you talking about purely fictional novels?
Yes. Straight fiction. Hemingway told me in Key West that I was not right in making this distinction, that there is no difference between a so-called fiction novel and a so-called biographical novel; all fictional novels are based on people and experience lived.

One could argue that point all the way around. Do you buy that?
In part, although in the fictional novel you can rearrange things. You can take 18 different people and situations and restructure them.

One article about your work said: "Only gradually, however, has a biographical novel based on sound research yet written with creative imagination been accepted by historians as a legitimate way to present past events to the reader. Now, the experts agree." Do they really? Or do you still get criticism?
Well sure, we get criticized. We get the back of the hand. For example, there was a novel being published last year about an artist, and the so-called critic or book reviewer of the *Saturday Review* said in very snide fashion, "This is an Irving Stone kind of book."

But if they don't beat you over the head with that, they'll find something else. Leaving aside the really first-rate critics, of whom we have a few, that's how they make a place for themselves.

When you first started writing, you put down on cards four little reminders on how to write: 1) Dramatize; 2) Plenty of dialogue; 3) Bring the characters to life; and 4) Use anecdotes and humor. Now you've discovered that it's a little more complicated.
Yes—now it comes to 250 pages of notes on how to do a certain book.

BY GARY PROVOST

ELLEN GOODMAN

*You can teach someone who cares to write columns,
but you can't teach someone who can write columns how to care.*

Ellen Goodman's desk at *The Boston Globe* is a mess. She works in a room big enough for a Frisbee tournament, except that it's furnished with dozens of other messy desks and the writers who own them, all pounding away at typewriters and video display terminals and shouting things like "Hey Sal, how do you spell *deciduous*?" And there's that odious trail of cigar smoke floating directly to her desk from the ashtrays of guys like columnist Mike Barnicle and other lovable newspaper types. ("They know who they are," she says.) It's a wonder she gets anything done.

But she gets quite a bit done. Twice a week, deadlines pop up like targets at a shooting gallery, and in 17 years of shooting, Ellen Goodman has never missed one. Most of those years she spent reporting the news, first for *Newsweek*, then for the *Detroit Free Press*, and then the *Globe*. But since 1974 her beat has been . . . well, the heart, because by every Tuesday and every Thursday, she has once again composed one of the best syndicated columns in America. It's about things like marriage, death, role-playing, friendship and kids. She hugs the human issues, not to the exclusion of momentous political and technological issues, but to their enhancement.

Her column—which won three major journalism awards in 1980, including the Pulitzer Prize for Distinguished Commentary—goes out to 225 newspapers around the country under the aegis of the Washington Post Writers Group, a syndicate that Goodman says is "small, classy, a nice group of people."

It goes to people like Linda Dolan, who lives in Shrewsbury, Massachusetts, on the western edge of *Globe* circulation. Linda Dolan, 30, is a housewife-mother-cum-freelance-writer. Twice a week she is amazed to discover that she and Ellen Goodman think alike.

When she's not typing someone else's letters as an office temporary to keep household finances in balance, Linda spends school mornings in front of her kitchen ta-

ble typing stories and poems she hopes will end up in *Redbook* or *Ms.* Like many new writers, Linda Dolan writes personal columns, too. Unlike most new writers, she has managed to sell several of them during her first year of trying, including a few to the *Globe*. Linda Dolan gives Ellen Goodman part of the credit for that, though the two have never met. Goodman is Dolan's idol, the embodiment of what a woman who writes can become. So every Tuesday and every Thursday, Linda snips Goodman's column out of the paper and presses it neatly into a box she keeps in her kitchen cabinet.

"Sometimes I think Ellen Goodman is tapping my phone," Linda once told me. "She says so many of the things in print that I'd like to say."

While Linda understands that Ellen Goodman would be out of business tomorrow if millions of other fans weren't saying exactly the same thing, on another level, Linda, like those others, suspects that Goodman is speaking directly to her.

Later I ask Ellen Goodman about this in a tiny, windowless storeroom at the *Globe* where we have gone to escape Barnicle's cigar smoke and the clacking typewriters.

At first, you'll probably wonder why Linda Dolan's butting into this profile. About midway through the piece, though, you'll start to appreciate Dolan: she's being brought closer to Ellen Goodman, and that brings Ellen Goodman closer to us.

Not that all of us have Goodman's credits—her three books (the most recent, Keeping In Touch, *published after this 1981 interview), her twice-a-week syndicated column (at one time the fastest-growing column in America), and her Pulitzer Prize. But we can dream about such success. And more important, aspire to it.*

Which is what this piece is all about.

"I've thought about this a lot," she says, pausing to think about it some more. At 39, she is more youthful than the well-seasoned oracle one would expect to produce such wise and authoritative columns. She smiles often when she speaks, and her eyes get wide and her hands brush through the air as if to clear away all previous thoughts.

"What I think happens," she says, "is that I respond the same way they respond. I mean I look at something like the Eleanor Roosevelt letters flap for example and I say 'Yuk.' My job is to say why *yuk*. News is divided into stories that tell you what happened and stories that tell you what it means. I face the world with as much confusion as everybody else, but once in a while it's nice to figure out what I think a few things mean."

And what about Linda Dolan out in Shrewsbury stubbornly lugging her typewriter to the kitchen table every morning? With two kids to raise and a husband who comes home hungry, can she ever even hope to be in the same league as Ellen Goodman?

"Certainly!" says Goodman, who graduated from Radcliffe College in 1963. "You don't have to go to journalism school. You have to live. Maybe at 20 you can write well, but I don't think you could do what I do. Some things have to happen to you first. My advice to writers who want to write columns is learn to think, learn about history, learn about economics, learn subjects. I'm not always writing in my head, but I'm always storing things like a computer. And then one day I press the button and there it is, more than I thought was there. You have to go through life with your head as sort of a vacuum cleaner.

"And you've got to have a view. Good columns are written by people with opinions, with a point of view on life. And the most important thing, you have to care. You can teach someone who cares to write columns, but you can't teach someone who can write columns how to care."

Caring got Goodman a syndicated column and a Pulitzer Prize. Six times during her first year at the *Globe*, she cared enough about issues to write columns for the opinion-editorial page. The *Globe* eventually made her a full-time columnist. Later, when she was approached by a syndication group, she and the *Globe* looked around for other takers and settled on The Washington Post Writers Group. Her Pulitzer entry, submitted by the *Globe*, was a selection of ten columns that illuminated some dark corners of issues as varied as the Lee Marvin case, and public distrust following the accident at Three Mile Island.

"Imagine, a Pulitzer Prize!" Linda Dolan said to me the day after Goodman won America's most prestigious journalism award. "It must make her feel so secure in what she's doing."

But when I ask Goodman about it, she says, "We're all insecure. Insecurity is the mainstream of every writer. You write two bad columns in a row and you think: 'Well that's it folks. I've lost it.'

"I think the Pulitzer has a half-life of 24 hours. All it means is that I now know the first line of my obituary. It hasn't changed my life. This is a slow-growth business, and you're in it for the long run. I mean, I was thrilled and excited. I'm not at all blase about it; I know I'm very lucky to have the job I have, and I've been rewarded, but I'm also aware of the truth in journalism that you're only as good as your next column. When you start writing drivel you get canceled. What you win in journalism constantly is the right to work."

Journalism is a word Goodman uses a lot. She describes herself as a journalist, not a writer, and though we could argue the difference until our hackles turn white with age, there are a few distinctions not to be denied. One of them is that a journalist is much more likely to have very little time between the event covered and the deadline. And Goodman, though her words reach the newsstands only twice a week, is very much tied to events.

"Your basic thing as a columnist is to write from the news," she says. "You can't make a syndicated column out of your life unless you're Erma Bombeck. That's one person who can do it three times a week. But I think most of us, including myself, have maybe ten personal columns in us. We run out of material quickly. I don't think of myself as writing what is, strictly speaking, a personal column. What I'm trying to do is make the link between a personal column and a public one. There's a lot of misunderstanding about what a columnist does. 'Would you rather be a reporter or a columnist?' is often the question. The fact is that as a columnist you do all the reporting you ever did, plus you have to make up your own mind. You have to figure out what you think because you're taking a stand."

As for those deadlines that Ellen Goodman has been meeting for 17 years? "Well, they're always there," she says. "You're not allowed writer's block in my business. Oh, you might arrive in the morning with the feeling that you don't know what it is you're going to write about, but by the time you leave, you've done it. Sometimes you've got to say to yourself the old journalist motto that at a certain time of day: 'You go with what you've got.' Of course, you're not going to bat a thousand every time out. It's the Woody Allen theory of life: 80 percent of life is showing up. You've got to show up. You have to meet deadlines. And you have to have a high tolerance for stress. I think I do. I never start screaming, throwing erasers, that sort of thing. My idea of pressure is to have to write a column in two hours."

Back in Shrewsbury, Linda Dolan—who never has to meet a deadline—is sitting in her kitchen grinding out one of those ten personal columns we each have in us, and thinking that lucky Ellen Goodman is a star with lots of freedom who can probably whip out a brilliant column by lunchtime, make it as long as she wants, turn it in whenever she feels like it, and have it read by several million adoring fans by the end of the week.

Goodman laughs at the image. "Freedom?" she says. "I have very little freedom in terms of space and none at all in terms of deadlines; 750 words is probably the shortest column I do, and 850 is maybe the longest. In newspaper writing, you're setting yourself up for the scalpel of the copy editor if you go over. I'm quite religious about staying with the word length. If anybody's going to cut me, I'd rather do it myself."

Goodman is also religious about the quality of her work, and though her desk may from time to time look as if someone has dropped it, sloppiness is something she will not abide in her writing.

"What makes me happy is rewriting," she says. "In the first draft, you get your ideas and your theme clear. If you're using some kind of metaphor you get that established, and certainly you have to know where you're coming out. But the next time through, it's like cleaning house, getting rid of all the junk, getting things in the right order, tightening things up. I like the process of making writing neat. When I read my column in the paper and I find I've used the same word twice close together or if I've got something dangling, I can't stand it."

Though most of her writing life is locked in the newspaper world of VDTs and city rooms and deadlines that sometimes rush her words into print before anyone can see that something is dangling, Goodman has known the calmer, slightly steadier world of the writer who has time to weigh words, and space to expand ideas. From 1975 to 1978, she interviewed 150 men and women about the social changes that seemed to be tampering with so many of their lives. She asked them about changing sex roles, about old assumptions, about new possibilities. These interviews became her first book, *Turning Points*, a book that was "somewhat humorlessly written and lacking a very clear focus at times," according to *The New York Times Book Review*, but "an eye-opening journey" according to *The Los Angeles Times*.

Good reviews or bad, *Turning Points* is clearly a book Goodman needed to write. With a divorce not far behind her and a daughter, Katie, to raise, Goodman says the theme of change caught her attention when she herself was being buffeted by it.

"I had just come out of a period of personal crises, the kind that often comes with divorce," she says. "It was

Maybe at 20 you can write well, but I don't think you could do what I do. Some things have to happen to you first.

a time when I was most aware of the weaknesses of my plans and how disruptive change can be."

From what she calls her "seat in the eye of the hurricane" as a news reporter, she had gaped wide-eyed at the wrenching social issues of the 1960s. So in 1974, she abandoned her newspaper beat for a year. She became a Nieman Fellow at Harvard and read everything she could find on the subject of change, "to see," she says, "if I could make some sense out of what seemed like chance." There, while she began the legwork for *Turning Points*, she acquired much of the intellectual background that leaves so strong a stamp of erudition on her work today.

Goodman's second book, *Close to Home*, is a collection of some of her best columns. There will probably be other books of columns, and even though Goodman is doing a lot of TV appearances these days and she has recently written for *Redbook* and *Life*, she doesn't see drastic changes in her life.

"I just don't have much time for much more than I'm doing," she says. "I can't think of a more congenial place to work. I like what I'm doing. I like the atmosphere. I like the energy and the structure of a newspaper office. I need the people around me. I could never work in a small room." She grins. "The only thing that bothers me is the cigar smoke from Barnicle and the others, but we're all good friends, and they're extremely good neighbors. I've had a very nice gradual growth as a writer, but I'm not 26 years old. I'm staying here at the *Globe*, where I'm happy."

When I ask Goodman if she's afraid of stagnating, of running out of ideas by staying in one place too long, she says "Not at all. I think there's a lot of material. I know there are some big gaps in my education, things I want to learn about and write about. I want to learn more about science. None of us has written much about the way technology affects our lives, for example. And there's the relationship between government and the person. That needs to be covered. And there's so much I want to explore between men and women. There's so much!"

A few days after I interviewed Ellen Goodman, I took my morning coffee in Linda Dolan's kitchen and she said the same thing.

"You know, there's so much to write about," she said. "So much!"

I could imagine Goodman speaking those same words years ago as a reporter, as a college student, even as a teenager. Maybe then it was she who wrote about values at the kitchen table and dreamed of having her own newspaper column. The dream came true.

"Ten years ago," Goodman says, "nobody was even remotely considered for a Pulitzer Prize for writing about values, women and children, love, guilt, responsibility, conflict. The whole category of things I write about was automatically excluded. But there is a change going on that journalism is finally noticing. I am profiting from that change, but I have been part of it, too. It wasn't easy getting my columns printed at first."

It isn't easy for Linda Dolan to get her columns printed, either. She is just starting out as a writer, and her columns don't get typed directly into a computer as Goodman's do. They get dropped off at the post office, accompanied by a self-addressed, stamped envelope, and, as any new writer can tell you, they almost always come back. Sometimes when too many have come back too soon, Linda starts to wonder about this whole crazy business of trying to get someone to publish what you write. So she goes into the kitchen and opens her cabinet and pulls out her box of Ellen Goodman columns.

Because every writer needs some inspiration.

BY LORETTA LEONE MCCABE

KURT VONNEGUT

*You can only be funny if you have matters of
great importance on your mind.*

For 23 years, Kurt Vonnegut agonized over the firebombing of Dresden, Germany, by American and British fighter planes in World War II. Twice the number killed in Hiroshima—135,000 people—were killed in Europe's largest massacre. Vonnegut had witnessed the event as a prisoner of war, with some 100 other American soldiers and a handful of German guards sheltered in the underground cold storage unit of a slaughterhouse.

Since that time, Vonnegut had turned out two short story collections, many articles and reviews, six books, and had remained largely unknown to the reading public.

Slaughterhouse-Five was published in March 1969. Now many people know about Kurt Vonnegut, but the book is out of his mind. "Once a book is done, it's gone," he says.

It is 2 P.M. this mellow autumn afternoon at the gray-and-white 14-room Vonnegut farmhouse in Barnstable on Cape Cod. We are sitting on metal lawn furniture in an Italianate garden with a brick-and-weed patio, a stone bust of a woman, a rusty anchor and a stone water fountain. Vonnegut, a tall (over six feet), lanky man of forty-seven, has tousled brown hair, deep brown eyes and a bristly moustache that sometimes camouflages his facial expressions—often a small, barely visible smile. He is dressed casually in an Irish knit cardigan, a red velour shirt, chinos, Navy blue socks and buckskin shoes. Jane Vonnegut, a pretty, prematurely-white-haired woman in Levis and Navy blue blouse is sitting nearby, hemming a wool skirt. They have just finished a liquid lunch. ("We are on a health food kick," says Jane.)

As we talk, Vonnegut buttons and unbuttons the sweater, chain-smokes Pall Mall cigarettes, and doodles on the covers of nearby magazines. He is alternately charming and irascible, mild-mannered and restless, funny and thoughtful. Conversation with him is an irrev-erent mixture of modesty and candor, sarcasm and sardonic wit and outbursts of grim humor.

"Dresden is a very nice city—except there are no natives there." Uproarious laughter.

Vonnegut could have been Kilgore Trout, the science fiction writer who appears in *Slaughterhouse-Five*. Trout "did not think of himself as a writer for the simple reason that the world had never allowed him to think of himself this way." For years, Vonnegut wrote, unsure of his talent, not knowing whether he was a writer or not. His work sold consistently, but not sensationally. One critic called him "the best least-read novelist in America."

There were chronic writer's blocks. He doesn't like to talk about them now, except to say, "It's like a faucet that gushes on and off. God turns the faucet."

One block came in 1956 after his father died, and lasted a year. Vonnegut worked for a Boston advertising agency. During another, he taught at a Cape Cod school for emotionally disturbed children. At one time, he talked about going into real estate. He swam, painted such diverse things as vivid flowers and a twentieth-century saint, and began to hammer into marble with a nail the last sentence from *Ulysses*, "And his heart was going like

---

This is the first of two interviews with Kurt Vonnegut—set 15 years apart—included in this book. The two interviews were included not just to highlight the differences the years make in Vonnegut himself, but also the differences in how Vonnegut is perceived. While the later profile casts Vonnegut as elder statesman, this interview sets Vonnegut in 1970, against the backdrop of his first big success—and it's somehow comforting to see one of our era's most influential writers as a generally quiet, relocated Midwesterner who bought a power mower with the proceeds from Slaughterhouse-Five.

mad and Yes I said, Yes I will, Yes."

In those days, Vonnegut was called a science fiction writer because of his books, *Player Piano* and *Sirens of Titan*. After *Mother Night*, *Cat's Cradle* and *God Bless You, Mr. Rosewater*, the label became *black humorist*. He dislikes all labels.

"I have always thought of myself as a novelist, not a science fiction writer, not a black humorist. Science fiction is a story with machines. There's no reason it should be a separate category, except that people who don't know anything about machines think it should be. They get embarrassed. They hope it's not really literature."

He says the term *black humorist* came about because "Bruce Jay Friedman decided all of a sudden there were black humorists. A big list was made up, and of course, Bruce Jay Friedman was on it. You could also make up a list of people and say they wear yellow roller skates."

With Vonnegut, everything is funny and nothing is funny. The put-on is ever-present. It is hard to separate it from the real. In his books, the put-on allows you to pierce to the heart of the subject. With Vonnegut, it holds you off. He is self-conscious about analyzing his writing.

"I am programmed to write. We are computers," he says evasively.

Then he reluctantly describes his writing this way: "Usually I begin with several ideas, start playing with them. They are authentic concerns about things in life that bother me. One way of my dealing with them is in writing.

"I play with these ideas until they start to feel right. It's something like oil painting. You lay on paint and lay on paint. Suddenly you have something and you frame it."

Vonnegut uses no outlines, no summary. He just sits down at the typewriter in his high-ceilinged workroom, farthest from the center of activity in the house, starts writing, and moves ahead.

"It's like watching a teletype machine in a newspaper office to see what comes out. I work seven days a week. Some days I hit. Other days I only waste time. Most days are like that, just throwing stuff away. I am not at all prolific. My published material is very small compared to what other people write."

Much of what he puts down in these daily sessions has been working and forming in his mind for days and perhaps months (or years, as with *Slaughterhouse-Five*). Three-quarters of the work has been done in his head already. He prefers to work this way, he says, because with other methods—such as outlines—writers begin responding to the outline or to other books or to other things their teachers have told them. "Their real function in society is to respond to life."

Because he is constantly revising and rethinking his material, Vonnegut sets no goals for numbers of written pages daily. He is so familiar with the material that he already has set down, he begins each session by picking up where he ended without benefit of rereading. And he never shows his unfinished material to anyone. "It stops you. Something I don't want to do is stop."

A few years ago, he showed part of *Slaughterhouse-Five* to Jane. She criticized certain portions. He couldn't write again for ten months.

Vonnegut generally gets up about 7 A.M., eats a light breakfast, and sits down at the typewriter from about 8:30 to noon. Sometimes, if the day is right, he works from 5 to 6 in the evening. If the spirit moves him at other times, he writes then, too.

His workroom is bright and airy. It is filled with shelves of books and memorabilia from his life. Among them are an Iowa license plate (he taught at a writer's workshop there for two years), an old black cast iron stove that used to supply him heat, a pair of antlers, and an avocado plant, which Jane says has never bloomed.

To get away and to get some exercise, he does errands at midday. Afternoons are usually spent answering fan letters or working in the yard. He gets about 70 letters a week. Despite the antiwar, antimilitary, antiorganized religion content of his books, he says he gets little hate mail.

When he writes, he sits on a padded Danish walnut easy chair. With his long legs drawn up and his back hunched, he leans forward to type on a machine set on a coffee table. Papers, folders and books are strewn about the table and on the floor.

"Writing is much easier this way," he says. "The floor is closer and you can put all sorts of reference materials all around. If you had a big desk, you'd have to crawl under it to get at the materials."

Vonnegut has been known to verbalize while writing. Jane says she frequently hears him talking in his workroom. He denies this. "I must be talking on the telephone."

He smiles.

Once settled for writing, the first thing Vonnegut does is give his characters names.

"You need a name right away. Otherwise, the character doesn't develop and grow or have much of a personality."

He picks the names out of phone books, and frequently from the mailboxes of his Barnstable neighbors. The names he seeks may be for people, philosophies, or communities. For example, the *karass* of *Cat's Cradle* is the name of a Greek family in West Barnstable. Vonnegut knew them only through their mailbox. Granfalloon, of the same book, "just sounded right." The Tralfamadorian aliens of *Slaughterhouse-Five* was "just made up."

When asked about his style, Vonnegut says, "It just comes out of the typewriter. You develop a style from writing a lot. I have been writing since adolescence. The style will change from book to book, according to subject material."

Like his recent books, *Slaughterhouse-Five* is short, 186 pages. "All my books are short now and will continue to be. Books should be. I hope to write books that men will read. The 500-page book was done for an idle person at a time when one specific purpose of a novel was to destroy time, particularly in winter. With books like that now, you reach only the idle rich or retired."

"A great amount of detail in those books was given to clothing, interior decoration, mail and transportation. There is no transportation in my books."

Vonnegut was born Nov. 11, 1922, Armistice Day, in Indianapolis. A fourth-generation American, his father was an architect, his mother a housewife, "but well educated." He has one brother, a physicist with a doctoral degree from the Massachusetts Institute of Technology. ("A humane scientist. He is working on the physics of clouds," says Vonnegut.) A sister died of cancer 12 years ago.

Vonnegut attended public schools and worked on his high school daily newspaper (one of the few such newspapers in American secondary education). After that came Cornell University, where he studied biochemistry because, as he says, "My father wanted me to take up something sensible." He wrote a column for the Cornell *Daily Sun* and was also the paper's managing editor.

In 1943, he joined the Army Student Officer Training Program. The Army sent him to Carnegie Tech to become a mechanical engineer. Later it trained him in artillery. Finally, it assigned him as a scout with the 106th Infantry Division, 2nd Battalion, 423rd Regiment, and sent him into the Battle of the Bulge. The outfit shattered, and he wandered around for about 11 days in the battle area, not knowing where the lines were. He was captured by the Germans and ultimately transported to a work unit in Dresden, an open city, which was supposed to be free from bombings. He was incarcerated in the slaughterhouse.

Vonnegut was decorated with a Purple Heart. After war, he attended several universities, finally settling at the University of Chicago. He studied anthropology days and worked nights as a reporter for the Chicago City News Bureau to support himself and his wife. He had married Jane Marie Cox ("I met her in kindergarten,") Sept. 1, 1945.

He finished his academic work for a master's degree and took the preliminary examinations. The full faculty committee turned his thesis down. The title was *Fluctuations between Good and Evil in Simple Tales*. Vonnegut dropped out of school.

It was never important to me to know whether I was a satirist or not.

"I picked up a lot of technical information on attitudes," he says now of his education. "Anthropology was wonderful. You surveyed the different ways men have lived all over the world, the relativism of culture."

He commented, too, that a science education had a wonderfully uncluttering quality when it came to literary matters. Though he has often been asked to define satire, he has never bothered to look the word up. "I've never worried about questions like that. It was never important to me to know whether I was a satirist or not."

For three years, from 1947-1950, Vonnegut was a public relations man for General Electric in Schenectady, New York. He did well ("I was able to get double-truck pictures in *Life*,") but left because he disliked the job, and because he was writing a book mocking GE. He didn't think it would be honorable to stay. The book, *Player Piano*, was published in 1951. In it, he mentioned an island where executives were sent for meritorious service to their company. GE phased out such an island shortly afterward.

He had already started writing and selling short stories. In 1950, he moved to Osterville on Cape Cod with his wife and family. Occupation: freelance writer. After a year of no returns, he went into a writer's mental block. Then the money began to come in. Not a lot. He has said of those years of short story writing that he earned what he would have made "being in charge of a cafeteria at a pretty good junior high school."

He was able to support his family, which eventually consisted of three Vonnegut children—Mark, Edith and Nanette—and three Adams children—James, Steven and Kurt Jonathan—who were nephews and children of his sister, and came to live with them when their mother died and their father was killed the same day in a train wreck. The family moved to the Barnstable farmhouse in 1956.

The stories he wrote crisscrossed our culture, touching on the themes of programmed happiness, the population explosion, the emotions of machines and a misplaced sense of values. Some were clearly tear-jerkers written for women's magazines. Some showed lovable human beings attempting to make their way in a zany world. Sometimes they created their own worlds. Most of his stories were printed in the *Saturday Evening Post* and *Colliers's*, now defunct. Others appeared in *The Atlantic, Esquire* and *Playboy*. Two collections of his short stories have been published.

Looking back over the short story years, Vonnegut calls that writing, a "hysterical effort. It was damn unpleasant for a number of years. I used to go hunting for something to write about. I would try to make up stories the way a cartoonist would make up cartoons." The experience left him feeling that writing was an industry. He has never since admitted that it is something he enjoys.

His second novel, *The Sirens of Titan*, appeared in 1959. It was tabbed science fiction. *Mother Night* came in 1961—the story of an American who served his country as a spy while posing as a Nazi propagandist, and later finds himself to be faceless and soulless. A moral was explicit: "We are what we pretend to be, so we'd better be careful what we pretend to be." The science fiction label did not apply.

In *Cat's Cradle*, published in 1963, war, weapons and religion were bunkoed. *God Bless You, Mr. Rosewater*, 1964, told about an eccentric philanthropist who lavishes love on useless people.

Vonnegut began to swing wider on contemporary society, on its shams and shibboleths, the everyday hokum that makes up our lives. There were no sacred cows, no safe categories of good guys. There was no room for self-pretension.

To get his point across, Vonnegut uses a potent system of indirection. His technique is to tread carefully between the horror and the humor, always maintaining a balance. In *Slaughterhouse-Five*, the technique reaches perfection as he treads gently between the pathetic and the ridiculous. The result is a subtle, unexpected, but solid punch in the emotional nose.

Because his writing probes some of life's basic questions, college students, as *Newsweek* said, see Vonnegut as "a prophet, if not quite of doom, then at least of some considerable unpleasantness."

But Vonnegut sees himself as neither philosopher nor seer, just "a middle-class man, a part of the establishment myself." He is concerned that people may read too much into his writings, take them too literally. "You see, all of this is a put-on. I don't have any more policy statements about life than I work on outlines."

But several statements about being kind are posted on the walls of the Vonnegut farmhouse. One writer quoted one inked on a wall, "God damn it, you've got to be kind," in a newspaper article. It drew an irate letter from a Midwesterner criticizing the author for trying to set himself up as a great humanitarian. Vonnegut now de-

liberately steers reporters and photographers away from the quotations.

Jane explains: "For years, he's blasted self-importance. He goes to an extreme in modesty and candor on his writing and views, and it comes off as arrogance. That statement has been on the wall for 15 years."

You say what you have to say. But you have to learn to say it in such a way that the reader can see what you mean.

He is not particularly interested in discussing writers or writing trends. He does a "fair amount" of reading, and after a minute of thought, he says contemporary writers he most respects are Donald Barthelme, Saul Bellow and Wilfred Sheed. Works of F. Scott Fitzgerald and Celine are on his workroom bookshelves, and he has said he likes the work of William Blake and J.D. Salinger. When he taught in the writer's workshop at the University of Iowa from 1965-1967, he assigned such works as *Alice in Wonderland*, *Candide* and *Journey to the End of Night*.

He deflects questions about the ideas or symbols in his books. Writing to him is simply a matter of communication. Talking about his books implies to him (besides a self-pretension) that he hasn't communicated very well to the reader.

"You don't ask writers to explain their books. The writer has already explained as best as he can what the book is about."

His advice to the beginning writer is "Face the audience of strangers," a statement he used to write on the blackboard as he began each writing class at the University of Iowa.

"That's what it is. You face the audience of strangers," he repeats now. "One part of writing well is writing something that can be read well. Otherwise, the link between the writer and the reader is broken. Anytime the reader fails to get the message, it's the writer's fault.

"You say what you have to say. But you have to learn to say it in such a way that the reader can see what you mean."

Vonnegut offers no sure-fire formulas for writing. He is as much against them as he is against outlines, or institutions. He does not believe that people can be taught to write. He does believe that writers can be taught to communicate.

"The real writer will write. He has something inside of him that must come out. If a person has a book in him, he will sit down and write it. There is no surgery approach through which this sort of thing can be examined."

What the real writer has to do, advises Vonnegut, is take a year out of his life to find out "what is inside of him. Even then, he wouldn't know. A writer's good book might be his seventh."

Critics frequently brushed the beginning Vonnegut off as a skillful, but slick, science fiction writer. He has been accused of having a snarl without a balanced perspective on the human condition, of being depressing, cynical and nihilistic. At the latter accusation, he bristles: "I don't like J. Edgar Hoover or General Lewis Hershey, but that doesn't mean I'm negative. I just don't like bugging."

But Vonnegut coteries existed in the Village on the East Coast and in San Francisco on the West, and with *Cat's Cradle*, literary figures began to take notice. Graham Greene called him one of the best living American writers. Cults sprang up on college campuses across the country. The kids saw in him someone who shared their anxiety, someone who spoke their language.

Critical opinion was not unanimous. Some considered him too precious. One review, in *Commonweal*, mocked the Vonnegut "formula. After the seal act, bring on the lyric tenor," and added, "Vonnegut seems bent on being loved not only as Class Cutup . . . but also as Most Sensitive Boy of 1922—that would explain the frequent feyness. He is an inventive, skillful author, working in a bad line. . . ."

With his growing popularity of the last few years, Vonnegut made room in his writing schedule for about ten lectures a year across the country. Many of these have been given on college campuses, but he points out that he has spoken for older groups, too.

"Lecturing can be a lucrative business, but I lecture to keep in touch. I charge modest fees and generally give the money to the American Friends Service Committee [a pacifist group]. I don't find lecturing interferes with my writing."

He found out that young people on his lecture tours weren't interested in hearing funny stories, but that what they really wanted to be told was, "What the hell should I do when I get out of this place?"

"So, I tell them what not to do," he says. "don't work for any company that harms the planet. There is a new concept of sin now. Anything which is damaging to the planet is sin. Young people are told to be terribly civil, to be responsible toward their elders, and they are told not to kill. Yet institutions and governments are largely set up to prevent people from realizing what they are doing. A good example is the high-altitude bombers in Vietnam, in which the men in the planes are killing people on the ground they cannot see. They are just turning dials."

His solitude has been broken frequently by writers and photographers who have descended on the Barnstable homesite to probe his life and his art. This is something unsettling to people unused to public attention.

On most days, however, life for the Vonneguts on the Cape is unchanged. He is usually busy, writing, tramping in and out of the many doors in their house, scraping at his boat hull, winding up garden hose or pushing a power mower.

Though he is a man of the Midwest, the Cape provides the creative environment he needs. "This is much more beautiful than Indiana. In the Middle West, they are not used to people in the arts. They are embarrassed and confused by them. There is a feeling that they don't pull their own weight. On either coast, writing is a recognized activity."

Their lifestyle hasn't changed with the financial success of *Slaughterhouse-Five*, though he "went out and bought a power mower, and Jane bought a new blender. We're not rich, just fortunate."

With the literary burden of *Slaughterhouse-Five* lifted from his mind, you wonder if the emotional burden has been lifted from his soul.

"Now that I've expiated it, life is always pleasant," he says.

And, with the creative tension of the big book removed, you ask if he worries about an erosion of writing talent. He says, "I have nothing to worry about now, I'm on easy street." He laughs uproariously.

Gets up.

Walks away.

With 15 years and Breakfast of Champions, Slapstick, Jailbird *and* Palm Sunday, *a divorce and remarriage between him and the previous interview, Kurt Vonnegut is much more deliberate in explaining his craft and thoughts. Or maybe he's just more practiced at interviews. Either way, keep an eye on the twists and turns he's put on ideas that were merely germinating in the previous interview. And every once in a while, forget the road and look at the scenery: the difference in how the two main types of interviews—the earlier profile and this question-and-answer—structure identical information.*

From the beginning of his career as a novelist, Kurt Vonnegut has been deeply concerned with the way the human race has addressed its potential, and with the price we have paid—in terms of lost faith, misplaced kindness, or even the escalation of cruelty—as we work our way along in time.

Like his precursor and model, Mark Twain, Vonnegut addresses these issues by making his readers laugh at their own stupidities or grit their teeth at the world's injustices. It is virtually impossible to read a Vonnegut novel without feeling exactly what Vonnegut wants you to feel, whether horror at the massive destruction and loss of lives at Dresden, Germany (*Slaughterhouse-Five*), desperation over the grim fate we face when confronting the ultimate in scientific and technological advancement (*Cat's Cradle*), or joy at watching an incredibly gentle and wealthy man, considered insane by his ladder-climbing peers, give away his kingdom to the salt of the earth (*God Bless You, Mr. Rosewater*). Compact and narrated in a style that seems simple, Vonnegut's books pack enormous emotional punches.

In October of 1985, Delacorte published *Galapagos*, Vonnegut's 11th novel. (He has also written a play—*Happy Birthday, Wanda June*—a collection of short stories—*Welcome to the Monkey House*—and two miscellanies of nonfiction—*Wampeters, Foma and Granfalloons* and *Palm Sunday.*) The story of a misbegotten cruise to the Galapagos Islands, the plot of *Galapagos* focuses on what happens when the ship's passengers are stranded and forced to face survival on an island 600 miles from the mainland. With its allegorical overtones, it is a particularly strong statement about the way we have evolved, not as much physically as socially.

Vonnegut explains: "The legend is that the Galapagos Islands were to Charles Darwin what the Road to Damascus was to Saint Paul: Saint Paul became a Christian on his way to Damascus, and the legend—which isn't particularly true—is that Darwin caught on to the theory of evolution when he visited the Galapagos Islands.

"*Galapagos* is about human evolution—where we might go next, what kind of animals we are now, and how we're doing. We aren't really surviving very well, having evolved in the direction we've taken."

Success has neither spoiled nor jaded Kurt Vonnegut. His Manhattan home, in the shadow of the United Nations building, is modest. One of the building's four floors is used as a studio/office by Vonnegut's wife, Jill Krementz, the well-known photographer; the top floor contains Vonnegut's office, with the other stories serving as living quarters. The second floor, where we talked, seemed spacious with its high ceiling and sprawling stuffed furniture.

In his cardigan sweater and baggy pants, which accentuate his long, angular form, Vonnegut comes off more like a favorite uncle than a bestselling author. His body language indicates a relaxed man, even when he's speaking on topics he considers important. He is soft-spoken and pleasant, occasionally self-depreciatory and always candid. He smiles often, transforming an almost tired-looking face into one of boyish mirth, and he laughs easily, starting with a chuckle that works its way into an explosive, wheezing, coughing sputter brought on from years of chain-smoking. It didn't take long for me to realize that this combination of straight-from-the-hip speech and easygoing mannerism would be hard to translate into a question-and-answer interview: words have a way of looking naked after they have been spoken and type-struck onto a blank sheet of paper.

So it goes.

In your Paris Review *interview, you were talking about being a scout during World War II, and you mentioned that your job was "to go out and look for enemy stuff. Things got so bad that we were finally looking for our own stuff." Sounds like an interesting summation of your career.*

What, that I've collapsed like the Battle of the Bulge? [smiles]

No, I'm saying that writers, especially the ones just starting out, are always looking for "stuff" out there, and the successful ones seem to find it within themselves. Don't you think that writers are much like scouts?

It all depends. For instance, my son, Mark, is a writer, and he wrote because he had something very much on his mind. It was as though *he* had been attacked, rather than his looking for a place to attack. He was responding to a whack from life. A lot of people, particularly readers of writers magazines, are looking for stuff to write about, because they want a job. They're out looking for any kind of idea, you know, that would get them into the profession, because they want this kind of job. They don't want a boss—they want to be free to travel, and all that. So, yeah, they're like scouts looking for something—*anything*. But there are a lot of writers, my son included, who felt a necessity to respond to life and not necessarily start a new professional career at it. Mark's a pediatrician now, and he's very busy with long work hours and his family.

How do you see yourself?

I've customarily responded to life as I've seen something that made me very much want to write about it—not that it made me very much want to get into the writing profession.

You've said that you have to have an ax to grind—

Well, you've got to have something to write about. I've taught writing at Iowa, Harvard and City College in New York. One big problem is that people don't have anything on their minds. They're not *concerned*—which isn't to say they need an ax to grind. Usually, a person with an ax to grind is a crank of some kind, or a partisan of some kind. So I reject the ax to grind. But you must be passionate about some aspect of life, because it's a high-energy performance to create something the size of a book. It takes energy and concentration. In a way, it's sort of like an athletic event: you have to have the same sort of energy that people are bringing into a basketball tournament, and the same sort of concentration—not an ax to grind. You should have something on your mind. You should have opinions on things. You should *care* about things.

A lot of creative writing courses teach you how to counterfeit concern, how to counterfeit energy, sincerity and involvement. You should care about things.

In an essay on writing with style, you said that caring was the main thing.

Yeah. English can be a fifth language, one way or the other. You can be quite eloquent at it. Of course, a lot of creative writing courses teach you how to counterfeit concern [laughs], how to counterfeit energy, sincerity and involvement. It's a little like going to modeling school to learn how to put on your makeup and always be beautiful [laughs]. People have succeeded going into the writing business as scouts, looking for any goddamned thing to write about and pretending concern for things they don't really care a hell of a lot about.

In a way, young writers almost have to be concerned about fitting into slots, as far as publishing goes, rather than writing about something that may not sell. Publishers are less than enthusiastic about publishing first novels these days.

Well, I knew John Irving when he was younger, and his books were simply so compelling that they were published. I knew Gail Godwin. Both of them were students of mine at Iowa, and their stories were so compelling. They really didn't fit into any formula that Random House or Simon & Schuster or anyone else had in mind, but their books were so goddamned compelling that they were readable; they were exciting. Publishers would be perfectly willing to have formulas in mind, but nobody knows what the formulas are. I would say that younger writers are being discriminated against because publishers are putting less money into them than they used to, and publishers aren't as patient to let writers develop now; but one thing is that writers themselves have been faithless.

In what way?

A young writer can be picked up by a Scribner's, say, for a small advance, and Scribner's says: "This guy is really very good, or this woman is really very good—or will be. There's a lot wrong with his first book, but we'll publish the second one, which is pretty good." But Simon & Schuster, say, offers this writer $180,000 for his third book. So does he stay with Scribner's, who developed him? No, he leaves. So any publisher who's looking at a young writer who is saying, "Invest some money in me, I'm going to get better"—any publisher in his right mind—knows that this person is going to jump immediately for a big raise. So publishers are wary of young writers, too, because they haven't been that faithful to the publishers who have invested money in them. America's a free-enterprise economy, and so there are these business considerations, but I am persuaded that anybody who writes awfully well is going to be published because readers are going to like these books. The thing is to write compellingly and you're going to do very well. Robert Stone [author of *Dog Soldiers* and *A Flag for Sunrise*] certainly didn't conform to any formula; he was responding to the Vietnam War. He wasn't a scout; he was responding to something which has happened to the whole country.

And this is what happened to you with the Dresden bombings?

Yes. In each case it wasn't an ax to grind; it was a matter of reporting something that hadn't been discussed before. Plus, it was very interesting, too. Deeply absorbing. The function for Stone, for me, and for a lot of writers is, in part, journalistic: We do often deal with the issues of the day, rather than merely characters or static situations.

Okay, let's say you care about something, such as you did with the firebombing of Dresden, and that you want to tell it in the best way possible, so readers are going to get exactly the way you feel about what happened. From there, you have so many different ways you can tell the story. You can tell it through black humor, or you can tell it straightforwardly, or in very flowery language . . .

You can try them all. I mean, take your time, you've got all the time in the world. On that particular book, I suppose I got into it a hundred pages several times and the tone was wrong. It didn't sound right to me.

What made you feel that your best method of writing was to write these fairly simple, declarative sentences, working in irony and humor as you did? How did you decide on that style?

Well, it's not something you can control very well, particularly if you've had an education. It's too visceral a matter. It's too intimate a matter, at least for somebody older than 25, to be controllable. I think by then the way you express yourself is bound right into your flesh and bones. I went to a wonderful high school—an elite high school—in Indianapolis. Such schools don't exist anymore, because they're considered undemocratic. . . . But, anyway, I went to a place called Shortridge, and the teachers I had were for straight, simple, forward writing. My intention was to become a journalist, and the high school had a daily paper. When I worked on that, it was simple, declarative sentences, saying as much as you knew, as quickly as possible, leaving yourself out of the story, and saying no more than you really could be sure of. Philosophically, this appealed to me very much; telling anything beyond that seemed to me like lying. Speculation is very suspect. So I was trained that way in high school, appreciated it, and thought it was right.

Then I went to Cornell and worked on the *Cornell Sun*, which was a daily morning paper, a business separate from the university. Again, it was this straightforwardness. Whenever I was spoken to about bad writing, it was because of a lack of clarity or for saying something that obviously pretended to know something I had no

right to know. That sort of thing. Ever since, I've found straightforwardness congenial, and it's made my books very short.

How did you come upon these kind of sighs of resignation that have become your trademark: "So it goes," "Imagine that," "Hi, ho," etc.?

Oh, you just try them. You're writing along, and all of a sudden you feel like saying it [smiles]. If it looks like a lousy idea, you can cross it out. I started doing it with *Slaughterhouse-Five*, every time anything died. I had one death in the book, and I dismissed it with "So it goes." Then I tried the invention that anytime anything died—including a bottle of champagne—I said, "So it goes," and I liked it. It seemed like a good idea. Again, it shortened the book—it didn't lengthen it. It was a comment on the finality of death and the inability to bring people back and the acknowledgment that we're all going to die someday and grieving probably doesn't help much, and so on. I could have had essays on those subjects; I could have gotten up to 800 pages with no trouble at all, with me ruminating on death. Another thing: It's very unlikely that I'd have any fresh ideas on death, since the subject has been discussed before [laughs]. After the death of somebody, people are ready to go to thousands of words before the action of the story starts up again.

That sort of simple understatement has a hysterically funny effect.

If you write in the baroque mode, like Henry James . . . it's so noisy. I mean, all these instruments playing, all at one time. It's difficult to stage surprises, because nothing is going to stand out. So if you do keep it down, you'll hear one solo instrument when it cuts in. It's possible to stage a surprise. Also if you're writing in the baroque manner—very complicated language and sentences and all that—jokes are going to be lost, because you can't time them. Jokes have to be quite naked to be understood. They have to be quite simple. There are gadgets for a joke to work—all parts have to be absolutely essential. You can't stray away from a joke to make an aside or anything else, you've got to go straight to the punchline as promptly as possible. So again, simplicity is essential. It's an important matter of style. In *Palm Sunday*, I said that the funniest joke in the world, if you tell it in King James English, comes out sounding like Charlton Heston [laughs].

> *Jokes have to be quite naked to be understood. They have to be quite simple.*

You grew up during the Golden Age of radio comedy. Those shows must have had quite an influence on your method of telling jokes.

They certainly did—and that was all based on sound, too. There was nothing to see along with the jokes. I consider Jack Benny one of the great men of our time, without question. And Stan Laurel, of Laurel and Hardy, too. Charlie Chaplin. Those people were geniuses, as great as anybody on the planet at that time. They knew how to construct jokes just exquisitely.

And their humor often commented on serious topics.

Of course. Charlie Chaplin played Hitler. You cannot be funny, I think, if you're not dealing with serious matters. That's one reason I find Bob Hope not a great comedian, because there's nothing troubled in anything he says. In fact, he does not allude to unhappiness or the tragedy in a situation, and so forth. Laurel and Hardy sure as hell did. There was a great sadness in Benny, who was able to bring forth the Jewish tragedy without really mentioning it, just by his presence and manner. You can only be funny—unless you're Bob Hope, and you want to be funny in that superficial way—if you have matters of great importance on your mind.

You're a person who makes people laugh, yet as a writer, you don't actually hear the laughter. Do you miss that? Is that the reason you go out on the lecture circuit and read your work?

I don't read the work; I lecture. If I read my work, nobody'd laugh. I lecture, I become sort of a vaudevillian. People do laugh. It's a very calculated performance. One problem with movies, incidentally, is that you can't pause for laughs. With any sort of live performance, if you really get the audience going, you can keep it going. When you start making jokes in the movies, the audience can still be laughing when you top the first joke, and they miss the topper. And when there's silence, they realize they've missed something. And they're stunned when you top it yet again: they're not in the mood for another joke, because they're still wondering what they missed. In theater, you can get an audience going and mug like hell.

I've seen that sort of thing happen in books, where a writer layers joke upon joke.

You can do that in a book, sure. You can pace yourself. The book has a certain advantage I hadn't thought of, which is instant replay, which virtually no other art form has.

You come from Indiana, and that seems to be important in the development of your humor and point of view. Your characters all have decent, middle-class values that are being challenged by a terribly complex, uncaring society. *Do you find that your having come from the Midwest has given you a different or unique outlook?*

Well, I might have become ethnocentric if I had come from someplace closer to the center of gravity. If I arrived in the East believing that Indianapolis was the center of the universe, it was very quickly cleared up for me [laughs]. There are people—and I, in fact, am talking about my neighbors, these native New Yorkers—who do feel at the center of things. You've seen that picture of the New Yorker view of the world: there's the East River, there's Jersey, and then you don't stop again until Los Angeles and San Francisco out there. No, socially, I haven't been in the position of being an explainer of things. I've been an outsider taking a look at it.

How does that make your writing different from that of insiders?

If you're an outsider—if you're roaming the world as an outsider, wherever you go, you're a rootless person—then you are an explorer and you write as an explorer, as a journalist, as an ethnographer. You're probably going to do a pretty good job reporting what you see, in the sense of coming into a strange situation and gaining some insight into it. If you are already at home—as so many New Yorkers are, or Bostonians are—you become an exemplar. I would write about what's best about Boston, and I would try to become better and better at that. As an Indianapolis person who left home, I'm a reporter everywhere, and I exemplify nothing except honest reporting. If you leave home, you become a reporter; if you stay home, you become an exemplar—particularly if you stay home in a town like San Francisco, Boston, New York or Baltimore. Chicago writers are exemplars.

I wanted to ask you a few questions about your career and writing habits, so let's start at the beginning. At first glance, you appear to be one of those rare writers who quit a steady job to write full time because writing was the thing you did best. What convinced you that you could do that?

I was making more money on the weekend and in evenings than I was making working for General Electric.

Still, writing full time is a tough, high-risk profession.

There's no question about it. It's an extremely high-risk situation. People are willing to take these extraordinary chances to become writers, musicians or painters, and because of them we have a culture. If this ever stops, our culture will die, because most of our culture, in fact, has been created by people who got paid nothing for it—people like Edgar Allan Poe, Vincent van Gogh or Mozart. So, yes, it's a very foolish thing to do, notoriously foolish, but it seems human to attempt it anyway. William Kennedy, who's very hot now, experienced many, many bad years, but he kept at it. Nelson Algren was a failure at the end of his life.

So was James T. Farrell.

Yes. They were no longer able to make a living. So that's it, the nature of that particular game. If you can go to work for American Motors or Dodge or International Harvester in order to be secure instead of being a writer . . .

You'll never get the job done.

No, and then the factory goes under [laughs]. And you've lost everything. In the Soviet Union, of course, if they figure you're a writer, you don't have piecework anymore. You get some kind of salary. I don't know quite how it works, but you get a house, you get a car, you get all this, and you don't have to produce that much. They don't notice it, unless you don't produce anything. My son is a pediatrician, and this is essentially long hours and low pay because his patients, by definition, are just starting out in life and don't have much money, and the big bucks are with people in the last two weeks of their lives or in the intensive care units. . . . So everything is a risk. A guy at American Motors can get his hands chopped off.

When you were starting out, you were in an un-enviable position, because you were trying to support a family on income earned writing paperback origi-nals and short stories. It must have been tough trying to keep things going.

Well, it really was. I mean, it's a young man's game, or a young woman's game, but you can survive as a writer on hustle: you get paid very little for each piece, but you write a lot of pieces. Christ, I did book reviews—I did anything. It was $85 here, $110 there—I was like Molly Bloom: "Yes I will, yes I will, yes." [laughs] Whatever any-body wanted done, I did it.

Is that one of the reasons you don't write short stories now?

Oh, they're very hard to do—they're much harder than a novel, I think, because they're far more artificial. Just to make a short story work, you have to misrepre-sent life. You've got to create a fist-like thing, a fist-like incident that's very clean and separate from the rest of life, like an egg, and there are no such instances in real life, so you're going to misrepresent life. I think an ordi-nary person reading a well-made short story is delighted, because you play emotional tricks on people with plot and so forth. You create expectations and you satisfy them—and you're doing things to their body chemistry, really. The brain, as it processes the material, is sending signals to the nervous system, circulatory system, and all that. So special things are happening. It's a very enter-taining thing for a writer to do—it's almost like doing crossword puzzles or something like that. It's a trick . . . like writing a sonnet. It's hard to do, it can be done, and when you do it, it's amazing that you got away with it. A typical short story is somewhere between 10 and 20 pages long. If you go to 40 pages, you can treat life very truthfully.

In the past, you've mentioned that you can't work with an outline. I wonder if we could talk about how you organize. Do you take a lot of notes? Do you spend a lot of time thinking out your novels?

It's like making a movie: All sorts of accidental things will happen after you've set up the cameras. So you get lucky. Something will happen at the edge of the set and perhaps you start to go with that; you get some footage of that. You come into it accidentally. You set the story in motion, and as you're watching this thing begin, all these opportunities will show up. So, in order to exploit one thing or another, you may have to do research. You may have to find out more about Chinese immigrants, or you may have to find out more about Halley's Comet, or what-ever, where you didn't realize that you were going to have Chinese or Halley's Comet in the story. So you do re-search on that, and it implies more, and the deeper you get into the story, the more it implies, the more sugges-tions it makes on the plot. Toward the end, the ending becomes inevitable.

But you do have specific things planned. You know that certain characters are going to do certain things.

I will pick a person, or a couple of people. . . . When I started this book, I knew that these people were going to go to the Galapagos Islands. When they arrived in Ecua-dor, I was sure they were going to be in Guayaquil, in a hotel, and that they would be able to see the ship a half a mile away at the waterfront. That much, I knew. After that, I also knew that hotels have managers and bellboys, and other people deliver news to the rooms—good news or bad news, whatever. There's also a cocktail lounge. Also, something's going to happen right away, because the ship is going to sail right away. So you're not going to have people milling around the hotel, saying, "Do you want to see the cathedral?" or "Do you want to go home?" No. They've got to go on that ship, because the damn cruise cost them $1,500 a head. So there's that much energy in the story, in the situation, to begin with.

Plus you knew that they were going to be stranded on the island.

Maybe they wouldn't be. Maybe I'd strand them, and if it seemed like a bad idea, bring them back home again. It's only paper, you know. Yeah, I tried it and it worked, but I might have had all sorts of things happen.

You once said that you wrote for an audience of one . . .

Everybody does.

Who is that audience now?

I don't know. I think it's probably still my sister, who died a long time ago. I wouldn't have started that if a psychiatrist hadn't said it—not about me, but about all writers. I read this psychiatrist's study that said that every writer, in fact, writes for one person. If you don't do this, your work won't have the unity. The secret of artistic unity, I think, is to create for one person; anyone else who comes to it will sense this focus in the book.

Who are you reading today? What do you find really exciting?

I read largely for social reasons now, because I know so many writers and I run into them and want to keep up with what they're doing. The exciting work that's going on in the country now is for the stage. There are some really exciting people, like Sam Shepard, writing for the stage. Novels are okay [laughs], but the high-energy stuff, in my mind, is happening on the stage.

There was a stage in your life when you were seriously considering writing plays.

Oh, I always wanted to, but there have been virtually no novelists who have written good plays, and also there have been virtually no playwrights who have written good novels. I think a young writer comes to a fork in the road

very early and becomes one sort of a writer or the other. When I was young, there were a lot of very good playwrights, people like Tennessee Williams and William Saroyan, and, God, I would get to New York to see what they were doing. That sort of thing is happening now . . . I envy those people. I'd rather be a playwright than a novelist now, because it seems to me that they're doing a lot more.

One last question about the literary scene: Many writers of your generation seemed hellbent on writing the so-called Great American Novel—almost to the point of making a competition out of it—yet three of the most popular novels in recent years— Slaughterhouse-Five, Catch-22 *and* The World According to Garp—*were unassuming novels that chose to explore the human condition in a humorous way. I don't think anyone set out to write the Great American Novel in those books, yet in many respects, they came damn close.*

No, only confused nuts would set out to do this, to regard it as a competitive enterprise. Writing isn't that sort of business. That hotel in Paris—the Ritz—is now going to give a huge cash prize every year for what they say was the best novel in the whole world [laughs]. I suppose we should be perfectly content with *Moby Dick* as the Great American Novel. We should let it go at that.

BY DUANE BEST

WILLIAM FAULKNER

A writer strives to express a universal truth in the way that rings the most bells in the shortest amount of time.

Do you aim your writing at the majority, or just intellectuals?

That question is difficult to answer. It's not the question of whether to write for an understanding by a particular audience but to write of what you believe and express it in the best way that you can. When you've finished, you hope that it is expressed so that everyone can understand it and derive some benefit from it.

Do you rewrite much, or do you leave a piece after one writing?

It depends on how well I express the idea that I am trying to get across. The craft is too fluid for any set pattern. One day you can do a certain thing and the next you need a complete change of pace. I do not rewrite unless I am absolutely sure that I can express the material better if I do rewrite it.

Do you find that revising tends to ruin a piece of material?

It can be overdone, but not ordinarily. You must wait, sometimes quite a long while, until you are sure that you want to make changes, before you meddle.

At what point do you decide a piece of writing is expressed well enough?

You will come back to it until you have decided that this is the best that you can do. If it still fails to express what you are striving for and is not good enough, then you must decide if it has enough to make it worth finishing.

Can you tell us a little of how you developed your style?

I am not a stylist. The necessity of the idea creates its own style. The material itself dictates how it should be written. A writer must express himself in the most honest, truthful manner that he can.

When you write, do you think of the words as being read aloud?

Yes. I'm sure that I hear every word. Some writers don't, but I definitely do.

Concerning your use of the long, long sentence as a device, what principal effects do you strive to achieve, especially concerning sentences where all punctuation is omitted, leaving only the naked words?

That is another difficult question to answer, and I am not sure that I can explain it so anybody will understand what I mean. I would also have to answer to another writer. A writer strives to express a universal truth in the best possible way that he can: in the way that rings the most bells in the shortest amount of time. He knows that he can't live forever and that each work might possibly be his last and also that the next time he may succeed in achieving his goal. It is almost like trying to write the Lord's Prayer on the head of a pin. It is an attempt to reduce all of the emotional capacities of the human heart into one phrase.

What good are universal truths if the writer cannot, or does not, live them himself?

In the world according to Yoknapatawpha County, there is no use talking: You put everything into your writing, and readers ask questions only if you fail.

Although the author of such classics as The Sound and the Fury *and* As I Lay Dying *compromised on that ideal as he grew older, his appearance at this University of Oregon question-and-answer session several years before his death in 1962 was still considered rare.*

Some of Faulkner's replies are unsatisfyingly terse, others brilliantly terse. But all strike at the truth of writing. Not even the young, reclusive Faulkner would argue with that.

Universal man strives to do better than that of which he is capable. A writer who lives a base or immoral life can say, "This is what I'd like to be if I could," hoping that someone else will read his material and see that truth and get some good from it.

What was your intention in writing the long middle part in A Fable, *dealing with three men on horseback who were crossing the country? I felt that it was far too long and distracted from the purpose of the story. Did I simply fail to get the significance of it?*

I had to justify, through the use of this passage, the reasons that caused a man to do a certain thing. I had to show the background which was responsible for this man's motivation to act as he did in the story. I wrote it once and it was three times that long. I rewrote it and it was half again as long. Finally I whacked it down to the length that was published, and that was still too long.

Which of your works gives you the most personal satisfaction?

I consider *The Sound and the Fury* my best work. If it had been given a better reception by the public, I might not have written another word.

How do you rank Absalom, Absalom!*?*

I can't really answer that because, to the writer, they all fail, which is the reason he writes another book. I rate *The Sound and the Fury* first because of the pain and grief it caused me to get it delivered. *Absalom, Absalom!* is number two.

Can you make a comparison between writing Sanctuary *and your other work?* Sanctuary *is so different.*

I wrote *Sanctuary* to sell, to make money. The publisher would not publish it because he said we'd both be put in jail. Finally, after it had lain around for some time, I rewrote it because I was ashamed of the first writing.

When you rewrote Sanctuary, *were you angered, or did you attempt to satirize the first version and others like it?*

No. I was ashamed of the first version because I had not given enough thought before writing it. The story itself is the same.

What is your greatest reward from writing? Is it monetary?

The reward, for me, is not monetary. It is the personal satisfaction that comes when you ring the bell and know it; when you know you have completely expressed your idea. It is in knowing that you have written the truth.

Do you think that turning out formula material for the popular magazines can work hand in hand with serious writing?

I don't see why not. If you have a piece of serious writing, a universal truth that you feel must be told, you will find some way to tell it to the best of your ability. The urge will eventually become so strong that a man will desert his wife or poison his grandmother, if need be, to get it told.

What do you think a good writer is? Is his ability a natural one or is it possible to acquire writing ability?

It is a little of both and varies with the individual. It is the result of sweat, hard work and a belief in truth; truth as a condition of the human heart, not the individual human heart but the composite heart of man. A writer uses what material he can to present truth in the best possible way. A good writer must be able to see that truth and believe in it.

What do you want people to get from your work?

If they can say, "Yes, that is true; that happened to me," then I am satisfied.

Do you find the physical act of writing difficult?

At first, no; I enjoyed it. Now I hate to sit down to write. I dislike it so much that I don't even write letters.

Then how do you get your inspiration?

I see something, or an idea comes to me, that needs to be told; and I think about it, putting off the physical act of writing until the urgency of the idea becomes so great that it demands that I write.

Usually first thoughts don't come right, and I hold off as long as possible without writing anything, not even notes, until that idea is clear.

What is the longest you ever wrote at one sitting?

About 5,000 words. It was the short story, "Red Leaves." I felt that I must write it, so I took pencil and paper, and a jug of corn whiskey, crawled up in my hayloft and didn't come down until the story was finished.

What do you think has most influenced your writing?

> *All the trash must be eliminated in the short story, whereas one can get away with some of it in a novel.*

A man cannot tell what influences him the most. Everything he has ever touched, read, tasted, smelled, heard or done since infancy influences him in some degree, and that is all reflected in the work which that man does. It is no more possible to isolate any single influence than it is to count the polliwogs in a Mississippi swamp.

How much reading do you do?
I do a great deal of reading because I feel that I must do a lot. I read everything, trash and all.

I always find time to read the Old Testament, *Moby Dick*, some of Shakespeare and about 12 other novels of that caliber at least once a year, because I learn something or see something of value that I had missed in the previous readings.

Do you enjoy reading your imitators?
Yes, because we are all imitators of one kind or another. I enjoy it if the story isn't written just to imitate. If they have a story to tell and it requires imitation, that is fine; and I'm flattered that they imitate me.

Have you ever made a formal study of dialect?
No. Without a formal education, or at least an education in dialectics, I don't think one is equipped to cope with the dialect. In every writer there is a certain amount of the scavenger. He remembers parts of dialect that he has heard and uses this without really knowing why he uses it.

How do you feel writers can be affected by a given geographic region?
A geographical environment is not important if the idea, the talent and the desire are there. If these are present, the writer will use the geographic region in which he lives or which he knows best merely as a tool to express himself. Moving to a particular geographic region just in order to be able to write does nothing more than put off the physical work and the mental anguish of writing.

What about writing in a university environment?
I'm not a university man, and my formal education was rather quick, but it seems that a university should be the best place of all to write, because to write one must be in contact with the emotional past of his society and his race. This is closest at hand in the books and art of a university.

What do you think of the short story form?
I like it very much. All the trash must be eliminated in the short story, whereas one can get away with some of it in a novel.

Do you feel, therefore, that there is no such thing as a poetic novel?
Not deliberately, although there are some that approach it.

What do you think of the different trends in the short story?
The short story doesn't permit any variation of trend. The short story must be entirely complete within itself. The form is too rigid to permit any trends as such; it is too much like the sonnet. The truths expressed through the short story will be the same a thousand years from now, no matter what the material.

Have you ever tried other forms of art?
I have tried a little painting, that's other than my barn. I have never done anything with music, although I do read about it.

Are you interested in the translations of your books into other languages?
Yes. I know only enough to read those translated into French, but I'm interested to see how the aroma that I intended does come through.

How does it come through?
It depends on the translator; sometimes not well and sometimes I discover things that I hadn't even realized were there.

To what do you credit your success?
I recognized something that was true and told it in a way that was moving to me; evidently it was to others, too.

How might it be possible for beginners at writing to make a living while learning the craft?
Do not look toward writing as a profession. Work at something else. Dig ditches if you have to, but keep writing in the status of a hobby that you can work at in your spare time. Writing, to me, is a hobby—by trade I'm a farmer.

BY LINDA BREVELLE

ROD SERLING

You can be a hunchback and a dwarf and what-all.
If you write beautifully, you can write beautifully.

I've never planned ahead," Rod Serling told me the spring before his sudden death. "I just sort of go through life checking the menu of three meals that day. I never worry about tomorrow. It's only since I've gotten older that I've begun to wonder about time running out. Is it sufficient unto itself that I don't plan? Because maybe next Thursday won't come one day. And then, I'm concerned about that. But that's not uniquely the writer's concern, that's the concern of every middle-aged man who looks in the mirror."

I spoke with Serling in the cocktail lounge he frequented at Franco's La Taverna on Sunset Strip. He was vibrant, as cooperative an interviewee as I had ever met. There was no prerehearsed or packaged dialogue issuing from his direction, no bored or weary let's-get-this-over-with routine. His allusions to death seemed more an intellectual exercise than prophecy.

Although I have regrets—I wish I had taped the pre-interview patter between us and listened more carefully to his second thoughts and verbal footnotes—I can't think of a more appropriate epitaph than what *was* said. Serling's reflective moments. A perspective. A looking back. Not too much in touch with the future. Locked into present time.

What better requiem for a heavyweight?

Where do you go from here? How can you top your accomplishments, if you have any real need to top yourself?
Well, first of all, I've never really topped myself, because awards in themselves don't really reflect major accomplishment. It's kind of a strange, backslapping ritual that we go through in this town where you get awards for almost everything. For surviving the day, you're going to get awards. So I can't suggest that those things represent any pinnacle or achievement. If indeed they did, I suppose I'd be worried about how do I top myself. But if in-

deed I'm a household name, it's a fortuitous event, really singularly undeserved.

But again, it's part of the business of really not caring about topping myself, because I really don't care what's going to happen. I think just surviving is a major thing. I'd like to write something that my peers, my colleagues, my fellow writers would find a source of respect. I think I'd rather win, for example, a Writers Guild award than almost anything on earth. And the few nominations I've had with the Guild, and the few awards I've had, represented to me a far more concrete achievement than anything. Emmys, for example, most of that's bull. Oscars are even worse. We have a strange, terrible affliction in this town. Everybody walks around bentbacked from slapping each other on the back so much. It looks like arthritis, but it isn't. It's hunger for recognition. And it's sort of like, "Well, I'll scratch you this time if you'll scratch me next time."

Is it really true what they say in Hollywood, that most of it is luck or a big push from the right person at the right time in the right direction?
I think a lot of it is luck and continues to be. That in no way discounts the terrible urgency that you have talent. It's always who you know, what marvelous moment in time that you find him or meet him. I think one of the

---

This interview—published in 1976 but given just before Rod Serling's death in June 1975—finds the 51-year-old creator of The Twilight Zone *and* Night Gallery *looking back at a lifetime of three Emmys (for* Patterns, Requiem for a Heavyweight—*probably his best known individual work—and another for the* Twilight Zone *series), taking common-sense potshots at the role of writing in both screenwriting and his own life, and describing every writer's "vaunting itch for immortality."*

problems sometimes with the writer is the personality of the writer, because it becomes a very personal medium. Selling yourself is sometimes almost half the problem. The producer doesn't like you, consequently he reads the script with a very negative view. But I wouldn't preoccupy myself with that, I don't give a damn. You can be a hunchback and a dwarf and what-all. If you write beautifully, you can write beautifully, that's all.

Do you recall your first sale?
It's an incredible event. The most important thing about the first sale is for the very first time in your life something written has value, and *proven* value because somebody has given you money for the words that you've written, and that's terribly important. It's a tremendous boon to the ego, to your sense of self-reliance, to your feeling about your own talent. I remember the first sale I made was a hundred and fifty dollars for a radio script and, as poor as I was, I didn't cash the check for three months. I kept showing it to people.

> *When I'm chosen to do an interview on writing, I think to myself, my God, what am I doing here?*

When you were starting out, how did you deal with rejection? Has it gotten any easier?
It's gotten easier because now it's only a blow to ego, it's no longer a blow to pocketbook. I'm sufficiently independent to know that I can live well and comfortably the rest of my life whether I'm rejected or not. In the old days, you were rejected and not only was a piece of your flesh cut to pieces, your pocketbook was destroyed.

Writers didn't get the same money for their work they get these days.
That's right, that's right. You can become much more independent, much more courageous with a bank account. And also much more independent and self-reliant when you know you have money still behind you. But rejection is still rejection. It's a very difficult, bleeding process.

Do you have any encouragement for writers who accumulate lots of rejection slips?
Only that somehow, some way, incredibly enough, good writing ultimately gets recognized. I don't know how that happens, but it does. It just works that way. If you're just a simple ordinary day-to-day craftsman, no different than most, then the likelihood is that you probably won't make it in writing. You're going to wind up either getting married, working for an insurance company, joining the regular army, or what-all. But if you have a spark in you, a cut above the average, I think ultimately you make it.

But a lot of writers don't make it, never reach the point where they're making a living, and quit writing. Generally they become producers. That way they can stop writing. It's the only way really to get the monkey off the back. In the last three months, I've been so busy writing that I really haven't been able to conjure up the luxury of excuses to keep from writing because I'm on a clock and I have a deadline. But there are millions of ways to not be writing. You say you're not in the mood, you'll pick it up tomorrow. You can take on interviews with pretty girls [grins].

That's a cop-out right there. That's natural and normal, because I don't think it's man's function to write. I don't think it's a normal thing like teeth-brushing and going to the bathroom. It's a supered position on the animal.

Do you ever get tired of talking about writing?
That essentially is my craft. If I don't know about that, I don't know about anything. My concern about it is that . . . Well, the other night I met William Goldman, who wrote *Boys and Girls Together*, and a few others, at a party. And I looked at him in awe, because he's written novels, brilliant novels that I've never been able to write, and when I'm chosen to do an an interview on writing, I think to myself, my God, what am I doing here, why isn't William Goldman sitting here with you?—who could tell you probably a helluva lot more than I can.

What causes you to write?
I never really thought about it. If I could really conjure up an answer to that, I suppose I'd be able to answer a lot of questions that bug me.

Why do I write. God, I guess that's been asked of every writer. I don't know. It isn't any massive compulsion. I don't feel, you know, God dictated that I should write, thunder rents the sky and a bony finger comes down from the clouds and says, "You. You write. You're the anointed." I never felt that. I suppose it's part compulsion, part a channel for what your brain is churning up.

But I don't subscribe to the "Know Thyself" theory. I'm afraid really if I started to ponder who I am and what I am, I might not like what I find. So I'd rather go along with this sense of illusion that I'm a neutral beast going along through life doing everything that's preordained. I'm out of control anyway, so why fight it.

I suppose we think euphemistically that all writers write because they have something to say that is truthful and honest and pointed and important. And I suppose I subscribe to that, too. But God knows when I look back over 30 years of professional writing, I'm hard-pressed to come up with anything that's important. Some things are literate, some things are interesting, some things are classy, but very damn little is important.

Are you saving any important projects, scripts you've been holding on to in your mind?
Nope. I've written all that I've wanted to write to date. This is not to say I might not find something. I mean, I'm not an old man. I'm not a young man, admittedly, but I'm not an old man, either.

Who do you write for?
Myself. I enjoy it.

What do you enjoy about writing?
I don't enjoy any of the process of writing. I enjoy it when it goes on and it's successful and it zings and it has great warmth and import and it's successful. Yeah, that's when I enjoy it, but during the desperate, tough time of creating it, there's not much I enjoy about it. It tries me and lays me out, which is sort of the way I feel now. Tired.

So it's a suffering process for you . . .
It is. Giving birth. Waiting, should we call the doctor, you know, for the caesarean. It's obviously not going to come out normally.

What's your system for writing?
I don't have any system. I dictate a lot, through a machine, and I also have a secretary, but I used to type just like everybody else. I find dictating in the mass media particularly good because you're writing for voice anyway, you're writing for people to say a line and, consequently, saying a line through a machine is quite a valid test. If it sounds good as you say it, likely as not it'll sound good when an actor's saying it. The tendency when you dictate is to overwrite, because you're not counting pages, you don't really know what the hell the page count is. But in terms of standing up when I write, what hour I write, that all relates very specifically to the individual. In my case, the only thing I would say is that I have to start writing quite early. I write much better in the nonconfines of the early morning than I do in the clutter of the day.

How much time do you actually spend writing?
I would guess three full hours a day. In terms of the pre-writing activity, God, that's endless, it's constant, almost constant.

Can you write when you are angry or depressed?
Yes, I think so, except very frequently—and I'm not alone—your depression and your anger find their way onto the page, and if you're writing a comedy, that can be damaging.

What was the lowest part of your writing life? Emotionally?
When I first went into freelancing, there was a period of about eight months when *nothing* happened. Everything that I wrote crumpled up, and then it became a self-destructive thing, when you begin to doubt yourself, when doubt turns into—it's sort of like impotence. Once impotent, you're forever impotent. Because you're always worried about being impotent.

How did you get out of that?
Well, I just got younger girls! [laughs] Oh, you mean the other, I see what you mean. It ran its course. I made a sale. It's as simple as that, a little funny external thing like that. And that's all it took.

If you could, would you go back to live TV instead of filmed TV?
No. I miss the camaraderie of live television, the fact that you were on the set, you worked closely with the director and the cast. That I miss. But, no, I'm happy doing film.

What was the transition from live to filmed TV like?
It wasn't very difficult. Essentially the scripts are not that different. In literary terms, it's the difference between writing horizontally and writing vertically. In live television, you wrote much more vertically. You had to prove people because you didn't have money or sets or any of the physical dimensions that film will allow you. Film writing is much more horizontal. You can insert anything you want: meadows, battlefields, the Taj Mahal, a cast of thousands.

But, essentially, writing a story is writing a story. And certainly there are differences in technique and attitude, God knows. The major difference frequently is in time. The motion picture, for example, gives you considerably more freedom of expression than does the 30-minute television show. But in essence, they're not that dissimilar.

Are teleplays as innovative and fresh as in the '50s?
Yes, I think they are, except that they have to hew to the line much more because most of them are series—unlike the old days, when the anthology ruled the roost, and you could write a different play each week.

Censorship is also a concern these days. Do you oppose the taboos enforced on the industry?
I haven't rebelled vehemently against any of them. I have compromised down the line. I disliked it intensely in the old days when you were trying to talk race relations and they would not allow you to. In the old days, you didn't talk about blacks, you talked Eskimos or American Indians.

I find it very difficult to live through the censorship of profanity on television. I find that the most ludicrous of the censorships. Damn. Hell. And all that. I find that it's part of our colloquial language, and that there's nothing sacrilegious or profane about any of it. It's the way we speak. What the hell is so dirty about *hell*? And you can say *death* all you want. You can say *kill*. You can even say *rape* now. And that's not supposed to be bad. You know, it's going to reach a point where you're going to do a travelogue on Holland and you'll say, "Well, here we are in Rottergosh and Amsterdarn."

Do you think you can say more about topics of social significance through a contemporary drama, or through the framework of science fiction and fantasy?
I think you can say more obviously in the framework of an honest contemporary piece so that you don't have to talk in parables, symbolisms and the rest of it. But this is not to say that you can't make a point of social criticism using science fiction or fantasy as your backdrop. We did that on *Twilight Zone* a lot, but there's no room for that kind of subtlety anymore. The problems are so much with us that they have to be attacked now.

Is a dramatist of your caliber expected to make script changes dictated by the producers and the networks?
Absolutely. You have to compromise all the way down the line no matter who you are. You say I'm an affluent screenwriter and all that—I'm a *known* screenwriter, but I'm not in the fraternity of the very, very major people. I would say a guy like Ernie Leman, William Goldman, and a few others are quite a cut above. There's a marvelous and unique man named Frank Gilroy. He's the only writer I know who absolutely, pointedly refuses to do any changes he doesn't feel are absolutely essential and totally in keeping with his own view and perspective. But not too many writers are that independent and that strong-willed.

Are there many teleplays that stand up well on paper, but not so well after they've been shot?
Jeez, there may be legion. On *Night Gallery*, for example, I did a show called "The Different Ones" about a boy who was a freak and ultimately was sent to a different planet where he would be more accepted.

It was beautiful, a very sensitive screenplay that became a kind of American International bug-eyed monster film, which it wasn't intended to be at all. Chuck Beaumont, God rest his soul, could tell you a lot about this because he had many shows on. *The Circus of Dr. Lao* was Chuck's, and he always deeply resented what they

did in the film. I would guess that Ray Bradbury would be equally resentful of what they did with *The Illustrated Man*, which, you know, took a central idea thesis of his and dumped all over it. Made it into one of the worst movies ever made. Aided and abetted by Rod Steiger, who literally destroyed it singlehandedly.

Do you have a script of your own that you have special feeling for?
Well, I guess *Requiem for a Heavyweight*, as old as it is, was as honest a piece as I've ever done. "Tearing Down Tim Riley's Bar" [from *Night Gallery*] was one of my favorites. And one that I just wrote, that CBS paid for and isn't going to use, called *The Stop Along the Way*, is, I think, a lovely script. But I don't know, there are a lot I'm proud of and a lot I wish the hell I'd never written.

How important is the screenplay to overall production?
You've got to be joking! I'd say . . . 60 percent of it. No, no, that varies. Let's pursue that a minute . . . An Ingmar Bergman film would probably owe a sizable bulk of its import and its direction and its quality to the directorial end and to the director because it's uniquely a Bergman film. But that again is not the general—no, that's much more the exception than the rule. Most screenplays, most motion pictures, owe much more to the screenplay. Bergman has such an economy of language, so little language in his pieces, it is so visual, his moods are introduced and buttressed by camera rather than by word and character. But that's, again, unique.

Are you ever surprised by the way actors interpret lines you've written?
I'm frequently surprised, sometimes bugged, and sometimes happy, depending on the actor. Often as not, an actor can breathe life into a line just as he can destroy it through misinterpretation. You get certain guys like Jack Klugman, Jack Warden, Marty Balsam—solid, dependable, consummately skilled men, who invariably take lines and breathe great life into them, and great vibrancy, great truth.

What do you think entering the TV arena does for a writer's sensitivities?
It probably bends them out of shape, it frustrates, it makes him feel inferior, it makes him deathly occupied with his own value and his own worth, and if he is even

I find dictating particularly good because you're writing for voice anyway, you're writing for people to say a line.

normally sensitive, he will very likely weep the rest of his life and also wind up with a terrible, terrible lack of awareness of his own worth. Because people are put down in television, now, not because they're not qualitative, not because they're not talented—because there's no room for them, and worse than that, there's nowhere they can find exposure. Their own good talent may die of mourning, just for want of having somebody read what they've written.

Now I can't, I don't presume to say how we can best provide platforms for new writers to get read. I don't know. But therein lies the major problem. I suppose it's very much like actors and actresses who trod pavements and get doors slammed in their faces. Well, the writer's no different. When he's rejected, when that paper is rejected, in a sense a sizeable fragment of the writer is rejected as well. It's a piece of himself that's being turned down. How often can this happen before suddenly you begin to question your own worth and your own value? And even worse, fundamentally, your own talent?

Then you don't think a writer can separate who he is from what he writes?
He can write completely different things from his own character, but it's nonetheless his creation, so an extension of his own mind. You know, he can write about the Foreign Legion without ever having been in the Foreign Legion, but that doesn't necessarily mean what he's written doesn't reflect the nature of him as an individual—or her. I'm using the male gender because it's me speaking. I don't mean to put down the female.

Do you envision a particular kind of TV audience when you write?
I don't. I choose to think of them as nameless, formless, faceless people who are all like me. And anything that I write, if I like it, they'll like it. I don't categorize them. I don't suggest that they're idiots with negative IQs or that they're massive intellectuals. I just think they are, quote, "an audience," like any audience. There're astute, thoughtful, sensitive people among them and then there are those who couldn't understand anything, no matter what you said.

Any regrets—if you're reincarnated, would you like to be another type of writer?
I suppose if I had it to do over again, I'd like it to be just as it's been. And to be able to make the decisions sometimes better than they've been made.

I don't believe in reincarnation. That's a cop-out, I know. I don't really want to be reincarnated. I think Willa Cather did a short story called "Paul's Case," and in it, when he finally commits suicide, it says, "He surrendered to the black design of things." And that's what I anticipate death will be: a totally unconscious void in which you float through eternity with no particular consciousness of anything. I think once around is enough. I don't want to start it all over again. She said, "What happens now if I come out as Louis XIV's donkey or something?" Or I come out as a rose. You know, in my case, with my kind of luck, I'll have rose bugs and things eating my leaves.

Ray Bradbury said, "All through history in every culture we've had to make up mythology to explain death to ourselves and to explain life to ourselves." Do you have any thoughts on that?
Very provocative statement. That may be, but now death is with us in such abundance and hovers over us in so massive a form that we don't have time to invent a mythology, nor is our creativity directed toward same. Now it's to prevent death. It matters not one whit what form it takes—whether it's an old man with a scythe, a pale rider on a horse, or whatever it is. Now it's become so omniscient and so constant that our major battle is warding it off. [long pause] I yield to no man in my respect for Ray Bradbury, however.

And what do you want people to say about writer Rod Serling a hundred years from now?
I don't care. I just want them to *remember* me a hundred years from now. I don't care that they're not able to quote any single line that I've written. But just that they can say, "Oh, he was a writer." That's sufficiently an honored position for me.

I guess that must be it. We all have a little vaunting itch for immortality.

BY LOIS ROSENTHAL

MAY SARTON

*I will never regret that I experienced failure so young.
It would never again frighten me so much.*

May Sarton has openly shared so much of her life with her readers (her bouts of illness in *After the Stroke*, her feelings about growing older in *At Seventy*) through her long career of writing poems, novels and journals, and has built such a strong bond with her avid audience, that visiting her in her house by the sea in York, Maine, feels like a homecoming. Those who have pictured her yellow-shingled Cape Cod, surrounded by the flower gardens she writes of tending with so much love and effort, will find it just as she has described it in her classic *Journal of a Solitude* and *House by the Sea*, as well as in one of her collections of poems, *Halfway to Silence*.

Now in her 76th year, plagued by health complications caused by a fibrillating heart, recovering from a stroke that kept her in near seclusion for most of the past year, Sarton is determinedly in the midst of a new novel—her 19th. In addition, she has written two children's books, fourteen books of poetry and nine books of nonfiction, which include the journals that have earned her a huge following.

She continues to live alone, fiercely protecting her independence, and she still rises at 6 each morning, writes from 8 until 11 when she feels well enough, then drives—through fog, freezing rain, snow or record heat—her Ford Escort station wagon over York's bumpy back roads to the post office to collect her mail. Though Sarton is small and now rather stooped, her presence is commanding. Her voice is rich and resonant, mirroring her Cambridge, Massachusetts, upbringing and her early adult years spent as an actress. When Sarton settles into a chair and begins to talk about her writing life, it is easy to see how her poetry readings captivate crowds from coast to coast.

"I never had any doubt that I wanted to be a poet," she says. "I wrote from the time I was 9 or 10, and was part of a family that encouraged deep thinking and creativity. My father, George Sarton, was a great international scholar. He was a pioneer in creating the subject of the history of science, and he wrote extensively about it. He was Belgian and my mother was English—an artist and an extraordinary woman. My parents were very radical, enormously idealistic in a way that no one has been able to be since World War I. Both of my parents read avidly, and we discussed books all the time at home. It was an exciting atmosphere.

"I was supposed to go to Vassar and get a good education as my family expected. But while I was in high school, my father took me to see Eva Le Gallienne—one of the most famous actresses of that era—and her Civic Repertory Company perform Martin Sierra's *The Cradle Song*. I haunted the theater in Boston where her company was performing other plays. I knew immediately I would never be the same. I wanted to become an actress, join Le Gallienne's company as an apprentice rather than go to Vassar—which, at first, made my father furious. Finally he agreed to let me have my own way and go to New York."

Though life in the theater was close to survival level for Sarton, she speaks of those years in New York with passion. "The company performed a different play every night, and Ibsen's *Hedda Gabler* might be followed by Barrie's *Peter Pan* and then perhaps Chekhov's *Three*

"Fame to me," says May Sarton, "is not writing a best-seller, but knowing someone, somewhere is reading one of my books."

Sarton's body of work—far exceeding that self-standard—is a group of cherished and intimate friends to her readers, and each new journal, novel or poetry collection is quickly made to feel at home.

In this 1989 profile, she invites you into her *home for a discussion on the fluid style and precise descriptions that have established such friendships.*

Sisters," she says. "I had an amazing education in the theater. There is nowhere in America today where it could be obtained to that rich and exciting extent."

However, in the middle of the Depression, Le Gallienne's theater failed. Sarton, as director of The Apprentice Group, tried keeping these earnest young actors together by forming The Apprentice Theatre, which was based at the New School for Social Research, and offering ten modern European plays as a course at this school. Because no scenery, makeup or costumes were used, critics were impressed that such illusions could be created with such meager means. Even so, after two more years of struggling to make ends meet at other theater locations, this troupe failed, as well.

"This was the Depression," says Sarton. "Though I only needed $5,000 a year to keep 12 people together, money finally ran out. But I will never regret that I experienced failure so young—I was 23. I had done more extraordinary things than I would have if I had gone to Vassar. Because I learned about failure, it would never again frighten me so much. And during all of that time, I never stopped writing poems."

Those poems were collected in a book published by Houghton Mifflin in 1937. Though they were critically acclaimed, Sarton was unable to live by writing poetry any more than she was by acting. Her father kept her going with an allowance of $100 a month.

"I lived on that $1,200-a-year allowance and the little bit I earned as a writer during the '30s and '40s. The New York women's club where I stayed cost $11 a week and included two meals a day. Though I never had any money left over, I was always able to make ends meet.

"I thought that a good way to supplement my income would be to sell short stories to popular magazines, but the ones I wrote were continually returned. Finally, my editor at Houghton Mifflin told me he felt I was a novelist rather than a short story writer, and he offered me a $250 advance to try one, which I eagerly accepted. *A Single Hound*, which was published in 1938, is about a poet I knew in Belgium and two of her friends. I was pleased because this book, too, was positively reviewed."

Poetry, however, seems to be at the core of Sarton's creativity. To Sarton, a poem is the result of a collision between an object and a state of awareness that registers sensation. This means poets must develop a sharp state of mind, must become an instrument to transform what they see around them into images about which they write poems. They must see what they see as if it had just been created, and they must write about it in such a way that it seems readers have never seen it before.

Sarton writes in her book *Writings on Writing* that poets must use discipline to create an extraordinarily sensitive state of mind. "I myself have found that a good deal more solitude and a good many empty hours than are usual in our 'busy' civilization are one of my own requirements. I have to induce the state of awareness by renouncing some pleasures—the pleasures of society, for instance. If I do go to a dinner party, I know that the next morning the edge will be a fraction less sharp. What is inspiration, so-called, but the successful wooing of a state of mind? You cannot write a poem by wanting to write a poem, but only by becoming an instrument, and that means not being knotted up to a purpose, but open to any accidental and fortuitous event.

"Here's an example of what I mean," says Sarton. "At the end of a very painful and marvelous five-year love affair, I found myself in Pocatello, Idaho. I was on a lecture trip in the middle of the winter, and I had the flu. I was in an absolutely miserable motel and was so sick I had to cancel my reading. But even though I had quite a high fever, I was forced out of my bed to write ten sonnets. They just came to me, and there was nothing I could do except catch them as they poured out.

"I had been thinking and feeling about this major love affair for about six months, and suddenly all of this came out. So these poems were about transcending an experience. I was somehow above what I was writing about and deep inside it at the same time.

"But people must realize that although deep feeling is important, you must also think a poem out, so it's the mixed combination of being able to think and feel at white heat that makes good poetry. And writing poetry can be quite a long process.

"So many people say, 'Oh, I feel everything so acutely and I've put it in my poem' and think that makes it a good one. But because you've felt something doesn't make your poetry good. There's the craft. There's the making. The beginner hugs his infant poem to him and does not want it to grow up. But you may have to break your poem to remake it. You must think and feel at the same time so that the thinking part of you can see why that particular line doesn't work, why it's too

> *The beginner hugs his infant poem to him and does not want it to grow up. But you may have to break your poem to remake it.*

trite, that you will have to work it over and over again.

"The revision process is fascinating to me. Some of my poems have gone through 60 or more drafts by the time I'm satisfied. I think it's very important for poets to have others read their work, get all the criticism they can as well as be extremely self-critical."

If Sarton's poetry comes from internal white heat, her novels come from questions to which she needs to find an answer. *Faithful Are the Wounds* is a good example of her trying to write about a subject she wanted to better understand. "This novel's main question is how can a man be wrong and right at the same time? It's set in the academic world of Harvard and Cambridge in the 1950s, and Edmund Cavan, the novel's main character, is an English professor who believed communists and socialists could work together in Czechoslovakia and was proved wrong. Yet his idealism and his belief that all people must work together was right. I was desperately trying to understand the forces during the McCarthy era that were tearing the United States apart by getting inside the problem and writing my way out of it. That Edmund Cavan commits suicide at the opening of the book has a dramatic effect on his friends and colleagues throughout the story. Years after the suicide, those most affected by this violent act are under investigation by the McCarthy Committee.

"I think I demonstrate another of my writing theories in *Faithful Are the Wounds*: If you create a sufficiently dramatic situation in a novel, you don't have to worry about plot. This book begins with a wallop—a suicide—and its effect on other people creates the plot. Something happens to everyone who is close to a suicide, and that is what this novel is about."

Sarton believes the first scene in a novel establishes the rhythm of the book. It should also suggest the theme, tell what the book is going to be about, introduce the major characters, and place them in their particular way of life. To Sarton, the first scene is a spell that pulls the reader into the book almost like the first line of a poem. The rest of the novel is a series of scenes, each rising to a climax; then the climax is resolved, which opens the door to the next scene.

Says Sarton in *Writings on Writing*: "At the end of each chapter or section, some precipitation must take place between the characters, something must have changed. Of course, some of this shaping is done when one has roughed out the whole thing and can revise for the dynamics of each scene in relation to the dynamics of the whole. I find myself cutting ruthlessly to keep the rising curve clean. It often happens that whole chunks can come out because what they convey is absorbed in the total drive of the book."

Still, Sarton feels that creating the design of a novel is an organic process and there is a danger in mapping it out too meticulously. That would destroy the pleasure of exploration and discovery in writing the story, of constructing a novel while letting it construct itself. There must be a delicate balance in maintaining creative fluidity while hanging on to the theme and not losing your way in the writing.

As for the worlds Sarton writes about in her novels, she says: "They very much reflect the world I live in. They are peopled by characters I know well—well-educated, cultivated men and women. Sometimes I've been sorry that my world has been so middle-class, so intellectual—in a way, so rarefied. But I think the proof is that writing about my world, I've been able to communicate with people way outside it, who feel strongly about what I do. I admire the style of Carolyn Chute, who wrote *The Beans of Egypt, Maine*, but my trying to do something like that would be grotesque. I couldn't."

What Sarton could do is reveal an innermost secret in one of her novels. *Mrs. Stevens Hears the Mermaids Singing*, written in the 1950s, is the novel in which Sarton told of being a lesbian long before it was acceptable to do so. "I wrote the book to understand myself," she says, "but I lost friends, even some jobs, as a result. However, as the women's movement came into its own, much of my work was swept up in a crest of popularity. *Mrs. Stevens* and many of my other books are now taught in women's studies programs in colleges throughout the United States.

"I wrote about homosexuality as a way of life, a kind of sensitivity. No one else had written about it in that fashion before I did, though I have never written graphic sexual scenes and think most of them are vulgar. I don't like graphic descriptions of bodily functions of any kind.

"Imagine someone eating an ice cream cone. Her tongue comes out of her mouth, laps up the ice cream, then swallows it. It's disgusting. It's much better to eat ice cream than watch someone eat it. The same is true of sex. The physical act is so mixed up with feelings, I think it's hard to separate the two.

"Many of my novels deal with the subject of friendship between women; women who stand up for their individuality is a recurring theme. *Self-actualization* is the term I like best to describe what my novels are about, and I think this element is most important to me in my own life, as well."

These same strong themes are woven through all of Sarton's journals, which ironically she considers the most minor of the mediums in which she writes, but is the genre that's earned her such a large following.

"The journals are not at all directed to lesbian women," says Sarton. "They appeal to all kinds of women because they explore what women's lives are like. I get so many letters from people all over the world who tell me that I've taught them how to look at everyday things in a different way, how to enjoy them.

"Someone recently wrote a master's thesis comparing my writing and Vermeer, the famous Flemish painter, and I wondered what she saw to put us together. She wrote that there were three things: the woman alone—Vermeer's paintings often have a single woman as their subject; the treatment of light, which is so important in all of my books and especially my journals—light in a room at different times of the day, light through flowers; and the sacramentalization of everyday life."

This passage—the entry for one entire day in *Journal of a Solitude*—is an excellent example of the way May Sarton looks at life:

A gray day . . . but strangely enough, a gray day makes the bunches of daffodils in the house have a particular radiance, a kind of white light. From my bed this morning I could look through at a bunch in the big room, in that old Dutch blue-and-white drug jar, and they glowed. I went out before seven in my pajamas, because it looked like rain, and picked a sampler of twenty-five different varieties. It was worth getting up early, because the first thing I saw was a scarlet tanager a few feet away on a lilac bush—stupendous sight! There is no scarlet so vivid, no black so black.

The mystical quality Sarton gives to what she sees around her moves readers of her journals to deluge her with letters telling her how much they identify with her feelings. As Sarton stops to revel in the beauty of a sunrise, as she is comforted by the warmth of a cat nestled next to her in bed during a worrisome night, she is able to propel these feelings straight to the heart of people who read her work. Then readers see their worlds as May Sarton sees hers—as poetry.

"Keeping a journal is much harder than it looks. I know that I have underrated its form compared to the novel and poetry and even the memoir, which is distilled, but there's no doubt it does have a discipline of its own. For any writer who wants to keep a journal, remember to be alive to everything, not just to what you're feeling, but also to your pets, to flowers, to what you are reading.

"Remember to write about what you are seeing every day, and if you are going to hold the reader's interest, you must write very well. And what does writing well mean? It means seeing very well, seeing in a totally original way.

"Look at the bowl of irises on the table in front of me. Five different people who are asked to draw them would produce five totally different works of art, which is good. In the same way, journal writers must be just as

> *For any writer who wants to keep a journal, be alive to everything, not just to what you're feeling.*

honest in what they see because it's the freshness that matters. Keeping a journal is exciting because it gives a certain edge to the ordinary things in life.

"Let's use another example. Say you've burned something in a pot, and you are standing at the sink scrubbing it. What comes to your mind as you are doing this? What does it mean to you in a funny way? Are you angry because you burn pots all too often? You can rage against the fact that it seems to be women who are mostly having to scrub pots, or you can ask yourself why are you bothering about this pot anyway. Why not throw it away if you can afford to get another? Is there something wrong with you that you are so compulsive you must try to clean something that is really beyond repair?

"Keeping a journal helps you get in touch with your own feelings. I think that's why I started the first one. I was in a depression when I began *Journal of a Solitude*; I was in the middle of a very unhappy love affair, and writing was my way of handling things.

"But a writer must always be perfectly honest. That's the key to people wanting to read a journal and that ingredient always astonishes me. When I've written things I felt were awfully weird and that no one would agree with, those are the very things that have made people say, 'you know, that's just how I feel.'

"My advice to any writer is never think of the effect of what you are doing while you are doing it. Don't project to a possible audience while you are writing. Hold on to your idea and get it down, and then maybe there'll be an audience, and maybe there won't. But have the courage to write whatever your dream is for yourself."

Sarton has lived these words, though she feels she has suffered because of it. Even though her audience is wide, even though Norton, her publisher, announces each of her new books with a full-page ad in the *New York Times Book Review*, the ingredient she misses is validation by the critics.

"Until about 20 years ago, when my audience was getting bigger and bigger, I was getting less and less critical attention," says Sarton. "I've never had a single important critic in back of me since the years in England when I received so much critical attention before I was 30.

"In America, I think I'm pushed aside as that awful thing called a sensitive feminine writer. The very ingredient that makes me universal has kept me from being interesting to the critics. You can't say that I'm a Maine writer, or a New England writer. I'm not regional. I can't be labeled as a lesbian writer because only one of my books deals with that subject.

"Poets consider me a novelist. Novelists consider me a poet. It sounds so dull, but I feel that what I write about is the human condition. I hope I'm a good writer, but the critics have no handle on what I am because not many distinguished writers work in as many forms as I do. That's why I feel I'm brushed aside by the most important reviewers, not taken as seriously as I'd like.

"I never went to college. Anne Sexton and Sylvia Plath did. Both of these women were enormously talented, so I'm not saying the people who get the prizes don't deserve them. I'm just saying that sometimes people who do deserve them don't get them, which is my case, I think.

"I've had a lot of blows and I feel I've been badly treated. Anyone but me would have stopped trying because these setbacks are hard to take. Still, I've never stopped writing, and my advice to young writers is that you must always keep trying. If you can't take the criticism, then you're not a writer. You've got to be able to take it. Hold on, trust your talent, and work hard."

Living by her own advice, Sarton writes prolifically, has continued to gather an even larger audience, and has accumulated more than a dozen honorary college doctorates. Though her advances from Norton are modest compared to the megabuck deals many authors of less reputation are able to negotiate, she says she is satisfied with her life. "Though I wasn't able to live from my writing alone until I was 65 years old, money isn't everything. I lectured, taught; in the early days, I even wrote 200 letters to schools offering to read my poetry for $25. Now I'm as comfortable as I need to be. I even have money to help other writers, to give to charities I care about, such as Amnesty International.

"Fame to me is not writing a bestseller, but knowing someone, somewhere is reading one of my books. Norton keeps 12-14 of my books in print at any one time. They've told me they've made a million dollars selling my work. As an example, *Journal of a Solitude* has sold 2,000 books a year for 20 years. I receive so many letters from people who tell me my books have changed their lives. I feel loved by so many people. Let's face it, that's better than money."

BY HAYES JACOBS

ARTHUR KOPIT

It's much more than just feeling that you have something to say.

*I*n the much-discussed, long-playing, long-titled off-Broadway play called *Oh, Dad, Poor Dad, Mamma's Hung You in the Closet and I'm Feelin' So Sad*, there are some highly unorthodox stage directions. Example: *He smashes the axe against the fish bowl. It breaks. The fish screams. (It goes "AAIEEEEEEE-EEEE!")* Another: *The Venus Flytraps have grown enormous. Their monstrous petals wave hungrily in the air while they growl.* Elsewhere in the play, which is described as "A Pseudoclassical Tragifarce in a Bastard French Tradition," a chair *slides out under its own power*, and a *cuckoo clock goes out of its mind*. And just before the final curtain, is this: *But as he staggers past the corpse of his father, his father's lifeless arms somehow come to life for an instant and, reaching out, grab Jonathan by the feet.*

The young man responsible for all this, Arthur L. Kopit, stood with me under the glittering chandelier that hangs, stage center, in his living room. "The reason you see these books all over the floor," he said, "is that . . . well, this place is a mess, *and* I haven't had any lunch. Could we go out and get something to eat? Do you mind?"

Hopping now and then to keep pace with his giant strides, I walked with him to a corner pizzeria, where he had a meatball hero sandwich and a root beer. A bachelor, Kopit cooks some of his own meals but often eats at the pizzeria, he said, to save time. We hopped and strode back to the apartment, a walk-up in a sedate brownstone near the western border of Central Park. "The reason for all the mess," Kopit said, continuing as though there'd been no intermission, "is that the other night, in the middle of the night, that whole bookshelf over there just came right off the wall—CURRRRRRRRRRRRRRR-ASH!"

I looked where he had pointed, to the left of a white marble fireplace, and saw two steel supports, bent into arcs, reaching out into the room. I got the uneasy feeling that they might grab me by the feet, so I moved quickly downstage and sat on a champagne-satin sofa, far away from the curling supports. Kopit placed his rangy, six-foot-three frame into, onto, over and around a small, helpless, nonsliding chair near the grand piano, and began to recall the distant past (he is 25) of his childhood.

"I began writing when I was just a little kid," he said. "I guess maybe it was because I was so allergic. I was allergic to *everything*! I'd go to school for two days, throw up, and then stay home for two weeks. I had to have something to do, so I read a lot, and wrote stories."

Kopit was born in Manhattan, but soon afterward moved with his parents and younger sister to Long Island. After conquering the allergies, he got through the public school system, and won a scholarship to Harvard, where he set aside his ambition to be a pro basketball player and plunged deep into the study of engineering.

"Engineering. That's right. After two or three years of the stuff, though, I began to wonder if it was really for me. All the other engineering students wore their slide

---

Watch out here not only for the advice given, but the advice-giver: the 26-year-old Wunderkind Kopit just might knock you down. Whirling around the room during an interview, waltzing to illustrate a point, Kopit demonstrates the same reckless creativity that resulted in the critically acclaimed plays Oh, Dad, Indians *(which Kopit says was inspired by his listening to Charles Ives's* Fourth Symphony *while reading a newspaper report of Gen. William Westmoreland's regret over killing Vietnam civilians), and the more recent* Wings *and* End of the World.

Since this 1963 profile, Kopit has grown from Wunderkind to major playwright, and the book he talks of writing was abandoned when he began Indians. *But his best plays are still an energetic waltz of imagination and brilliant plotting.*

rules on their belts, you know, like some kind of cavalry sword, or something. I always hid mine in my jacket pocket. I began to think that if I always hid my slide rule, then maybe I wasn't the engineer type."

Kopit had enrolled in a drama course under Robert Chapman, and before he graduated in 1959, Harvard dramatic groups had produced nine Kopit plays, including one titled *On the Runway of Life You Never Know What's Coming Off Next*. Kopit finally decided he was definitely the playwright, not the engineer, type. After graduation he won a Shaw Traveling Fellowship, spent nine months in Europe, wrote *Oh, Dad*, and "sent it back to Harvard and let them worry about how to do it." They worried successfully, and the play created a stir that Cambridge and neighboring Boston hadn't seen for years. From then on, it's been pretty smooth sailing.

"I've been lucky. I haven't had to go through all the agonies of looking for a producer, and trying to get my work performed, and so on," he said. This is because producers—big ones such as Roger Stevens—sought him out. Stevens produced *Oh, Dad* first in London, where it closed after 13 performances ("Thirteen too many," says Kopit), then at the Phoenix in New York, where it has been one of the biggest, brightest, longest-running hits in off-Broadway history. It has since opened in France, Sweden, and Germany, and oddly enough, may be done again in England.

Listening to Kopit talk of his work, I concluded that despite his reference to luck, he was not the sort who would sit around waiting for a stroke of it. There is an earnestness in the handsomely sculptured face, from the firm set of the jaw, the rise of the cheekbones and the faintly green glint of his light brown eyes, up to the high forehead, marked off by dark, mobile brows. There is a boyishness about him still—the kind reminiscent of early Gershwin photographs—but there is a mature, organized quality there, too.

"While we were getting *Oh, Dad* ready, I was pulled away from writing," he said. "It was chaos, and I had a hard time trying to get back on the job. Now I'm working, though, and I really enjoy it. I keep to a pretty close schedule. The best thing is to get a telephone that you can shut off." (When his phone rings, there is no ring— only a flashing light signal. The light is in the living room, the phone is in the kitchen, and Kopit is in the bedroom, which is where he works.) "I write standing up, or sitting in front of that drafting table you see in there. Hangover from engineering, I guess. And I do quite a lot of writing

lying down, with a clipboard. The danger there, though, is that you often fall asleep. But I put on a big eight-cup percolator of coffee and sharpen about 35 pencils and I'm all set. I have to have sharp pencils."

He writes in three- to four-hour stretches, usually in the mornings. Afternoons, he plays tennis in Central Park, sprints around the reservoir, or goes to movies.

When working, he may take ten-minute breaks now and then to sit on the terrace that leads off his bedroom, or to play Mozart, Chopin or contemporary classics on the piano. There was a time when he had to have music going in order to write. "For a long time it had to be Bartok's *Concerto for Orchestra*, but I got off that finally." Sometimes, Kopit may get up and walk around, clipboard in hand, to write. "There's a waltz scene in *Oh, Dad* and I was actually waltzing while I wrote it," he said. He got up and demonstrated. There before us, in Ivy League flannels and jacket, was Commodore Roseabove from the play. We could almost hear him: "Ah, the waltz. How exquisite it is, madame, don't you think? *One*-two-three, *one*-two-three. Ahhhhh, madame, how classically simple. How mathematically simple . . . " (At the end of that scene, Commodore grows dizzy, breaks free from his partner, Madame Rosepettle, and collapses from an attack of asthma.) Kopit, undizzy, and full of energy, assaulted the chair again and went on talking.

"I love movies, particularly old ones, and bad ones, down on 42nd. Science fiction and horror stuff I really adore. Sometimes I see three and four a week. Movies are great. There are better things being done in movies today than in the theater. Why? Because movies are a director's medium; he can control everything. In the theater, you know, there are too many people who think they have to get involved. Everyone takes a hand, and many of them don't know what they're doing. It ends up a committee. I'm embarrassed, you know, when I meet a novelist, and I have to say I'm a playwright. Being a playwright is really a silly thing to be, in this country. In France it's a great thing to be. The American theater is still in its infancy, and it's too much mixed up with show business, which is entertainment, not art."

Kopit has a Harper's contract for a novel, outlined but yet unwritten. "I'll write it, though," he said, and we didn't doubt it for a second. "I'll probably do novels as a kind of diversion from playwriting." His next play, all completed, will be *Asylum*, which he said takes place in "what seems to be a very strange kind of mental hospital, but one is never quite sure."

> *There's a waltz scene in* Oh, Dad, *and I was actually waltzing while I wrote it.*

Did he have advice for young writers? "Well . . . read as much as possible, and while you're reading, try to see why the writing works. And—very important—don't wait to write when you 'feel like it.' Keep a schedule. And start with fundamentals. A writer has to master his craft and learn the rules before he tries to break them. It's much more than just feeling that you have something to say. You have to learn how to say it."

The trouble, he feels, with too many would-be playwrights, is that they work too hard at trying to be avant-garde; their minds are "full of dreams about living on the Left Bank," and not on the writing craft.

"The first thing you should do is try to write *real people*. Try to write what they see. Try to write a simple breakfast scene, say, between a husband and wife who are about to break up. Try to write a simple scene in which a young girl tells her lover she's pregnant. And make it *real*, and *believable*."

BY MICHAEL SCHUMACHER

JAY MCINERNEY

*The only sensible approach is not to take it
too seriously. What counts is the writing.*

You are not the kind of guy who would be at a place like this at this time of the morning. But here you are, and you cannot say the terrain is entirely unfamiliar, although the details are fuzzy. . . .

These words, thoughts of the unnamed protagonist in Jay McInerney's bestselling *Bright Lights, Big City*, also describe the author's own Road to Damascus. For McInerney, there were no flashes of light or auditory displays—only fading neon lights in early Manhattan predawn and an internal whisper that told him he was on the wrong path.

It was 1981. McInerney was a 26-year-old aspiring novelist with a list of failed attempts in his near past. His first wife, a model, had packed her bags and left. A nine-month stint as a fact-checker at *The New Yorker* had been an unhappy tenure, winding down with a "quit or be fired" understanding. The short stories he wrote were returned with form rejection slips. After the *New Yorker* fiasco, he took a job at Random House as a manuscript reader, but the position only fortified his growing doubts about his direction: the manuscripts he read, often offered by respected New York agencies, were losers—worse, he felt, than the efforts he was having turned down. He didn't have an agent, any published credits or, by all indications, much of a future as a writer.

He *did* have a good sense of where the party was, and spent many nights in New York's after-hours clubs, with their milieu of drugs and alcohol.

But he wasn't *really* that kind of guy. The thought gnawed at him off and on over the months, but it struck home particularly hard one evening—make that *early-morning*, 5 A.M.—as he prepared to leave the now-defunct Berlin Club in Manhattan. His drinking buddy had already left with a woman he'd met on the dance floor and McInerney, sick and dazed, realized that he was again about to step from a night's partying into daylight.

You are not the kind of guy . . .

The words formed in his head, and he went home and wrote them down. They would eventually be the opening words of a short story titled "It's Six A.M. Do You Know Where You Are?" The story would then become the first chapter of *Bright Lights, Big City*, one of the most astonishing first novels of the 1980s. In the novel, written entirely in the second person, the protagonist, not unlike McInerney, drives himself to the brink of self-destruction before he sees the light.

There is a koan-like quality to McInerney's "dark night of the soul": to find the way, one must be lost beyond hope, caught in a territory without guideposts or map, where sheer survival becomes a test of will.

It's a road, McInerney now believes, that most writers travel, though the way is usually less extreme.

"There are no guarantees," McInerney says of the writing life. "When one goes to law school, one pretty much knows he is going to practice law at the end of it all, whereas in setting forth to be a writer of fiction, not only are there no guarantees, but the route isn't even mapped out. You know: do you work as a lumberjack, or do you go to creative writing graduate school, or do you

Not knowing Jay McInerney, it might be easy to dislike what you know about him: bestselling author of Bright Lights, Big City *at age 26, with all the attendant hoopla and celebrity and guaranteed book contracts, and all while most writers have to struggle for years for only a modicum of respect, and you just know he's only another Brat Packer stable-bred—*

Nah. In this 1987 profile, McInerney reminds himself—and us—that he isn't a success, just someone who wrote a success. Written before the release of McInerney's third book, The Story of My Life, *this story of his life is disarming and charming, careful to deal with failure as well as fame, and leaves both paths open to all writers.*

try to go to Paris to see if you can discover the ambience Hemingway sought out?"

Success has afforded McInerney the opportunity to look back at the options with less frenzied, more detached insight than he experienced while he was living the Question. Though confident, he is far from cocky, and you get the feeling his failures, personal and professional, serve as reminders. He admits to his somewhat hedonistic past, but he's quick to point out that he has not only reformed, but also that he was never as extreme as the protagonist of *Bright Lights*. He had, he claims, a romantic's view of the writing profession that years of trial and error, coupled with his experiences in the magazine and book trades, honed to a far more realistic attitude.

"When I first got out of college, I had a sort of unfounded faith that I would be a self-supporting writer. As the years went by, I felt that I had to be more realistic about it. I never lost *faith*, but at the same time, this whole idea about becoming Hemingway or something, of being a writer who had a big audience and could support himself, was one that seemed a little unrealistic to me.

"I can't help but be tremendously grateful that my long apprenticeship paid off in the way I'd always hoped—but never believed—that it would. I had worked in New York in publishing long enough to know that authors' adolescent fantasies were seldom fulfilled. I'd seen friends publish books and almost expect, despite their better instincts, to be mobbed on the streets the day after publication. Of course, this hardly ever happens. So I had lowered my expectations to a point where I was just eager to publish a book. I hoped to get some critical attention and reach some readers, but I wasn't expecting to reach all that many."

But McInerney hit the jackpot with both readers and critics. *Bright Lights* has sold more than 300,000 copies—a remarkable achievement for a first novel, and even more impressive because the book was a paperback original. As for the critics, who tend to ignore both first novels and paperback originals, their reviews were slow in arriving, but once the word was out, they virtually fell over each other in praising the book.

Even today, McInerney is cautious in his assessment of the publicity and critical acclaim. While he's now being courted by magazines that wouldn't have considered his work or returned his phone calls two years ago, he knows there are no guarantees his celebrity will last.

I fell in love with the image of being a writer—this Dylan Thomas, this roustabout, this bad boy, this perennial adolescent.

"There's a terrible tendency in this country to consume art and culture, to try to package it in the same way that all our other familiar products are packaged, and that can be terribly distorting to the work, to objects of art and culture. Every once in a while, a writer does get processed by this machine. All of us can think of writers who have been distracted and who, perhaps, have taken the publicity more seriously than they should have—perhaps, eventually, more seriously than their writing. I feel like it could all be gone tomorrow, so the only sensible approach is not to take it too seriously. What counts is the writing."

The humor of this literary rags-to-riches story is not lost on McInerney. When interviewed by *USA Today*, McInerney quipped that the success of *Bright Lights* even affected the way people looked at his age: all of a sudden, he had transformed from an aging, unpublished writer to a young, published one.

As if, when the dues are paid, one forgets the cost.

"Writing is something I've wanted to do since I could remember, aside from a brief notion of being a trapper in the Hudson Bay, or a mercenary, or something. . . ." McInerney says, laughing, the unspoken understanding being that writing a book, to a child, might have seemed as accessible as the life of Lewis and Clark. "When I was a kid, we moved a lot, and I'd find more companionship in books, when I was the new kid in school, than I would elsewhere. I was also an insomniac, so I read an awful lot. I read the Hardy Boys and that kind of stuff. I sort of stumbled on Dylan Thomas—he was the first literary author I discovered, I guess. What he did with words seemed incredibly imaginative to me. He's a natural for adolescents, because he's so word-drunk and romantic. At that point, I fell in love with the image of being a writer—you know, this Dylan Thomas, this roustabout, this bad boy, this perennial adolescent. I guess I've just gotten more pleasure from reading than from almost anything else, and it seemed that the most interesting thing I could do would be to be a writer."

Writers such as Hemingway and Fitzgerald strengthened McInerney's romanticized vision of the writing profession. McInerney notes that, as an apprentice writer, Hemingway had considered moving to Japan (where McInerney spent two years as a young expatriate writer), although he chose to go to Paris instead. "The myth of Hemingway the writer is very powerful," he says. "I think it's hard to be an American male writer, even now, and not feel the shadow of Hemingway. The myth shapes one's conception of the nobility of the calling. I also learned a great deal about storytelling because Hemingway's work is so clean and stark. It's very easy to learn from him, to overcome some of the traditional defects of apprentice writing, such as being very florid, overly-emotional and underly concrete, showing off. It's easy to imagine and build your conception of how a sentence works if you start with Hemingway.

Ultimately, though, Fitzgerald proved to be a greater influence. Fitzgerald's public image as a powerful figure in the imagination of American literature, like Hemingway's, intrigued McInerney, but Fitzgerald offered more stylistic possibility. "I love Hemingway's prose, but it doesn't do as many things as Fitzgerald's does. In one sentence, Fitzgerald can be wistful, intelligent, funny and sad—that's pretty remarkable. I love Fitzgerald's lyricism and his ability to see the poetry at the same time as he somehow maintains his critical faculties.

"I recently reread *The Great Gatsby*, which I hadn't read in a long time, and one of the things I admired, about the book and about Fitzgerald, is how, in a book like *Gatsby*, he can show the massive illusion of Gatsby's dream, which is essentially a version of the American Dream, and expose it as an illusion while at the same time he lyrically celebrates its power. He once said, in an essay, the mark of a great mind is the ability to hold two contrary and opposing ideas at once, and I think *Gatsby* is like that: it's a critique of Gatsby's dream and, at the same time, a sort of celebration of it. Fitzgerald figures specifically in *Bright Lights, Big City*, I think, in that the young Fitzgerald is exactly who the protagonist wants to be. He wants to be successful and good-looking, and sort of jump into the fountain of the Plaza—and do it all with his left hand."

In some respects, that was what McInerney hoped for in the literary life. Writing, he felt, could be a romantic adventure with both temporal and immortal qualities that even failure couldn't diminish. (The tragic demises of Hemingway, Fitzgerald and Jack Kerouac—another influence, to a lesser extent—were treated kindly by most biographers and critics.) Wealth and fame were the rewards for creation, McInerney sensed when he studied fiction at Williams College. As he would learn, the struggle to reach any level of success is one that has to be experienced, not read about, to make a lasting impression. If the spirit of good literature is pure, it is nonetheless far from perfect.

"When I was in college," he says, "I wanted this literary world to be immune from the kind of petty motives and shortsightedness that I thought were characterized by the world of commerce. I subsequently grew up and learned that the literary world is imperfect, too, that some of the same principles operate here as operate elsewhere. I realized that I might not ever make it as a writer,

that it might be because I wasn't good enough, or that it might be because the odds were just too long and I didn't get the right kind of help or attention."

Upon graduating from college, McInerney packed his Volkswagen, and with Gary Fisketjon, a classmate and eventually his editor, embarked on a Kerouacesque journey across America. He intended to write a novel about the experience, but nothing ever came of it. When his money ran out, he returned to the East, taking a job with a weekly newspaper in New Jersey, the *Hunterdon County Democrat*. His apprenticeship had begun.

"It was a small newspaper, where I did everything from school board meetings to dog shows," McInerney says. "I could write features on anything interesting that I could dig up. My editor used to weigh copy bags at the end of the week, and mine would always be light. Other people would have, like, ten pounds of stories that they'd written, and I'd have three or four stories."

McInerney tells the story with good humor, preferring to write off the job as ancient history, although he admits it had a benefit or two. "It was very good for me, I think, in that it loosened me up a lot at a time when I was sitting and rewriting first sentences, over and over again, like some kind of precious poet. It forced me to think about beginning and ending—something that, at the time, I was not very good at."

Though he now has more time to plan his projects than his weekly newspaper deadlines allowed, McInerney still finds the two ends of a project—the beginning and ending—the most difficult aspects of writing. "I'm always afraid, when I sit down, that nothing is going to come out. That's a scary feeling when you're about to embark on a novel or a short story, wondering if you're ever going to finish it, wondering how you're going to get started and what you're going to do. If I'm in doubt, I'll sometimes make myself go farther along a certain road, to see if it will work. I find that I actually have to write in order to discover my ideas. I think you could allow yourself to never get started if you tried to guess in advance what was going to inspire you.

"I also find it difficult to let go of my fiction without worrying about whether I'll be revising it for another three years. I like to tinker. Every sentence is potentially revisable in 30 directions, and it's tough to stop doing that, to know when you've ended."

The newspaper business taught him the discipline of working under deadlines and since, by his own admission, he is the type of writer who needs the pressure of a timetable, he continues to work under artificial, self-imposed deadlines. The first draft of *Bright Lights* was written in six weeks to accommodate one of these deadlines.

Newspaper writing, however, was not McInerney's idea of the proper program for a future novelist. In 1978, as his tenure at the paper wound down, McInerney began looking around for another type of employment and was told of a fellowship, sponsored by Princeton, that would send him overseas for two years. He applied and was granted the fellowship. Not yet exposed to the formalities of the publishing world, he still had an idealized notion of the expatriate writer who finds his voice, while gaining valuable experience and the time to write, in an exotic setting.

Like Christopher Ransom, the expatriate American character in *Ransom*, his second novel, McInerney found assimilation into Japanese culture impossible, despite his efforts. He pursued the trappings, going to the public baths, studying karate (for which he received a black belt), and taking Japanese courses at the Institute for International Studies near Tokyo. But he soon realized that he was as much a prisoner of the myths about Japan as others were of the myths about New York. He wound up teaching English to Japanese businessmen—an irony that didn't escape him.

The experience gave him plenty of material to write about, even after his two-year stay expired and he moved back to New York. He spent the next five years, off and on, trying to write a novel that proved to be as elusive as the one about his cross-county trip. Both journeys had found him searching, but he wasn't prepared to write about what he might have found. In many respects, his taking a job at the *New Yorker* was also a quest; what he gained was an education unlike any he'd receive in his formal schooling.

"When I came to New York, I was looking for the center of the literary world," McInerney begins, quipping that *The New Yorker* is a sort of stand-in for the center of the literary world, although it's a very insular place. It seemed like the closest thing I could find."

It was a logical, if not accurate, assumption. Long regarded for its commitment to excellence in prose, *The New Yorker* offered a literary history especially attractive to the serious fiction writer. One could not walk the halls without feeling the tradition of Salinger, Thurber, Updike and E.B. White.

McInerney, however, was not employed to write (nor, like his *Bright Lights* alter-ego, did he send unsolicited short stories to the magazine's fiction editor, only to find them rejected in stiff, formal terms). McInerney was a fact-checker, and that carried an unwritten yet enormous responsibility. No fact was too small or unimportant to check, and the tedium of the job eventually worked on McInerney's nerves.

"It was interesting, and I enjoyed the experience very much," he says, "but fact-checking was not for the aspiring fiction writer and an absent-minded space cadet such as myself. Its demand for strict attention to detail just wasn't my forte." According to McInerney, he made a mistake—like his *Bright Lights* character, again, with far less consequence—that led to his demise.

His next job, as a reader for Random House, was also useful for a future novelist, McInerney believes today, adding that E.L. Doctorow held a similar job for two years when he was just starting out. "It was interesting to see what was being submitted and, in a negative way, it was probably instructive, because I did not feel that most of what I read was eminently publishable. Some people told me that, if something wasn't too good, you didn't have to read the whole thing. But I can hardly ever start a story without finishing it, so I would always finish these things and then think about what I would do with them if I were writing them. That was an interesting exercise. There was a way, in seeing those completed manuscripts and seeing how they worked or didn't work, that I could view the novel as not quite such a daunting object. With these less than perfect manuscripts, it was easy to see the seams."

McInerney will always remember this period as bittersweet. He was learning the ropes of the publishing business, establishing contacts, and supplementing his income by helping to edit *The Random Review*, a literary anthology originally intended to be an annual publication, but which died after its initial issue. But the schedule was less disciplined than McInerney had encountered in his newspaper and magazine days, and he began to take advantage of it. He began his "party period," recalling now that there were many days when he barely made it to work. His brief marriage failed, and he wasn't producing any good writing.

Shortly after his "revelation" outside the Berlin, he caught his first big break. Raymond Carver, the critically acclaimed short story writer and a model to McInerney, was in New York. McInerney met him and they spent an afternoon discussing fiction. At the time, Carver was teaching fiction at Syracuse University.

"We developed a correspondence," says McInerney, "and he said to me, 'Living in New York and working in publishing doesn't look like it's doing much for your fiction. Why don't you come study with me at Syracuse?'

"I was torn, but I applied. It was a way of going for broke, of making a decision to stop straddling and trying to have it both ways—have a publishing career and write. I figured that sooner or later you had to make a commitment, one way or the other, and I decided that removing myself from New York City and going to upstate New York, to a campus that I had never seen before, leaving a lot of things behind, was a way of going for broke and demonstrating my commitment to fiction. Not having developed my writing habits and having to work somehow to make a living in a very expensive city, it was important for me, at that stage, to get myself into an environment that was more conducive to writing, where I didn't have a high overhead that required a full-time job."

When he returned to New York City four years later, he was the literary toast of the town.

E.L. Doctorow, author of *The Book of Daniel, Ragtime*

and *World's Fair*, once compared the process of writing a novel to driving at night. It's an analogy McInerney remembers and likes to repeat. "You can only see as far as the headlights," McInerney recalls the saying, "but you can make the whole trip that way."

The idea describes McInerney's method of creating a novel. "I think a set of themes or an intricate plot design that pre-exists the work itself is not going to result in an organic work of the imagination. I'm not saying that I don't *try* to figure out what I'm doing, but usually I only figure it out by doing it. That's the excitement of writing. If I didn't constantly get surprised by the material and the configurations I was stumbling onto in my writing, I don't think I'd be able to keep my interest up to finish a book."

McInerney's life, like his writing, might be seen as a matter of his driving at night, and when he followed his instincts to Syracuse, he was heading in the right direction. Raymond Carver turned out to be a remarkable teacher and friend.

"He's a very, very patient teacher," says McInerney. "He believes in finding the strength in everyone's work, because he says he can never be sure: one of his worst students, when he first started teaching, he subsequently came across 15 years later and recommended for publication. It's somebody who's quite well known as a short story writer now. Carver's approach is to try to encourage everyone's strengths, and since there's so little encouragement out there when you're trying to become a writer, having someone like Ray—encouraging you and egging you on—can be psychologically invaluable. One of the great advantages of creative writing programs is that you're in an environment of support, and you're with people engaged in the same enterprise—people you don't have to explain yourself to."

Despite the more tranquil, academic environment, McInerney continued to feel frustration when he submitted his short stories for publication. "I think I had the kind of luck that many aspiring writers would be familiar with—not much," he says, laughing. "I would send out stories to magazines, and I always got form rejections. I once got a nice note from *Redbook*, but I never had any luck.

"The first story that I did have published was in the *Paris Review*. I'd had something rejected by them right before that, but they said, 'We liked this story, but we're not quite sure it's right for us. Do you have anything else?' "

McInerney looked around for a story to submit; in one of his drawers, he found the fragment he'd written, a one-page scrap about a young man, dazed and lost in the wee hours of the morning. Intrigued by the second-person voice, he decided to expand the story, and within two days he had completed "It's Six A.M. Do You Know Where You Are?" *Paris Review* accepted it immediately.

"I just flipped," McInerney says. "It was the first positive response I'd had from an official source. I'd had my friends and teachers encouraging me all along—which, I think, is the only thing that keeps a young writer going."

Writing an entire book in the second-person, present tense, was an especially noteworthy risk for a first novelist, but McInerney claims the actual writing presented no special problem. "It's a common form of interior monologue, which I think somehow makes the story more ironic. I tried rewriting parts of it in the first- and third-person, but some aspects, like humor and irony, disappeared entirely. The voice must have been appropriate for that character in that situation. What actually happened was that it became difficult for me to start writing in the first- and third-person again when I finished the book."

McInerney's irreverent humor, placed in the mind of his protagonist, smoothed the rough edges of what might have become, given the nature of second-person narrative, an exercise in excessive self-consciousness. The result was a character of sharp wit and insight who is never dragged down by the undertow of his predicament:

> *I realized that I might not ever make it as a writer, that it might be because I wasn't good enough, or that it might be because the odds were just too long.*

You wake up with a cat on your chest. You are on a couch, wrapped in a quilt. After a few minutes you recognize Megan's apartment. Her bed is empty. The clock on the nightstand says 11:13. That would be A.M., judging by the sunlight. The last thing you remember is an amorous lunge at Megan somewhere in the P.M.; presumably unsuccessful. You have the feeling you have made a fool out of yourself.

To the unpublished writer, using this style is like working with a safety net: you will be applauded for your courage while being criticized for being foolhardy. There are, after all, easier ways to publish a first novel.

The McInerney-Vintage Contemporaries marriage was, in the beginning, as touch-and-go as McInerney's writing career. Gary Fisketjon, McInerney's old college buddy who became an editor at Random House, had a plan for publishing paperback originals and reprints under a cover designed to give the books the look of being part of a continuing series. The literature had to be of high quality, the cover graphics sharp enough to command the attention of book buyers who were eye-weary from looking at titles. When the idea started to take form in 1983, the fiction book market was, at best, questionable. Fisketjon hoped to launch the series, which he called Vintage Contemporaries, with six reprints and one original.

Fisketjon thought of McInerney and asked if he'd like to contribute the original. McInerney was less than enthusiastic. Publishing tradition calls for a book's being printed first in hardcover, then in paperback. The book, McInerney felt, might not be taken seriously as literature by critics and readers, and sales to libraries might also be difficult. Fisketjon argued that readers just couldn't afford to buy a lot of books each year—especially first novels. McInerney finally agreed.

In hindsight, McInerney sees the idea as brilliant. "It's applying some good marketing sense to an industry that hasn't changed in a hundred years," he mentions. "We're in a very vital period of fiction, and it's important to reach general readers—not just the 5,000 who are always going to pick up a book that's reviewed by *The New York Times*. If you think of the way you read Dostoevski or Hemingway, it was in a paperback edition. That's the way we consume books now. It's impossible to guess what would have happened to *Bright Lights* if it hadn't come out that way, but it clearly worked, and I'm glad to have been a part of it."

Indeed, it did work. There was an enormous "word of mouth" factor in *Bright Lights*'s early success, and once the belated reviews started rolling in, the book took off at breakneck pace. At one point, the book was selling more than 5,000 copies per week.

McInerney had found the literary Fountain of Youth and, as a young bestseller rather than an aging, unpub-lished writer, he completed his long apprenticeship with a final, important lesson: If you prove to be a power hitter in your rookie season, critics will watch closely for signs of sophomore jinx. They will search for weaknesses, rather than ignore them or write them off to immaturity. They will be especially interested in finding out if success went to your head.

Predictably, the reviews were restrained when *Ransom* was published. The book, in part a fictionalization of McInerney's experiences in Japan, was more traditional in style and narrative, leaving McInerney open to the comparative criticism he had not encountered with *Bright Lights*. Many reviewers wound up writing as much about *Bright Lights* as about *Ransom*.

This may bother McInerney more than he lets on, but he's not showing his hand. He shrugs off the response to *Ransom* as being part of the territory.

"There's a way that a book that has any sort of success assumes an identity over which you don't have any control, which becomes something that people feel they have to take a stand on. I *did* publish *Ransom* pretty quickly, right on the heels of *Bright Lights*, when people were just getting around to reading my first book, so a number of the reviews of *Ransom* were actually reviews of *Bright Lights*, by people who wanted to review *Bright Lights*. *Ransom* will probably be reviewed more when I write my third book."

In looking back on his apprenticeship and comparing who he was then with who he is now, McInerney finds no conflict. "I suppose, in a lot of ways, I've experienced a radical change, but, at the same time, I don't feel that I've changed as a person or writer. One doesn't develop a new personality after 30 years. The other years are the important ones.

"What has changed are my material circumstances. I'm now in the enviable position of being creatively unemployed, devoting all my time to writing. That's the greatest benefit. I no longer have to pretend to be something I'm not—whether it's a Ph.D. candidate in English or a bartender or a newspaper reporter—when all I ever wanted to do was write fiction."

BY MICHAEL SCHUMACHER

NORMAN MAILER

You're gambling with something vital. Most writers get smashed egos.

In April of 1983, Norman Mailer unveiled *Ancient Evenings*, his first work of pure fiction since 1967, a novel that took him ten years to write. An epic set in Egypt during the reign of Ramses II, *Ancient Evenings* is a multi-layered tale of startling creativity, its sweeping plot including battle scenes, ghosts and gods, a six-year-old prodigy with telepathic powers, magic, one of the most varied and detailed lists of sexual encounters anywhere, and an exquisite, 100-plus-page banquet scene at the tables of the pharaoh. The main character dies and is reincarnated three times in the course of the novel, each life testing his sense of honor and courage in a series of spirited scenarios.

Critics normally pay Mailer a lot of attention, but *Ancient Evenings* elicited a response so vigorous that it thrust the book into *event* status. The reviews praised and damned the work as if the critical word could *will* the book to live or die. When the brouhaha ground down to an exhausted whisper, one thing was clear: people were reading the book. As in the past, Mailer had wrestled with his devils, preserved them in the amber of the printed page, and virtually challenged his readers to work through the 709 pages of what he termed "my riskiest book yet."

Though Mailer downplays it, the key word to understanding the author appears to be *risk*. Norman Mailer has not gained his literary status and reputation by sitting ringside and watching the fight. Like with Hemingway, one of Mailer's early influences, the matter has always been decided by testing courage. For Mailer, the scene of the contest could as easily be a social event as it could be his office, where he devotes two three-hour shifts a day to writing out his visions in longhand on plain, unlined paper.

One approaches an interview with Norman Mailer cautiously. Mailer is known to dislike the interview format, claiming that the ideas he expresses in such encounters might be better put in his own written form. Mailer is also known as a skilled counter-puncher with a keen eye for his opponent's weaknesses, and I wouldn't have been surprised to find him in a combative mood when we met. *Ancient Evenings* had been getting some pretty tough reviews.

With this in mind, I did everything within my power to be prepared. I read through most of his books, took copious notes, wrote down a number of questions, and to assure a good first impression, showed up ten minutes late for the interview.

Happily, Mailer was not the mad-brained bear he is sometimes depicted as; to the contrary, he was warmly receptive and willing to answer any question tossed in his direction. Dressed in a well-worn blue sweater, gray slacks and blue sneakers, he exuded a casual, friendly tone, the only hint of his literary interests being a copy of *Vanity Fair* on his dresser. He smiled and laughed heartily throughout our session.

After we exchanged pleasantries, Mailer noted the time and mentioned that he had to watch the clock because of a very tight schedule. "There's plenty of time," he assured me. "I talk quickly, as you'll see."

Mailer is an animated speaker, using his hands to punctuate or underscore his words and moving around freely

---

People are used to finding Norman Mailer in the vortex of the hurricane: writing monumental works such as The Naked and the Dead, The Armies of the Night *and* The Executioner's Song; *running for mayor of New York; campaigning for the prison release of murderer Jack Henry Abbott; appearing as Stanford White in the movie* Ragtime . . . *he may be America's most visible literary figure. As a result, readers feel they know Mailer.*

Until they meet him. Then usually, as in this 1983 interview, he smashes a few public conceptions, and reinforces some of his favorites.

as he talks. His speech captures the dialects of Brooklyn, where he lives, and Harvard, where he went to college. He comes off confident but not aggressive, and extends a sense of humor and irony often lost in translation.

Like Hemingway's writing, your work has spent a great deal of time considering courage and the way an individual confronts his demons. Since your risk-taking has become some sort of personal trademark, I wonder if we could begin with your definition of courage.
I think courage is relative, absolutely relative. Say you have a man who was raised in a West Point family. He's brave as hell, trained for combat, he's *professionally* brave, he's been in training all his life. You won't be able to measure his true bravery until he gets into a situation that extends him beyond his limits. Now you get someone who's terribly timid, some little old lady who's terrified of being mugged, and one time she'll get out of her bed and go out to the street and walk over to the corner to buy a newspaper and come back, in terror of being mugged every step of the way. That can be a great act of courage, in a funny way. See, it is relative. You have to measure it by the content. To talk about somebody being courageous, as an absolute quality, is meaningless. Once in a great while, you will find somebody who's sort of a genius in courage, who keeps transcending the given, but those are very few people.

You've labeled Ancient Evenings *your riskiest book to date. What is the greatest risk a writer can take?*
I'd say it's probably to take a risk that punctures his working ego so that he can't recover from the attacks that are made on his work, and he then loses confidence in his abilities. If you take those risks, you're really gambling with something vital. This is the story for most writers, sooner or later. Most writers get smashed egos. They become like race car drivers in that sense. What happens is sooner or later the punishment they take stops them. And it may be that they write less well, or they stop writing, or they take a tremendously long time to write, or they lose the desire to write. No matter how it happens, it stops. If you've been going along as many years as I have, I suppose the only true risk you could take would be to write the kind of book that gets so bad a reception that you lose faith in yourself.

Should a writer be concerned about looking foolish when taking risks?
I don't see it as a risk when I'm doing it. Afterward, I can recognize that risks have been taken. Once in a great while, you'll think, "This is going to get the world's worst reviews." You're getting into something that's going to make no one happy, or is going to make certain people very unhappy. Then you feel a little fear, sort of like going into an alley. But that's not the major part of it. The main part of it is that you're dealing with something that is

exciting as you do it. Then afterward, you realize that you were taking risks.

Sometimes you can tell just on the face of it. Obviously, with a book about ancient Egypt, everyone would have been happier if some unknown author had written it. There would have been an incredible curiosity about who the author was. People would have read the book more easily. One hurdle I had to overcome with this book was knowing that a lot of people would pick it up and spend the first 50 pages saying, "What the hell does this have to do with Norman Mailer?" It irritates them because one of the things about modern life in America is we all pride ourselves on our acumen. You know, we think we're in control of the scene, we know what's going on. So if someone refuses our expectations, it irritates the hell out of us and we turn on people. Just for an example: Herschel Walker was hired by the New Jersey Generals. Everybody was terribly excited about that. Then he had a couple of bad games, and everybody was ready to say he was a terribly overrated player.

But the mark of a pro, whether you're talking about an athlete or a writer, is that he never does lose that faith in himself. He always comes back.
Yeah. They lose faith in their *luck*. Pros almost always believe in luck. You feel a favorable tide, or you're bucking a tough tide, and all that.

Do you feel that way?
I'm almost more comfortable with a tough tide. I get nervous when I'm on a good tide, because I figure prosperity is something I've never steered too well. That's when I start to lose my rudder.

Does your name get in your way? Do you find your critics judging your work more harshly because *you're Norman Mailer?*
They'll work me on a tight collar, no question. That's the given. If you want to be a big writer, that's the obvious price you've got to pay. You're there to be shot at, and that's part of it.

How do you deal with it?
I'm pretty tough now about a bad review. This isn't even arrogance any longer. It's just professional confidence, the same way a dentist would look at a dental student and say, "If I'm not any better than he is at filling teeth, then heaven help not only our patients but ourselves." By the same token, if I'm not smarter, in the literary sense, than the reviewer, then we're both in a lot of trouble. After all, I have to know more about my book than a reviewer does. They come across it and have an impression, a reaction. Generally, they're reading something quickly. So I can read a very bad review and shut it off, just say, "Well, he read the book in two days and he isn't getting it." Now, that works until it *doesn't* work, and the moment it

doesn't work, you've got a catastrophe on your hands. You know, if all the reviews are bad, I'd have to wonder.

I would think it could go the other way, too, if you took your good notices too seriously.
That's very dangerous in another way, because you can get terribly spoiled. You get softened for the next book.

Did that ever happen to you?
Sure. *The Naked and the Dead* softened me. *Barbary Shore* almost knocked me out.

It must have really brought you down, being proclaimed a major writer for your first book, then being nailed by the critics for your next two.
It brought me down a lot. It not only brought me down, but it also brought everyone around me down. I changed, in people's eyes, from being a Wunderkind to being "poor Norman, he had one book in him." That's not something you like to walk around with when you're 28 and 30. It tends to eat at you badly. You know, what if they're right? That's a terrifying thought, especially if your third book's not going well at all.

> *I changed, in people's eyes, from Wunderkind to "poor Norman, he had one book in him." That's not something you like to walk around with.*

Maybe that's why Advertisements for Myself *came off as a primal scream of sorts. It was like telling your critics, "This is who I am and what I'm all about."*
Yeah, but I think that came out of writing *The Deer Park*, because that is the book where I became a man. And I mean this modestly as a male, because everybody of the male gender is going to find himself a man, sooner or later. *The Deer Park* is the one I wrote with my liver and had to keep getting off my own floor. The nearest I came to having a crackup, as far as writing goes, was those years after *Barbary Shore*. *The Deer Park* was written very much as an act of will from all stretches, and it didn't work at first, didn't come out right. And then it got bounced by the publisher, and I rewrote it in a year and all that. When it was done, I felt strong about it. I felt that it was a good book. In fact, I was so sure of it, I even made an ad of all the bad reviews, which I think is one of the funnier ads that have been written in the last 50 years. *Advertisements*, I think, came out of the truculence but also the exuberance of having been able to finish *The Deer Park*. It's something to my satisfaction. As I look back on it, that was a fairly good time. With *Advertisements*, I began to find my style, so these two books are very important to me.

There is a noticeable evolution in your style, especially once you began writing nonfiction. You employed many fiction techniques in your journalism, which was a new thing at the time. How did you decide on that style?
All that "new journalism" came about almost by accident. I didn't start with the idea of doing a certain kind of journalism. I went out to cover the Democratic Convention in 1960, and I just wrote about it without thinking particularly about the style. This was just the way I wrote about it. A lot of people reacted well to it and were excited about that kind of journalism, and I thought, "Well, if they like this, this is the easiest thing in the world for me." I'd always had terrible trouble with plot, and here the plots were marvelous. They were written by events, and those were always the good plots, and I have no trouble writing if I know where I'm going. The problem for me is finding my own plots. They take a long time.

Because you don't know where they're going?
Yes, but also because I don't like to decide too quickly, either. I like to have it happen, just like in our own lives. We don't always know where we're going, and if we make formal decisions on a given night, if we sit down and put a list of things we're going to do on a piece of paper, they almost never work out right.

In Pieces and Pontifications, *your most recent collection of essays and interviews, you claimed that "journalism makes opera singers of novelists. We've got the story, now all we've got to do is go on and show our vocal chords." Now that's true in light of what you just noted about plot and journalism, but there's something disquieting in the current suggestion that style may be as important—if not more important—than the story itself.*
Well, style must always have an organic relation with the story. If you're telling a simple tale, then the style should be simple, but if you're dealing with very complex people, I don't think you can capture the quality of their minds without a style that is, syntactically speaking, complex. So it's not automatic. When I'm talking about finding a style, that's saying a lot, but it's different than having to create something out of whole cloth.

You've been known to change styles frequently, bring-

ing to mind your statement in The Deer Park, *which reads, "One must grow or else pay more for remaining the same." Would you advise writers to change styles from time to time?*

I think it's meaningless advice. There are writers who will change styles and ones who won't. It bears a great relation to one's identity. For certain writers, their style is their identity. They're two and the same. We can't think of Hemingway without thinking of his style, and if you think of his style, you think of his identity. They're all the same; they never shift. The same is true of Faulkner.

In writing, you don't have too many examples of the opposite. In painting, you do. There are certain painters who paint the same way throughout their lives. Their style is their identity. On the other hand, you have Picasso, who went through 20 styles and loved each one in different ways. He showed us different things with them, and he learned different things from them. They stimulated him and kept him young. I've always been captured by Picasso's example. I felt if you can change style, why stick to one style? Style is a vanity because it gives you product identification, but we've got an awful lot of products now that stay the same when they shouldn't.

Changing style also makes it hard for people to pigeonhole a writer and put him up against the inevitable comparisons.

It makes for a more orderly life—but it's also trench warfare—when you stay in one style. If you change styles, it makes for a certain chaos in your life on one hand, but it can have its own curious pleasures, too.

Probably the biggest example of combining fiction techniques with a nonfiction story was The Executioner's Song, *which wound up winning a Pulitzer Prize for fiction. Did you ever suspect, in the beginning, that the project would evolve into something so massive that you would be devoting a thousand pages to the subject?*

No, I wouldn't have started it if I'd known. I thought I'd write a 300-page book and be out fast. It would be an interesting story and, fine, I'd make some money, get ahead, and have money for the Egyptian novel. So there I was, in paradise with two expensive women on hand [laughs].

Considering the length and scope of the book, I think

> *If you can change style, why stick to one style? Style is a vanity because it gives you product identification.*

you might have had a love-hate relationship with The Executioner's Song. *Did you?*

I didn't have a deep one with *The Executioner's Song*, because I never felt that it was altogether my book. One remark I made then, that I'd like to repeat, is: "God's a better novelist than the novelist." It was almost as if someone was handing this to me, chapter by chapter, and I just kept clucking to myself, saying "My God, this is a fascinating story."

The only hate I had toward the book was it kept me working so hard. It was a prodigious mining operation. There were so many interviews. Lawrence Schiller did a lot of the interviews first, but then I'd study them and very often go out and interview the people to follow up the interviews. Then I'd have to adjust my interviews, boil down the interviews, and decide what was there to be used. And then I'd have to start shaping it artistically a little. The man-hours were prodigious. It was a book that was written in two years—counting the research, the interviews, and the writing—but it was really a five-year job compressed into two years because I was so broke.

The love-hate relationship comes when the book is just treating you like a bitch. The book reveals herself to you one day and hides herself the next. And you're just running around and you don't know what your relation is to the book. That starts a love-hate relationship. But with *The Executioner's Song*, it was just like I had a good, strong woman there working for me, I'm working for her, and we're having a relatively simple life together. Once in a while, I might say, "Goddamn it, she's working me too hard," but that was the only hatred I felt toward it.

Ancient Evenings *was another massive work demanding a lot of research. I read somewhere that you read 75 to 100 books on the subject.*

I never counted them, but it must have been something like a hundred books.

What kind of method did you use? How did you join history and fiction?

I wanted to keep it as accurate as I could, but in Egyptian research, Egyptologists have left a lot of holes. It's not that they left a lot of holes—there *are* a lot of holes. They recover what they recover, but there are gaping spaces missing. So there are places where I had to make up the material to a degree. There's other stuff that is highly accurate. The battle of Kadesh, for instance, is very accurate. It comes from any number of descriptions that were made of it on the temple walls of Ramses II's various mausoleums. The harem stuff in the book is, to a great degree, made up. I had very little more to rely on than drawings.

It's especially noteworthy that you wrote several other books in the ten-year stretch you spent on Ancient Evenings. *How did you keep a sense of continuity when you were always being interrupted?*
Well, when I'd go back, I'd have to psyche up again, find the book. I had to do that three or four times, but it was there. I put a lot of care into sanding the joints, and I defy people to find the spots where I'd broken it.

When reviewing the book for Time, *Paul Gray seemed to scoff at the notion of pursuing the Great American Novel today. He pointed to your generation of writers as primary offenders—*
He's right, we were. I think he's right both times. I think it's impossible today. One of the reasons I went back to Egypt—one of many reasons—was knowing that you can no longer write an all-encompassing novel about America. It can't be done. It is crucial now to have the kind of mind that can learn much about many different occupations. See, we live in an age when there's an awful lot of high-tech writing. If somebody writes about the advertising meeting of a board of corporation executives, you're going to get some extraordinary dialogue there. So somebody from the milieu, from the way of life, will come out with a great short story. There are an awful lot of people around who can write one great short story that has extraordinary dialogue and detail of place. But if you want to write a panoramic novel about America, you have to know all these places, and you can't do it. If you come in with dialogue that's not as fair or as good as all these special treatments, the reader, who is very sophisticated, loses respect for you and what you're doing. It's very difficult to do a panoramic novel about America now. I think it's just about impossible.

But to balance that dream out, I also remember reading an account of your early working days, when you supposedly said you would be content to be a hack writer if it meant making a living.
Part of that is from the Mills biography [*A Biography*, by Hilary Mills]. I think she stuck to every story at face value. None of them are adjusted or weighed. You know, when you're doing a biography, you really have to check out the stories against one another. You have to assume that one person's lying and another can't remember properly, and that a third person has a vested interest in it. Out of the distortions that all three bring, you try to find your way to what the reality might be. But you don't throw in all three sources and say, "Gee, which one can it be?"

No, I once said darkly to an editor, when I was writing *The Naked and the Dead*, "Do you realize that if I can't make a living from this, I'm going to have to write pot-boilers?" [laughs] As if, weep, it's the most terrible fate that could befall anyone. But I never seriously thought of writing that way.

Yet I'm also reminded of a quote in Pieces and Pontifications, *where you mentioned that your books may have turned out more "polished and well-rubbed" if you had more time to work on them.*
Well, it's something you do if you can do it. I didn't start off doing it. I couldn't have done it when I was a young writer. I wrote *The Naked and the Dead* quickly. It wasn't that I was in control of the pace—it just happened to come quickly, and that was wonderful. But *Barbary Shore* took four years, and *Advertisements for Myself* took another four years. I didn't start writing *Advertisements* the day after I finished *The Deer Park*, but it was four years before it came out. I'd written some other short pieces in the meantime. Some of them took me a year to write. The new stuff from *Advertisements* was only about 100 pages, so I was writing very slowly in those days. But as I got older, I could write more quickly.

An American Dream *appears to be the ultimate marriage between writing for art and writing for money, since you wrote the novel on a month-to-month basis as installments for* Esquire. *What kind of effect were you aiming for when you wrote the book this way?*
I felt it would push me in the direction of plot and fast action, that it would force me to make decisions—which on the whole it did—and that it would be a certain kind of book. Maybe I made a mistake. I might have had a much bigger book and a much deeper and better book if I had taken my time, found it, and taken it another way. I'll never know and I don't care anymore, but at the time, I used to wonder if I made a big mistake. Of course, if I had more time, I would have probably dealt with the contents of the anthropology professor's mind. It would have been a much slower, much richer, novel. But then, it might have gotten top-heavy the other way, with the parts of the book that had to do with murder and spies and all that. Looking back on it, I was probably trying to take a crazy movie story and make it work.

It didn't make much of a movie.
It made a terrible movie, I hear. I never saw it. Any time you take a novel like that, which depends so much on taking place in New York, and the first thing you hear is they're going to film it in Los Angeles, you know that the movie is not worth looking at. Because anybody who could make that kind of movie is capable of anything.

How do you feel about looking back at your books? Some writers feel that their books are like their off-

spring: they created and raised them, but they don't want to be explaining them now that they're grown up.
They're there, they're mine, they're my children—everything you say. They'll have to fend for themselves. I'm not going to go out there and write critical pieces supporting them. That's a fair way of putting it.

In Genius and Lust, *your work on Henry Miller, you spoke of a genius as being the person who comes to grips with all his contradictions. How do you cope with them?*
It's easier than it sounds. Finally, you're just the result of the factors that work on you. On a given day, you're doing what you're doing. . . . See, I probably think about myself a lot less than you'd expect, because I'm bored with myself. It's the only thing I'm an expert on, and I'm weary of my expertise [laughs]. I really don't spend time thinking about myself. You'd be amazed how often my mind is simply empty. I've become a great believer in emptying one's brain and saving it. In Provincetown, there are sometimes a lot of Portuguese fishermen, and I have a longstanding joke with a few of them. I'll pass them in the winter, and I haven't seen them in a year, and they'll say, "Hey, Norman, are you still writing?" And I'll say, "Oh yeah, I'm still writ-

ing. When I'm not writing, I keep this arm on a green silk pillow." [laughs] So when I'm not thinking, I keep this mind on a green silk pillow.

Sounds like you're mellowing with age.
Yeah, but I'm not happy about it.

The session ended. Mailer signed my books. While he was doing so, I mentioned that I was working on a novel.
   "Oh yeah?" he said, looking up for a moment. "Can you see an end to it?"
   I told him that I could, but that it was a distance away. The temptation, I noted, was to move too quickly in order to finish.
   "Don't rush it," was his suggestion. He scribbled a note wishing me luck on the inside cover of *The Executioner's Song.*
   We shook hands, and as I started from the room, Mailer said, "You never know, maybe someday I'll be reading your book."
   "It'll probably be a potboiler," I used as a parting shot. I was waiting by the hotel's elevator when the door to Mailer's room opened again and he poked his head outside.
   "Hey, Mike," he called. "Better you than me."
   Rumors start in the damndest places.

BY BRUCE JOEL HILLMAN

JAMES DICKEY

What I want is to be willing to fail rather than stagnate.

There are so many different selves in the poet. He must try to get more of these selves to speak up in different voices. When I first began to give poetry readings—now, this was when my first wife and I were starting the family, and though we weren't exactly poverty stricken there wasn't any extra money, either—I was rather shy about reading my own work. So I thought I'd do just as well reading somebody else's, which I sometimes did. And my wife said to me, 'You shouldn't worry about it. After all, you teach classes and it's sort of the same thing. Just get out there and be yourself,' which sounded pretty fine to me. Then I began to ponder it a bit. 'Be myself,' indeed; but which self?"

Jim Dickey indeed is a man of many selves. There's the poet known for the 1966 National Book Award winner, *Buckdancer's Choice*, and the novelist/screenwriter even better known for the book and movie *Deliverance* (and the actor who played the small-town Georgia sheriff). There's the deer- and rattlesnake-hunter in the field armed with bow and arrow or blowgun.

("I don't like guns and explosions," he says. "I had enough of that in the war, and I'm far too nervous for that." Dickey flew 100 combat missions with the 418th Night Fighters in the Pacific.)

There's the intellectual who speaks the better parts of five languages and is at home in Washington as the Consultant in Poetry to the Library of Congress; and there is the softspoken, Georgia-accented voice of the South reading "The Strength of Fields" at Jimmy Carter's inauguration in early 1977.

There are other voices, too. The New York ad exec who quit and went on welfare because he felt corrupted and corrupting; the musician who plays bang-up, knock-me-down hillbilly guitar; the college professor in the beat-up old buffalo hunter's hat and the poet-in-residence at the University of South Carolina. There is the loving husband and father, totally devoted to his young wife, Deborah, and the memory of his dead wife, Maxine—the romantic who calls the period between his marriages a time of "dreadful freedom." And the man, whose drinking was almost a trademark, who doesn't drink any more.

But primarily there is the poet: James Dickey, author of 12-plus books of poetry; the first, *Into the Stone*, in 1961, the latest *Puella*, written consciously for Deborah ("They all come back to rest in the ones we love the most"), off to his publisher last August.

I got a chance to hear most of James Dickey's voices in a series of interviews over several days that resulted in more than ten hours of conversation. Dickey lives in a wooded Columbia, South Carolina, neighborhood in a comfortable home with a lake for a backyard. Inside, the furnishings are modern in a timeless sense: chrome-and-glass, low leather chairs, contemporarily patterned opposing sofas. There are career mementos on the walls. A framed page from *Variety* attests that *Deliverance* was the number-one box-office hit for that particular week in 1972. A metal mask of Dickey, used as an *Esquire* cover, hangs guard. He almost lost his eyesight posing for the

---

The riskiest thing James Dickey could ever do would be to quit taking risks. Like Norman Mailer, Dickey thrives on challenge, and has built his reputation as one of today's major poets not only on his poetic skill, but on how he adapts that skill to each individual poem.

And Dickey transfers that writing skill to living. Through more than 20 poetry collections, the acclaimed novel and *screenplay* Deliverance, *hundreds of essays and articles, and even jingles for Coca-Cola, the 66-year-old poet has continued to pit himself against himself.*

In this 1981 interview, he talks about the results.

mask; acid used in making the cast dripped into his eyes, causing temporary blindness.

The house boasts four typewriters, home to as many projects, and just half as many clocks—none in the living room or library. There are literally as many books as would be found in a one-horse-town branch library. The books spill over everywhere. The shelves can't hold them all; they are taking over the house. Dickey had to move a stack of them to make room for us to sit and talk, over Coca-Colas, on the opposing sofas with a paperback copy of *Deliverance* and a hardbound edition of *Jericho: The South Beheld*, on the coffee table between us.

Listen to some of the voices.

You have said that you don't agree with T.S. Eliot's theory that the work and its creator are separate. Does this imply that your work leads us to you personally?
Well, in a way it does. There should be an aura of a distinct human personality that hovers around the words in some way. Maybe this is an illusion, but it is one of the basic illusions of art. Everyone has his own personal idea of Shakespeare, as they do of Jesus Christ.

Satisfy these criteria: something that only you could say; and that you judge it good even though it's something only you could say.

somewhat analogous to that, but not exactly. Words are a different sort of medium. They are extremely private in that when you read a poem, you're forming your own inner vision of what the poem gives you to form a vision about. In a movie, everything is right here in front of you. The poem gives you something that by means of the poem you give yourself. If I say *tree*, and you call an image of a tree to mind, your tree and mine would not be the same, probably not even the same sort.

It's interesting that you mention Robert Lowell. The Atlantic *called you two the only major poets working in English today and—* Somebody else said that; *we* most certainly didn't. I really don't like those pieces where they compare you to some other writer. There really is no competition among poets, at least not between the poems. There may be a bit of ego competition among the poets, because they're human, but it really is not much of a competitive thing. After all, Robert Lowell and I are not running in the Olympic games against each other. We're trying to say something that is unique to us. He says things his way and I mine. People go to either poet for what may be in it for them, the readers.

So a careful reading of your work would give us a good idea of what you are like as a man?
I think so. But it's important that it be different for different people. There should be for everybody some feeling that you're talking to an actual person instead of reading poems that have been arranged by a computer. You can read the poetry of Robert Lowell and tell exactly what he's like: very nervous, sort of uncertain, but a man with very violent emotions, and all torn-up and divided within himself—all this from the *way* he writes, aside from his choice of subject matter. You can tell a great deal from how a writer writes. You can tell almost as much about what he is trying to hide, maybe, as what he actually does get out. But the sense of the man, the enduring part of him, is in the poem.

So your enduring quality . . .
Well, every poet hopes there is going to be something that will be enduring, but it has to be in the words. It is not like an actor or a movie star. So much of the actor's personality, someone like Burt Reynolds, is in the fact that he is a movie star, that he's around *right now*. The actor's lot is very time-bound. The poet's situation is

Are you disciplined?
In some ways, yes. Not so much in the day-to-day routine of living, and I believe that the entity of chance is very strong in any poet's writing. Even a mistake of some sort will lead to something that's maybe not a mistake, or at least not as much of a mistake.

As far as working on things in a sort of determined way for a long time, that I do have. I will not let a subject go until I have gotten it as close to what I think it ought to be as is humanly possible. I work by successive drafts. You never finish a poem; you abandon it. You should work hard to get as close as you can, not to some idea of perfection you had before the poem was begun, but an idea of perfection that develops as you work and work on the poem. It's different and usually better than what you had originally conceived.

I use the same approach on all works, whether poetry or prose: I tacitly assume that the first 50 ways I try it are going to be wrong. Yet, the essential thing is to make it seem inevitable, to take all the sense of labor out of it. I very much believe in the principle of superabundance and the attendant principle of cutting back. You can always take out or change, but you cannot always put in.

I write out of subjects. Some poets urge you to give the initiative to words, to go where words take you. I generally will work out of situations and bring the words to that situation, instead of working from the words outward to the situation.

I am experience-oriented, rather than word-oriented. Or rather, I have been up until now. I'm sort of interested in trying the other way to see what there might be in that.

Are you working on that now?
Yes, some. The new book has at least partly the other approach to it.

That would be Deborah Puella
Yeah, but it's just *Puella* now. It began as *Flowering*, when I thought I was going to be working with an artist on it, then changed it to *Deborah Puella*, and now *Puella*. It's unusual, not at all like the other books. In it, I undertook a difficult, but fascinating, task, which was to write a series of 19 poems about young girls moving from childhood through the gateway into womanhood, to try to catch the changes in their lives, their thinking, the things they do. I can't really *imagine* what a boy would feel like in that time of life, because I *know* it too well. It's good because I have to imagine the world of the young girl. To a poet, at least for my kind of poet, that's much better. To have to create the effect entirely from imagination.

Some people occasionally say, "Why don't you write more poems like were in *Buckdancer's Choice*?" I don't want to write like that. All the poems I wanted to write that were like I wanted to write when I wrote *Buckdancer's Choice* are in *Buckdancer's Choice*. Self-imitation is not right for me. I would rather make some mistakes—give up the reputation—than be repetitive. If I can't take a chance on what I write, do something different, well, then writing has no interest for me at all.

You have said, "Failure is the most creative thing about the poetic process, if you learn what to do with it." How do you turn it from disadvantage to advantage?
Well, this will only happen after you've been writing—and failing—for a good long time. Then you develop a kind of critical sense about what you write. You can tell when something is good, but it would be just as good in somebody else's work, too. You want to hold out for those things *only* you can say. You satisfy these two criteria: one, something that only you could say; and two, that you judge it good *even though* it's something only you could say. These are rare times when you get something like that, but you can tell. You know it when you think to yourself, "Did I say that?" And then the other part of your brain answers, "Yes, I did. And nobody else could have." That's when you know you're on to something.

I have heard you say that you believe in a poet writing a great deal and publishing a comparatively small fragment of it.
Yes, I believe in that very much. The main thing is to write a lot, to keep yourself immersed in the element of poetry, to stay in deep in the creative possibilities.

How much unpublished Jim Dickey material is there?
Oh, God, thousands and thousands of items. One of the universities is bidding on my papers, my correspondence, my literary remains. My executor was showing them through the files, and there are 20 or 25 full boxes of unpublished manuscripts. I had saved them all because I thought I would eventually go back through them and be able to use the ideas on some other basis. But now I know I can't do that. The new stuff is coming in at such a great rate that I don't need to go back to the old stuff. I wish I could; I wish there was that much time. I had some ideas that I flubbed very badly, and I might not do so badly on them now, maybe. But I've got new things that are always coming in, and I've got to give the best of them a chance.

How do you choose that which you're going to publish?
I publish the things that seem to me to have solved some of the problems I set up for myself, or which have a particular distinctiveness about them. I ask myself if I can truthfully say I had initially a good idea for a poem, and that I did fairly well by it. So many times I end up thinking: "God, I never found the form for this one. This was initially a good concept, but I was not able to realize it." That happens a good deal to me. But you can't know what will eventually work out until you try. And you should try a lot, and very hard, and very long.

You say the process goes on all the time, even in sleep. That you never have any layoff periods, and that you are "one of those slow, plodding, searching writers."
Amen. Amen. I think the tragedy of my poetic generation is that people are willing to let stuff go and be published simply because there are people who can and will publish it. The bookstores are flooded with forgettable books that are good, but not good enough. They just don't make it around the bend into the area of being good, or memorable, or with luck, even unforgettable. Many are called the good books, but few are chosen.

You told me that when you were asked to read "The Strength of Fields" at Jimmy Carter's inauguration, you considered it an obligation to use it as a forum for promoting poetry, the "neglected art," and that it would have been an act of cowardice not to take the opportunity. Do you still feel a continuing obligation to promote poetry?
No, no I don't. Of course, it is the discipline I live by, and to a certain extent for, and naturally I have an interest in what happens to it. Poetry is, I think, the highest medium

that mankind has ever come up with. It's language itself, which is a miraculous medium that makes everything else man has ever done possible.

You have written just about every kind of writing there is—poetry, advertising, novels, screenplays . . .
Yeah, I guess so, including a little music. I haven't written any outright journalism; that is, I don't believe I've *reported* anything.

Although you did cover the Apollo moonshot for Life *magazine.*
I did that, that's true, but I did it as an exercise in poetry.

Perhaps that's just another kind of journalism, adapted to your own way of reporting.
Maybe it is. I'd like to think it is because some of my best literary friends think that journalism, particularly the interview, is the great art form of our time. Norman Mailer does, and so does George Plimpton, and they are both superb at it, as is Tom Wolfe.

You have called poets "more human" than other people.
Well, maybe; but they *are* more attuned to the connections between language and things, existence and experience. Words have the capacity for these people to change reality, to deepen it, to make it more meaningful and perhaps mysterious. For the poet, composition is a form of ritual magic, a spell of some sort.

Can you be a part-time poet?
Yes, I think so. Of course, the composition of poetry is different for different people. Myself, I couldn't be anything but a full-time poet. But someone—Max Beerbohm I believe—said the difficult thing about being a poet is finding what to do with the other 23-1/2 hours in the day.

But that isn't the way it is with me. Sitting and staring at a manuscript in the same place and in the same physical position is not right for me. I need to have something in the typewriter that I have gotten down in white heat, and then leave it for a while and go on to something else before going back to it. It is amazing how quickly you can then see what to do with it: this should come out, you shouldn't encourage that to happen in this poem, but this other thing would be okay to try out a little bit in this direction. It's kind of a shakedown process.

Which is why you keep three and four typewriters with three and four projects scattered around the house?
Yeah, sure. Because in some weird way, the projects will tend to cross-pollinate with each other. The best artists I've known wouldn't work on just one canvas at a time, either. They'd have four or five right in line in their studios.

You make a lot of connections between the visual arts

and poetry, not to mention your collaborations with artists like Jericho. *Is there some relation here for you?*
Well, no, except that painters are makers of visual images, and poets make mental ones. I like images; I love pictures. I am very visually oriented. But I would be a very good blind man, too. Because the tactile sense is very strong in me. Hearing is also important, but on the other hand, I have no sense of smell at all. None. So I am a blind man in my nose.

In Self-Interviews, *you wrote that you have only one criterion for what will eventually become the subject of a poem: something that keeps recurring for no apparent reason. Do you mean your poems sort of filter up from subconsciousness into conscious thought?*
Yeah, I think so. You drop something, say an incident that will eventually become a poem or a novel, either deliberately or undeliberately into what Henry James calls "the deep well of unconscious celebration." And later on, you bring it back up and it has undergone a metamorphosis. The unconscious has worked on it some way, transformed it.

Is that work, part of the writing strategy?
I think it is. It's not a conscious part. I can remember so many things in my work that were that way, and they come out different from what the actual experience was. In fact, there is not anything I've ever written, in verse or in prose, that is actually a literal transcription of anything I ever did or saw. It's a commentary, sort of. Like the war poetry, some of them are based on actual incidents. A long poem of mine, "The Firebombing," for instance, is not based on any one mission I flew. It is a composite of several different ones, plus a lot of invention that seemed to go with the other stuff.

Does that sort of process lead to a lot of 3 a.m. wake-ups to get something down?
Yes, yes it does. I do that often. If it wouldn't wake my wife, I would use a recorder where I could talk out the essential things. But I don't usually sit up all night. One of the essential ingredients for a writer, particularly a writer like myself, is to keep the energy level fairly high. My first orientation into adult life was athletics, and there is so much that can be learned from sports. Especially about pacing yourself.

To relate to that, you have said that when something looks close to being finished, you're capable of 17-hour stretches at the typewriter.
Yeah, then I want to go full-blast on that and nothing else. When I see, or think I see, the well-known light at the end of the tunnel, I want to *get* there. Even so, when I do think I've gotten there, I sit on it for a while and chances are I'll fiddle and fool with it some more. But if the essential of it is down, that's a great, great feeling, boy. And you know it's got the qualities of being good all the way

through. You see that with luck, and a lot more work, you can get the thing where no word can be changed without diminishing the piece. And when you see you have a situation like that, you want to push. You want to get it like that because you see it can be done.

You have mentioned that you're pacing yourself better these days . . .
Yes, I'm always falling back on that notion of pacing, which I used to feel was not so important as I do now. Today, no tomorrow—I was born February 2, 1923, I will be 57½ years old. I'm at the age where you count half-birthdays. If you haven't learned to pace yourself in a creative way by that time, your days are numbered. That is what burned Ted Roethke out.

Also, another element ends up being part of the scene—drinking. When you go hard and constantly, liquor is going to enter into your efforts to keep things going. It is a good short-range stimulant, but it's death and damnation if you apply it as medicine. Your body cannot stand up under giving all-out, and you're wearing out physically, and you're getting older and trying to hold it all together with alcohol. James Agee was a great all-night talker and drinker, and that's what killed him at the age of 45. I used to drink a lot, which I enjoyed enormously. And if I had it to do over again and I didn't injure my health, I would do it again—or twice as much. But it begins to get to the point where there *is* harm, and you can tell. But when you get to that point, you're usually in too deep to get out of it easily. And so, when I saw that was likely to happen in my case, I left it. I don't drink anything now, not even beer, wine, nothing.

So it's only fairly recently that you have been so taken with the idea of pacing yourself.
Yeah, and I'm getting more down on the page. That's where my immortality is going to lie—in what I've put down, not what I've said at some bull session or cocktail party. Besides, I love to write. Writing is an obsession with me. I have a plain-and-simple fascination with words. There are so many combinations of possibilities that can be done. I love the sound of words. The English language is the greatest medium for communication in-depth or in any other way that has ever been devised. It is the perfect language for poetry; you couldn't get a better one. It's got all the advantages and only one or two disadvantages.

> *There are so many selves in everybody, and just to explore and exploit one is wrong, dead wrong, for the creative person.*

And what would those be?
The main disadvantage is that it's rhyme-poor compared to something like French or Italian. But if you don't write rhyming poetry, that's not much of a disadvantage. And even if you do write rhyme verse, there are poets who feel, like Auden, stimulated and challenged by the very fact that there is a paucity of rhymes in English. He thinks that's a source of strength to the formal poet.

Do you use the tools of the trade, say like rhyming dictionaries?
I'm sparing in the use of such things, although a thesaurus is a different matter entirely. I also will read through dictionaries for fun, particularly that huge thing that comes with a magnifying glass attached because the entries are so small. That's one of the best gifts I ever received. Reading a dictionary, or just perusing it, locks you into words. To be immersed in the element—words—is extremely important for a poet.

I am an inveterate notebook keeper because it is rich and good practice. But I also read a great deal, and I am very interested in interviews with poets as a good way to gain insight. This is kind of the age of the interview and nobody likes to give out interviews better than poets do. Consequently, there are hundreds of interviews with poets on this side of the Atlantic and in England and elsewhere. Some surprising things come out.

I also advise poets to become great readers of newspapers. Every issue is full of items of such bizarre interest. This is the sort of thing that engages my attention for a potential poem: I read once, years ago, about this guy in the nineteenth century who had just been married and had a son. He was exploring up around Upper Siberia where they found that mammoth in the glacier. Now, this is almost too pat to be true, but it is true. Well, he fell into a crevasse, and his body was left in glacier ice. Years later, at 36, the son was exploring the same area and found the father. He, too, like the mammoth, was preserved. You have this curious situation of the son getting the father out of the ice, and the father is 15 years younger than the son is in appearance. Now that would make for a good idea for a poem. You never know where they come from.

You have said that you have a horror of backsliding, of not being as good in whatever you're doing this year as you were last year.
Yes, I've thought about that, and you can never really tell.

And when you've published as much as I have, and you get to be about my age, there are going to be people who want you to do what they are familiar with. They inevitably say, "He's slipping, he's not as good as he used to be," or "His early work was so much better," and so on. But I really don't care that much anymore about being as good as, or not as good as, or better than. That is not my primary consideration. My primary consideration is to *change*. I dare not use the word *grow*; there may or may not be growth involved, but to change. To still keep that openness, that chance taking-ness as part of the work. Not to be afraid to make a mistake, even if it's a long and costly mistake.

The whole tragedy of the American poets of my generation is that they didn't do it. Lowell did it to some extent. Roethke did it, but even he was beginning to repeat himself badly at the end. What I want is to be willing to fail, even if it costs in reputation, rather than stagnate. That's what keeps it exciting for me. Not only to do something that nobody else has done before, but to do something that *I* haven't done before. There are so many selves in everybody, and to explore and exploit just one is *wrong*, dead wrong, for the creative person. He must get more selves to speak up in different voices.

BY NANCY NICHOLS

CAROLYN CHUTE

*If I can be writing, I can take a certain amount of control
when so much around me is upsetting.*

arolyn Chute lumbers across the wooden floor of her tiny house, her new green-and-yellow workboots making a flat squeak. She is wearing a peasant skirt and man's workshirt. Her long hair, drawn back with a bandana, sways side to side as she crosses the room. "It's been crazy with reporters," she says, shaking her head. "I don't understand it."

Chute has just become a celebrity. Her first novel, *The Beans of Egypt, Maine*, was in its third printing only a month after its debut, and reviewers had already compared Chute to William Faulkner and Erskine Caldwell. Appearances on *Good Morning America* and feature articles in *The New York Times* and *The Boston Globe* followed.

Before the book was published, Chute (the *ch* is hard, as in *choose*) and her husband, Michael, were often desperately poor, living without food and fuel during Maine's winters. The small house near Portland doesn't have an automatic flush toilet, and their truck was bought in parts at the junkyard where Michael worked. When she received her first advance check, Chute wrote her agent: "It was like a dream. We all took turns holding it. Even my neighbors."

In her novel, Chute chronicles the loneliness and isolation of poverty in the backwoods of Maine (she jokingly calls herself the "Woody Allen of the rural poor"). She tells the story of Earlene, a little girl who watches the Bean family across the way through a large picture window at the front of her house. The Beans live in a trailer. "One of them old ones, looks like a turquoise-blue submarine," writes Chute. "In and out of the submarine-like structure come tons of Beans." They are a loud, incestuous lot with rough exteriors and poor educations. They have occasional run-ins with the law. They know the frustration of poverty.

"Daddy says the Beans are uncivilized animals. *Predators* he calls 'em. 'If it runs, a Bean will shoot it. If it

falls, a Bean will eat it,' Daddy says and his lip curls. A million times Daddy says, 'Earlene, don't go over on the Beans' side of the right-of-way not ever!' " In the course of the novel, Earlene grows up and leaves her father, eventually marrying a Bean and bearing the fruit of the once forbidden family.

The New York Times called the novel "a triumph of art out of life, art over life," because in many ways it reflects Chute's life. Chute is 38 and the veteran of one failed marriage. She left high school at age 16 and later passed a high school equivalency test.

She suffered through any number of demanding and demeaning jobs before succeeding as a writer. She worked in a chicken processing plant, in a shoe manufacturing plant, and as a correspondent for the local paper (a job she calls "boot camp for writers"). Chute defends her decision to leave school at such an early age; she says it gave her the freedom to write. The decision also left her and Michael on the verge of poverty. Michael struggles at jobs that pay only minimum wage.

As Chute writes: "This book was involuntarily re-

Carolyn Chute's life is a slap in the face to less-disciplined writers: high-school dropout, waitress, floor scrubber, potato farmer, living at poverty level, writing without electricity, writing in a cellar. . . . But writing. Always writing.

Chute was 38 when The Beans of Egypt, Maine— *written about poverty, out of experience—was published in 1985 to both critical and commercial success (five hardcover printings in the first three months).*

In this 1986 profile, Chute is working on her second novel (then called Metal Man, *published in 1988 as* Letourneau's Used Auto Parts*). "It is work," she said after the interview. "Plain and simple. There's no shortcut. You spend 11 hours a day, 7 days a week for 10 years on every book and it might succeed."*

searched. I have lived poverty. I didn't *choose* it. No one would choose humiliation, pain and rage."

She writes to control her hostile world. "If I can be writing," she says, "I can take a certain amount of control when so much around me is upsetting." In the world that Chute lives in, poor people "either don't exist or they're to blame for everything." But in the world that Chute creates, they are strong characters trying to live as best they can in a world they are not all that prepared to cope with.

Chute wrote to her editor: "My greatest wish is that readers will *feel* with the Beans and will see the humiliation and frustration that comes with minimum-wage-type work . . . my deepest wish [is] to educate people on something that people since the beginning of time don't want to feel . . . they'd rather blame poverty on the poor . . . and then just forget about it."

She spent three years writing her novel and many more working with the characters. "It's crazy, I know. I feel at times that, wow, I'm making up these little people and I've lost my mind. But if that's what it takes . . . You know, if I wasn't a writer, I'd be locked up probably. You know, they'd go, 'Well, she doesn't write—she just sits over there and makes up these little characters.' They probably would have the wagon pulling up outside now and off I'd go.

"I believe, I actually believe—and Michael believes—that [my characters] are real, and we talk about them at the table when we eat, and we really kind of pretend that they're real. Before I can convince the reader that they're real, I have to kind of believe it, too."

Chute says she does some of her best work while telling stories to Michael. Often when he was out of work and they were alone on a cold winter night, they would act out the scenes from her novel. "No pencils, no word processors, just telling. Something happens when you're doing that that doesn't happen when you have tools in your hands.

"Writing is not writing skills, but knowing how to see." She tells new novelists to "tune in and notice all the details. There are people who can't read and write who are novelists. They've got two lenses. A telephoto lens for big pictures and a lens a dentist would use. What they do to show the big picture is to use those details they see with the small lens."

That kind of thinking led Chute to write passages like this:

I know the way Beal's beard spreads over the sheet. He don't never cut it. It's like one of those dinky houseplants you get with good intentions, but it takes over, needs a bigger and bigger pot every time you look. The beard fills our bed at night, lies between us, and sometimes I feel it try to grip me.

Chute gets up at 4:30 in the morning, and does housework until 8, then packs her husband and their dog into the truck. Only after they have left does Chute begin to write. She writes until they come home, usually at 9 or 10 at night.

When Chute was working on *The Beans*, she was living in a borrowed cabin in Vermont without electricity. She could work only during the daylight hours. Later, when she and Michael returned to Maine, they lived in a shed. Because a neighbor boy pestered her there, she finished writing her novel in the cellar. She recalls it being "very gruesome" in there, but she never gave up.

"I'm a perfectionist," says Chute. "I do a first draft of my story. I naturally assume my first, second, third drafts stink. I work on it. I never feel it is perfect." She has even changed some passages in her published copy of *The Beans*. "I love writing so much. I have to force other people to let me write. It is always something. I get bombarded." To stop the constant interruptions, Chute has turned off her phone; a poster with a skull and crossbones sits on her door with the warning, "Bother This Writer and You'll Be Sorry."

Chute has been writing since she was eight. She sold her first story to *Ploughshares* magazine for $50. It was called "Ollie, oh," and it described the different ways two people have of grieving. Anne Tyler selected it for a collection of *The Best American Short Stories*.

Chute polished her writing skills at the Stonecoast Writers Conference at the University of Southern Vermont. Her instructor was Madison Smartt Bell, who has said of Chute: "She was just wonderful. Every year she would come out of the woods with these wonderful stories." He encouraged her to shape her stories into a novel so he could introduce her to his agent.

In 1983, Chute had *The Beans* ready for review, but could not afford to photocopy it. Bell convinced her to send the original copy and loaned her $10 to cover the cost. When Jane Gelfman of Farquharson Ltd. in New York saw the manuscript, typed on lined schoolbook paper and illustrated by hand, she found it "charming." She

> *I*t's crazy, I know. I feel at times that I'm making up these little people and I've lost my mind. But if that's what it takes . . .

took her on as a client.

Few editors saw the book, says Gelfman. Cork Smith, an editor who had just moved to Ticknor & Fields from Viking, bought it. "It seemed like a fresh, distinctive voice, but I had no idea it would be so successful," Smith says. It was his idea to bring the book out in both hardcover and trade paperback editions, an uncommon practice. "If the book was going to get started, it had to find an audience that could pay for it."

The book sold an "absolutely colossal" number of copies, hard- and soft-cover—almost 200,000 books in its first eight months. It was also sold to Warner Books for $100,000 in a subsequent mass-market paperback sale.

Chute is at work on her new book, tentatively titled *Metal Man*, about life in a junkyard. Because Michael worked for three years in a junkyard, Chute was able to get a feel for the life. She often takes ventures to the junkyard to take pictures and observe the routine. "If you're doing a junkyard story, there is nothing more inspiring than junkyard pictures," she says.

Life has changed for the Chutes. They are using the money from *The Beans* to build a house, and things are becoming more comfortable. But old fears borne in poverty linger: because she is afraid her first novel might have been luck, she continues to write 12 hours a day.

BY ROSE ADKINS

ROD MCKUEN

A poet can't afford to be aloof. The tools of his trade
are the people he bumps up against.

With more than 40 million copies of his books in print, Rod McKuen is the only author to place three books on *Publishers Weekly*'s year-end bestseller list in a single year. His poetry is studied in more than 5,000 schools, colleges, seminaries and universities in this country, and his poetry and recordings are used as therapy in hospitals and health-care centers.

McKuen has recorded more than 200 albums. His film scores have twice been nominated for Oscars (*The Prime of Miss Jean Brodie* and *A Boy Named Charlie Brown*—the latter in collaboration with Vince Guaraldi and John Scott Trotter). His classical music includes symphonies, concertos and ballet suites. He was nominated for the Pulitzer Prize in music for his composition, "The City," for *Orchestra, Narrator and Soprano*, commissioned by The Louisville Orchestra.

Among his awards and degrees is the Carl Sandburg Award as "The People's Poet, for making poetry so much a part of our daily lives" and in 1981 he was honored by Brandeis University for "Continuing Excellence and Contribution to Contemporary Poetry." In 1983, the Freedoms Foundation at Valley Forge gave him its highest award, The Patriots Medal, and invited him to join its board of governors.

McKuen has traveled extensively throughout the world, giving concerts, lectures and poetry readings, and his works have been translated into more than 30 languages.

He lives in southern California in a Spanish house built in 1928-1929. The house has thick walls, large rooms filled with books and recordings, and privacy. McKuen has his own recording studio and projection room, sauna and barber shop. Books, mostly poetry and literature, line McKuen's upstairs office. Downstairs in the den are books on theater, film, architecture and the other arts. Another library, containing books on politics, science, environment and social studies, is in the living room. A collection of framed signatures and manuscripts adorns the walls.

Most of the art McKuen has collected over the years is modern; the unlikely combination of Mao Tse-tung, Richard Nixon and Jane Fonda in outsized portraits by Andy Warhol stretches across one wall. Above a staircase is a painting of William Faulkner.

Most of the rooms have fireplaces that McKuen uses even in summer. The kitchen is functional, because McKuen likes to cook, even though he considers eating "a necessary waste of time," and doesn't like food very much.

McKuen's New York apartment is quite the opposite. McKuen lives vertically as opposed to living horizontally in California. Three apartments in a high-rise have been made into one, designed by his brother Edward. It's really his brother's place. The view is extraordinary and the decor modern. McKuen was in New York off and on for seven months last year, but this year he'll spend much more time in California. In New York he's nearer to his publisher—although now he has publishers on both coasts. And in New York are theaters, lots of concerts, recitals and poetry readings to go to. "I'm becoming more and more withdrawn," he says, "so I don't go out much even in New York. Maybe a love affair or some other cosmic change will change all that," he adds wryly.

Although Rod McKuen continues to be generally scorned by critics and serious poets, the critics who pay—readers—continue to testify to his popularity. He's been America's most-read poet since 1954's And Autumn Comes, *and carried the tradition through with 1984's* Valentines.

This 1984 interview was the first in-depth interview Rod McKuen had granted in more than five years, and the biggest since then. "There's more of me in it," he said at the time, "than I'd ever planned or ever expected to let go of."

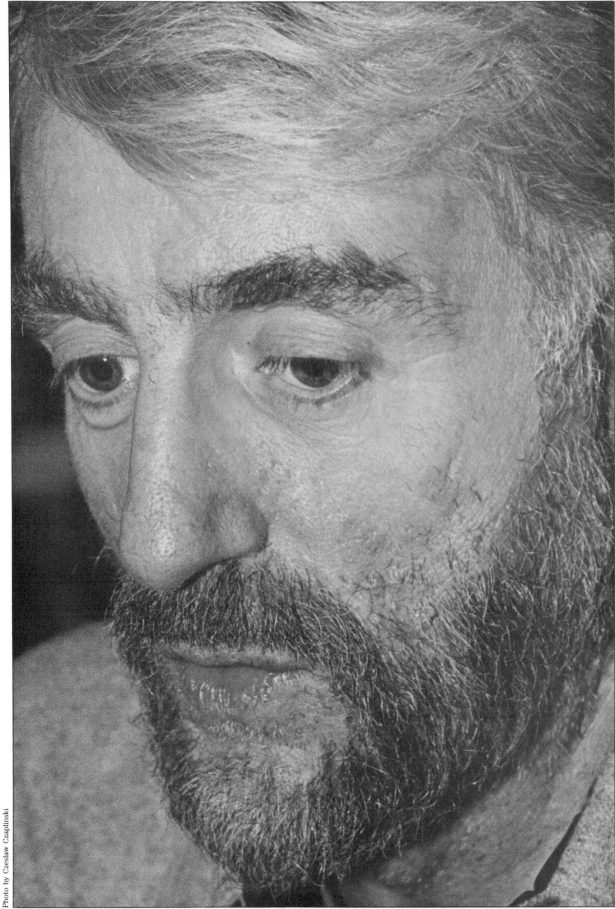

McKuen describes himself as "curious, anxious." His brother Edward says he's "complicated."

"Maybe so," McKuen adds, "but isn't everyone?"

You've reached more readers than most poets ever will or do. Are the possible rewards worth the sacrifice most poets make, struggling in obscurity?
Absolutely. Poetry is not a luxury; it's a necessity. The poetry in our lives separates sanity from savagery. The poet, by relating honestly his or her experiences, views, thoughts, wishes, and even bigotry, helps us articulate our own feelings. Man would not only starve without poetry, but he would also turn on himself and be lost. By *poetry*, I mean gentleness, understanding, truth and illumination. A verse need not be *written* to be a poem. It can exist in the way clouds are arranged on a certain day. It can be a fragment of music that for only seconds fills the ear to overflowing and changes the way we feel for a moment. Poetry is transportation, taking us out of ourselves. It need not be a vehicle, but it is definitely transportation.

In terms of self-worth, few jobs are more rewarding. From a monetary standpoint, most successful poets have a second occupation. William Carlos Williams was a fine country doctor. T.S. Eliot was a publisher; Walt Whitman, a journalist and editor. Many poets teach. Even if economics weren't involved, it's not a bad idea to be doing something else. Another occupation usually forces us to write and often provides us with fresh ideas.

I'm a total product of this time and this age. I've worked on the railroad, split logs and danced log jams free on the river out of lumber camps. I've dug ditches and dug graves, worked in a cookie factory, been a shoe salesman, a theater doorman, a disc jockey, broke both legs in the rodeo, again in the army, and a third time in the backyard horsing around. I've held jobs that don't exist anymore. Lived through half a dozen depressions without knowing it, watched radio turn to television, television to video, found myself smack in the middle of the electronics revolution. And if out of all that I couldn't be observant enough to write a couple of thousand songs, make 200 albums, write 35 books, and give a few thousand concerts that mirrored how people during my lifetime felt and lived, I wouldn't have much to show for all those earlier years of preparation.

Did you know during those "years of preparation" that you wanted to be a writer?
I never planned on being a poet. I started writing by keeping a notebook. Actually, that's how my two *Book of Days* had their beginnings. They're only about 30 years late being published. I wanted to paint. To be a painter encompasses everything. I draw and paint every day now—with word and brush.

What was your first poem in print?
I can't remember, but it was published by the *Portland Oregonian* when I was a kid working in the north woods. I remember that being published felt good, but I wasn't about to blow my cover by showing it to my fellow lumberjacks.

How close do you come to writing from life?
I write almost totally from life experiences. That doesn't always please my friends or family. My brother Edward understands my need to write this way better than anyone, and he turns up undisguised in many of my books. Much of my work is confessional. My newest book, *The Sound of Solitude*, is so autobiographical it hurts—and it was the hardest book to get down right. To be able to say that being alone, even lonely, is a plus in life takes work to believe. Solitude is safety. I did 34 rewrites, and then threw out roughly half of the book and started again.

In truth, I'm an outsider. I always have been. No one invites me in, so I know alienation and neglect by their first names.

Do you think a successful writer must be a bit reclusive?
Yes, although I wish it weren't so. Writing is the loneliest occupation in the world. But a poet can't afford to be aloof. Part of the tools of his trade are the people he bumps up against, the situations he encounters, the observations he makes from everyday living.

I have never been able to reconcile social obligations with writing. If work is going well, I miss appointments, ignore long-standing dates. And worse, I've run out of apologies. It's a wonder I have any friends left. Those who don't know me very well must sometimes find me rude, unfeeling, and not worth the time it takes for understanding to settle in.

Tell me about your writing habits.
My writing habits run in cycles. I used to write best at night. When I'm home, my animals [cats and dogs] get me up around 5:30 or 6 a.m. I wake up easily, drink coffee, and swallow half my intake of vitamins while waiting for the first newspaper to arrive. If the paper's late, I start writing or reread the evening paper from the night before. I eat one meal a day (usually breakfast) unless I'm going out later. Breakfast could take place any time between 7 a.m. and 7 p.m. I have to remember to eat. My secretary arrives at 10; we work together, on and off, on mail and other projects, from about noon till 6. If my writing is going well, I don't stop till the evening news on television.

Do you work at the typewriter? Handwrite? Dictate?
I used to write directly on the typewriter. Now I work in longhand. My friend and concert manager, Wade Alexander, usually types the final manuscript for my editor, mainly because my spelling is so bad. A copy is delivered to my agent at the same time. When I'm working in Cal-

ifornia, Eve Kronfeld, who's worked with me since 1968, usually types the final version.

Do you need a special place in which to write?
I write everywhere, but I write best at home. In a hotel room or some such foreign place, I have to get to the point where I take the paintings on the wall, the view from the window, whatever, for granted before I can settle down to write.

The greatest luxury of writing at home, in addition to familiar surroundings, is being able to leave things where they are between spells of writing. Even my animals respect my clutter.

How do you organize your writing day?
The prose writer has an easier time of sticking to any kind of writing routine than poets. Most poets are lazy. That's why I write songs and film scores and extended classical works. Whenever I have writer's block in a certain area, I switch to something else.

What do you think generates writer's block, and how can a writer handle it?
Usually fatigue or maybe something isn't going right in other areas of your life. But a writer must be able to disassociate himself from all of that or even take advantage of it. In the case of my recent block, I stared at the wall for a while, blankly watched television, and tried other projects not involved with poetry. Finally, after not leaving my room for nearly three weeks, I ventured outside and into the street. That did it. I ran back home and words started gushing out. All of them weren't good or of use, but I was writing again. Usually, if something isn't going smoothly, I switch to something else. Play with the animals. Take a walk.

But I try to write every day. That way I stay in training. Developing good writing habits is a must if you're serious about your work. I envy Gay Talese. He's the best-organized writer I know. He's methodical in his preparation and completes almost all of his research before writing a single word. That's probably why his finished product seems so effortless.

When you're writing a poem, which comes first— character, idea, structure or theme?
The idea always seems to sort out the structure. If the theme and character are very far away from the idea,

the poem won't work, or it splits and becomes another poem or several poems, or nothing but fodder for the wastebasket.

Do you keep notes on ideas?
I'm deadly afraid of being caught without a pencil and paper. I may start something on the back of a magazine, misplace it, and finish it years later. Once the situation or the emotion is set, it's easily recaptured if it's valid. Lots of scraps of paper get thrown away.

Do you outline a poem before you write it?
I suppose if I were to work on an epic poem, an outline on paper would be a must. Nearly all of my books are thematic, so before I commit anything to paper, I have a mental outline of the work as a whole. Sometimes a group of poems I've written over an extended period of time will compile themselves for me. I can't honestly admit outlining individual poems very often. As far as lyrics for songs go, outlines are the rule, not the exception. As it stands now, *A Soldier of the Heart* is an outlined poem because it has been germinating for three or four years.

How vivid are individual characters in your mind before you begin a poem?
Very vivid. "Tom & Andrew Enter the Eighties," from *The Beautiful Strangers*, and "Spencer's Mountain," a long poem in *The Sound of Solitude*, are straight jobs of reporting. I only left out the last names. "A Cat Named Sloopy" might be a better poem if it *didn't* have its basis in as much reality as it does. More and more I like to work from fragments, because fleshing something out, developing it, while it's really unexplainable, is fun and good, hard work.

How do you feel about rewriting?
The older I get, the more I rewrite. *The Power Bright and Shining* had seven complete revisions. *The Book of Days* represents years of work. As an example, one edition had about 75 revisions after it was published.

I do a lot of rewriting while a poem is in progress. But there always comes a time when you have to let go, leave the work alone. Auden rewrote his poems all his life. He told me once that a poet should never be satisfied. I agree.

Have you ever abandoned a piece of work?

> *Unless your desire to be published overrides everything in your life, poetry is one field you can forget about. I can't say the sacrifices are worth it.*

I completed a book entitled *The Morning of My Life*. It had been advertised and carried in the Simon & Schuster catalog for two years. Nan Talese, my editor at the time, read it and pronounced it "the most depressing book I've ever read." She was absolutely right. That same year, I substituted a more upbeat work, *Celebrations of the Heart*, which became one of my biggest sellers. Now and again I read *The Morning of My Life* and take something from it. But I doubt that I'll ever have the courage or the folly to publish the whole work.

Is there an easy answer to being successful as a poet?
No, other than to work hard and care about what you do. There are contests that offer publication of your work as a prize, but beware of any that charge an entry fee. Some of the university presses will take a chance on new poets. Far from diminishing, the market for poetry of all kinds seems to be expanding. Not only do we have the regional poetry and literary magazines, but national publications as diverse as *Playboy* and *The New York Times* use poetry. And they use poems by the nonestablished or little-known poet. Local newspapers publish poetry as fillers. *Writer's Market* is updated each year, and it provides the names and addresses of a number of periodicals that publish poetry. Your local librarian probably knows of poetry societies in your town and can give you an idea of local publications that foster new poets.

Talent is never enough in any field; it must be coupled with perseverance and the need for recognition. Unless your desire to be published overrides everything in your life, poetry is one field you can forget about.

I can't honestly say the sacrifices are worth it. Every individual must decide for himself. But the sacrifices do outweigh the rewards, monetary and otherwise, unless you're very, very lucky. More to the point of your question, you're successful if you feel you are.

Do you think formal education has much effect on a writer's success?
I've had less than four years of formal education, though the honorary degrees are beginning to pile up, which is nice. I prefer work to study. But I don't recommend my way of life for anyone else.

Writing can't be taught, but if the natural talent is there, it can be improved. A grasp of language never hurt anyone. Writing courses are fine as long as they don't take away individuality. The best thing about workshops

is that they are supportive. The young writer needs encouragement, especially from a successful peer. But if native talent is missing, it's the instructor's duty to say so.

Any other advice?
Keep themes and characters separate from yourself as much as possible, give them individual voice, watch out for self-pity. Don't get so close to the imagined accident or love affair that it actually happens to you. Care about the characters and situations—but let them interact by themselves; don't join in on the action.

> *The world needs writers. We will always be necessary. There are few professions that can claim that distinction.*

The poet, if he or she wants to be understood, should write in the language of today. While I've had no formal training in psychology, I find it easy to identify with the average human being. A great many of us have common hopes, desires and needs. I write about what I know, but I'm not afraid to explore the unknown. Human nature is complicated, but each of us sets up a number of those complications. The trick is to reduce each of them to basics. There are roots from which the complications and appendages in everyone stem. It isn't difficult to find those roots or initial premises once you've set up certain rules for your own thinking and writing. For instance, no matter how smart you think you are, how gifted or intellectual, never write over, under or around people. Write straight ahead. The only way to protect the language is to use it simply and straightforwardly. Writers are only communicators. We are not some lofty breed meant to speak only to other writers. If we are given the gift to communicate, we should not abuse it.

When should a poet begin to think in terms of a book, rather than individual poems and submissions to magazines and journals?
Once you've had poetry published in magazines, journals and newspapers, it's much easier to get a publishing house to look at your collection. You can argue persuasively that the combined circulation of the periodicals you've been published in might warrant a book. Publishers want to make money, and you have to persuade them that your collection is a money-maker. Most publishing houses even discourage their name authors who write in other media from writing poetry. Or if they do publish a prose author's book of sonnets, they do so out of accommodation. Nan Talese saw to it that Margaret Atwood's work had a larger audience. If I could find an interested publishing house, I'd lend my name and work hard at ed-

iting and promoting new poets in a special series every year. I know how to market poetry, and I know what's needed in the marketplace. I believe poetry can make money for publishers, and I'd love to have the opportunity to prove it with some enterprising publisher not afraid of new ideas.

How can a poet today reach a mass audience?
To reach a mass audience, a poet should give readings, go on book tours and meet his public, appear on television (there are many more arenas open in this area now that we've entered what I call the "Electric '80s" with pay and cable TV). Hang out. Make friends with other poets just beginning. Pester successful poets. Most of us won't like it, but you can try. In short, a poet should be accessible and willing to be self-promoting.

What writers have influenced your work?
It is impossible to be a successful American writer and not have been influenced by what I call the four cornerstones of the American language: Walt Whitman, Henry Thoreau, Langston Hughes and Carl Sandburg. They helped invent and influence our native speech. The real American language.

Walt Whitman, first and foremost. I've been tagged "the people's poet," but that distinction always belongs to Whitman. Robinson Jeffers, E.E. Cummings, William Carlos Williams, Dag Hammarskjold, Thomas Merton. Mao Tse-tung's poems on The Long March are very nonpolitical, depending on whose translation you read. Homer, Robert Burns, Eliot, Robert Frost, Ezra Pound, James Dickey, Pablo Neruda. Certainly Truman Capote's prose and that of Hemingway. Charles Plymell—a more recent influence—writes with such immediacy you feel each poem will be his last. Byron, some of the San Francisco group, Indian, Chinese and Japanese poetry, American Indian poetry and journalists whose names I've long forgotten who remembered the who, what, where and why commandment in the first paragraph of articles in every newspaper or magazine I picked up when I was a kid. I've read several translations of Michelangelo's poetry that stayed with me. Early German poetry and prose had great style and feeling.

I like contemporary novels, but I'm easily bored by them. None approach the early Dickens understanding of the human psyche. The first works of American southern writers I find almost flawless—only when they drift north do some begin to lose their individuality. Russell Baker's *Growing Up* is one of the best autobiographies ever.

I've left out more than I've mentioned, but there's a start. Even if you don't come away with an individual style after reading the authors listed, you'll have developed a set of prejudices (which is good for any author), and you'll be better read than most of us who write for a living. For God's sake, stay away from Kahlil Gibran and Robert Service. Everyone's imitating them. The same probably goes for early Rod McKuen. Sometimes I think I have nearly as many imitators as readers.

What are your long-range plans?
Every year I promise myself this will be the year I take some time off. I think by now I've earned a vacation, since I've been working more or less constantly since I was 11. But new things come up. A film score. An idea for a book. A friend needs a song for an album. I get a classical commission.

I suppose that after so many years of the telephone not ringing, now when calls come in offering the chance for new fantasies to be lived out or an opportunity to prove something to myself that seems important at the time, I'm reluctant to say no.

I made a list not long ago of things I wanted to write about: ideas, book titles, outlines. The list was 14 double-spaced pages, covering 80 separate items. If I were to remake that list today, some projects would be dropped, others added. But I confess there are times when I wake up in the morning and the tension in my head and back is so great, I feel like packing it all in. It's as if a great weight were pulling me down and under. Those times don't come often, but when they do, they are real and they are hell.

Some*one*, somebody, will come along one day soon and lift that weight permanently—or help me carry it. I believe that, because I believe in love. Whatever it is I did with my life or am doing with it, it wasn't for me, so it figures that somewhere down the line someone waits that I can turn it over to. Why do I go on seeking new adventures of the heart? Why not? I may be set about my ways, but a shakeup couldn't hurt.

Writing is a privilege. A joy. A pain in the ass. The easiest thing in the world to do. The most difficult feat to pull off. It is profound. It is ridiculous. Better than making love. Akin to dying. More trouble than it's worth. Like rolling down a hill. Like scaling the Alps. Whatever it is— and it's all of the above—it's not for amateurs. You really have to want to write, to write. The world needs writers. There has been no world known to us that didn't have poets. We will always be necessary. There are few professions that can claim that distinction.

BY MICHAEL SCHUMACHER

JOSEPH HELLER

I've not written one book in which humor was the intention.

*I*n December 1981, Joseph Heller, in the middle of writing the book that would become *God Knows*, was stricken with Guillain-Barre syndrome, a virus that attacked his central nervous system and left him virtually paralyzed. The disease rendered him helpless, unable to hold a pencil or sheet of paper, to stand or walk. His swallowing was so impeded that he was fed through a tube in his nose. He spent nearly six weeks in an intensive care unit, another six months working with physical and occupational therapists.

It was the sort of illness that Capt. Yossarian, the bombardier in *Catch-22*, could appreciate; Yossarian periodically checked into hospitals to avoid bombing missions. Heller's "painless" ailment, however, afforded him anything but an unofficial period of R&R. Besides his physical problems, Heller was going through a particularly rough stretch that found him financially depleted and saw the bitter legal struggle that terminated a marriage that began in 1945.

In 1986, Putnam published *No Laughing Matter*, Heller's detailed, touching and occasionally very funny account of his illness and its aftermath. Co-written with Speed Vogel, Heller's longtime friend and indispensable companion during the illness, the book was Heller's first work of nonfiction. It was a challenge: denied the novelist's array of stylistic quirks and tricks (especially his trademark habits of exaggerating event and looping time structure within his books), Heller found himself concerned with presenting the occasionally gruesome facts in a manner that might be instructive, inspirational and entertaining; furthermore, he had to do so while working with someone who had never written a book. The result received the response that has, by now, become customary with any Joseph Heller book: the critics were divided and vocal about its merits, and the public bought it briskly.

Heller has said that he always wanted to be a writer, but his career took a long time to develop. Born in 1923, the youngest of three children, Heller spent his childhood in the largely Jewish and Italian Coney Island section of Brooklyn. At eleven, he was writing imitative short stories and submitting them, without success, to magazines like *Collier's* and *Liberty*, and to the *New York Daily News*, which then published short fiction every day. After high school, he joined the Army Air Corps, where he flew 60 missions, as a bombardier, during the Italian Campaign of World War II.

The army sent paperbacks to GIs overseas; Heller read a great deal, and he began to write again. By the time he returned to the U.S. and was attending N.Y.U. on the GI Bill, he was a polished enough writer to have some short stories accepted by *Esquire*, *The Atlantic Monthly*, *Gentleman's Quarterly* and *Story*. One of his stories, "Castle of Snow," a piece about an impoverished Jewish family living in the United States during the Depression, was reprinted in *The Best Short Stories of 1949*, establishing Heller as one of the bright new talents of his generation. Despite his early success, Heller remained

---

"I'm out of answers anymore," Joseph Heller told Michael Schumacher just before this 1987 interview began, "having to do with being a writer, about a writer's place in society and all that. I no longer have answers for them."

Fortunately, the 66-year-old author of Catch-22—*the novel so successful it's become part of our language—found a few answers. Heller, at work on what would become the 1988 release* Picture This, *prefaced the above comment by saying—as neither complaint nor apology—that he was uncomfortable with long, detailed discussions about a creative process he doesn't fully understand. What emerged was a friendly discussion about humor (of course), writers' objectives and* survival.

skeptical of what he considered to be his imitations of the popular writers of the day, stories designed to fit into editorial slots. "By the time I finished college," he said, "I had a critical sense, and I was intelligent enough to know that what I was writing was not much good. I wasn't even writing out of my own experience as much as writing out of my experience of reading other people's work."

He continued his education, receiving a master's degree in American Literature at Columbia, studying English literature on a Fulbright scholarship at Oxford. For a decade after his graduation, Heller worked his way through a series of jobs. He worked at his fiction off and on, but little became of it until a pair of sentences—"It was love at first sight. The first time he saw the chaplain, Someone fell madly in love with him"—gave him the seed of an idea for a novel. The unnamed Someone became Yossarian, and by working out his story on a series of 3x5 index cards, a practice he still employs today, Heller conceived the twisting, wandering, poignant and painfully funny novel that became *Catch-22*.

The hardcover book was published in 1961, to a generally apathetic public, receiving notice only after S.J. Perelman cited its merits, but the paperback edition of the book, hitting the stands about the time the fledgling anti-Vietnam War movement was developing, became an ideological textbook for the New Left—*required* reading. Along with Kurt Vonnegut and Thomas Pynchon, Heller became one of *the* voices of a literature of the absurd that decried the immorality of war and the hypocrisy of modern American life.

Thirteen years passed between the publication of Heller's first and second books. During that period, he taught creative writing. His first play, *We Bombed in New Haven*, went nowhere, though it was well received by critics. He wrote the screenplay for the film version of Helen Gurley Brown's *Sex and the Single Girl*. An excerpt from a novel-in-progress, *Something Happened*, appeared in *Esquire* in September 1966, but as the years advanced without Heller's producing the book, there was speculation that he may have been a "one-book wonder."

Alfred Knopf's publication of *Something Happened* became one of the literary events of 1974. The book club and paperback deals, established prior to publication, afforded Heller the luxury of becoming a full-time writer. The novel, a dark, first-person account of the psychological disintegration of Bob Slocum, corporate and family man and, arguably, one of the most detestable main characters of his day, was as different from *Catch-22* as one could have imagined. Many critics, perhaps expecting the short and outrageous episodes that gave *Catch-22* its charm, tore into the new book.

In *Good as Gold* (1979) Heller returned to a more outrageous style of humor, detailing the farcical political aspirations of Bruce Gold, Jewish writer, product of Coney Island, family scapegoat, and social climber. As in *Catch-22*, the absurd characters in *Good as Gold* were often contemptible but given to moments of painful lucidity.

God Knows (1984), an irreverent accounting of the life of the Bible's King David, easily became Heller's most controversial work. Based on the Old Testament books of Samuel and Kings, *God Knows* began with David on his deathbed, ruminating about his life, his running feud with God, his failed relationship with Bathsheba, and his contempt for their son, Solomon, who David saw as little more than a money-grubbing, mentally bumbling *klutz*. Heller's technique of adding one-liners to actual Biblical quotes, as well as his use of anachronism to underscore his humor, angered his book attackers.

Only a few lingering aftereffects of GBS—a slight trembling of his hands and a difficulty pronouncing certain words being the most noticeable—remain as reminders of the trauma that gave him the subject of his most recent book. He seems at ease with his life and career, and while he admits to becoming exhausted after an hour or so of talking for the record, he is candid and direct—a man who looks at you when he speaks, offers straightforward answers, and punctuates many of his remarks with the laughter you would expect from a man who has built a career on making others laugh.

When I was reading No Laughing Matter, *I had this picture in my mind of you in this* Johnny-Got-His-Gun *scenario, and I thought that that has to be the biggest fear an artist can have: to have your creative mind active and fertile, but not be able to execute it.*
If I had ever thought of that as a permanent condition, it would have been appalling to me, perhaps unbearable. But I was in the middle of a book, and I do most of my writing in my head, anyway. I did not realize that I would be invalid for as long as I would be, so that didn't become my most pressing concern in the beginning. The ironic part to me was that, on the day I decided to call the doctor, I got a phone call from the woman who was typing for me, and she had 200 pages and offered to deliver them to my apartment. I told her to wait. I had a feeling that what I was experiencing was mysterious enough that I'd probably have to go to the hospital. Then I called her from the hospital and said for her to bring it up to the medical intensive care unit—I wanted to work on it there, while I was lying in bed. And, of course, I couldn't hold the pages by the next day.

At that time you were a couple hundred pages into God Knows—
Exactly 325 typewritten pages. I had 125, and she brought exactly 200.

And you were pretty confident that you were going to finish this book, even when you were debilitated?
I was not confident once I began to understand the illness. No, that didn't come until I began improving and

was out of medical danger. Then it was just given to me in a very gentle way that I would need a rehabilitation hospital. When I got to the rehabilitation hospital and realized how long it was going to take and saw that there was no guarantee of recovery, then I began to wonder. I was fortunate in this respect, also: the more typical case affects the extremities severely in what they call the praxal muscles; with me, it was the reverse. I never lost complete use of my fingers or my hands. When I got to the rehabilitation hospital and they looked at me and asked a few questions, they could tell by the way I could move my hands and arms that I would be able to work again, be able to use a typewriter and a pencil. So, by the time I realized the potential seriousness of it, the permanent seriousness of it, I'd already escaped most of the dangers.

Would you have been satisfied if that had been it as far as your career was concerned?
No. To begin with, I wouldn't have been able to pay the medical expenses. I was in bad financial shape, even before this happened. There were two bad years with income. One of the things that Anthony Burgess touched on, in his review in the Sunday *Times*, is the misconception that people have about how much money a successful novelist makes. I would not have had enough money, if I were to remain permanently crippled. I had no wife to go back to, no home to go back to. I don't know how I would have lived. I was thinking of a veteran's hospital. I also know this: I could not be a writer and dictate. It's so remote. Possibly I could conceive television plots and dictate dialogue, but I don't really have a television mind. It would've been the end.

Even before I left the hospital, I was able to read those pages—start reading and thinking. I was using a pencil to make the changes I wanted. By August, I was rewriting those 200 pages. But if I didn't have my arms or hands, I don't know what I would've done.

Did you feel a compelling need to write about your illness?
No, no—not at all.

It seems that writers need to write about matters that gravely affect them, which may, for example, explain the glut of novels that came out after World War II.
I don't think it's that; I was not gravely affected by World

War II. What happens is they're given an experience that lends itself to dramatization or novelization. I think most writers—and I'm excluding now the adventure and mystery writers—will write about episodes meaningful to them in terms of their own imaginations. Now that would include a great deal of what they experienced, but I'm not sure there was an autobiographical intention so much as the use of experience. That's been true in my case: I believe I'm telling the truth when I say that, when I wrote *Catch-22*, I was not particularly interested in war; I was mainly interested in writing a novel, and that was a subject for it. That's been true of all my books. Now what goes into these books does reflect a great deal of my more morbid nature—the fear of dying, a great deal of social awareness and social protest, which is part of my personality. None of that is the objective of writing. Take five writers who have experienced the same thing, and they will be completely different as people, and they'd be completely different in what they do write, what they're *able* to write.

When *No Laughing Matter* came up, it was an unusual opportunity for me to write something different than I had written, to write nonfiction. I never thought I could delude myself into thinking I was presenting anything of value to people. People don't write books to benefit humanity [laughs]; they're doing it to satisfy, I believe, an exhibitionist . . .

A creative urge?
Yeah. It's *respectable*. Writing's a respectable occupation, and for me, it's the best form of occupation to have. Very few people do the work they want to do. I'm one of the fortunate ones. I'm doing the work I want to do, and it's also what I'd be doing if I were retired.

This was a rather unusual nonfiction project in that you had experienced what you were writing, yet you had to double back and research it all over again, by obtaining your medical charts, and so forth. What was that like?
The hardest part was reading it, because they don't have good photocopies [laughs]. I was surprised and greatly impressed—I thought more of my doctors and the hospitals when I went over the records than I did at the time, although the attitude I had was not a derogatory one. In sifting out what I would need and what I didn't need, I

> *I* never thought I could delude myself into thinking I was presenting anything of value to people. People don't write books to benefit humanity.

was surprised to find certain reports showing that things happened more slowly or rapidly than they seemed to. But there was not much emotion until I read the book after it was published, and then I would be affected, I began to sympathize with myself and what I went through [laughs]. In the course of writing it, it was just writing. There is that objectivity that I always find in writing; I think of it as being almost ruthlessly indifferent to what the characters experience. To me, to portray effectively some of the most touching scenes—the scenes I *want* to be touching—really requires my not having those feelings in the course of writing it. The effect I have is different from what I want the effect to be on the reader.

You've written some extremely moving scenes. There's that scene in Rome in Catch-22.
Oh, sure. But in writing that, I knew what I wanted to do. There's something manipulating about it, and I don't think an author can do it if he's experiencing, at the time of the writing, what he may have experienced in his imagination or in his life, if it's based on experience. Way back, when I used to read a lot of Shakespeare criticism, I read a critic. . . . Others have said that Shakespeare went through periods of depression when he wrote *Hamlet*, *King Lear* and *Macbeth*, and they said it's because his child died. But this person said that a depressed person cannot write *Hamlet*, *King Lear* and *Macbeth* because the depressed person doesn't work. Imagine Shakespeare writing: he's thinking of the crowds—what will make the scene, what will make them laugh, what will make them cheer.

It surely seems like a manipulative process in your books, such as in Good as Gold, *where you have a moving scene with Sid and Bruce Gold talking seriously and sentimentally about their childhoods, followed by an outrageous scene at one of their family get-togethers. All in a matter of a few pages.*
That was a very quick change, yeah.

And you used humor to heighten your more serious intentions.
I usually do. I contrast with humor and exaggeration and juxtapositions. I don't see life as simple, I don't see characters as simple.
   I don't see people that way. Well, there are people who

> *To portray effectively some of the most touching scenes requires my not having those feelings in the course of writing it.*

are bad and people who are not bad, but my view of the people I experience is usually complex and ambiguous, and that is often what I try to present in the books. A subtle touch, I think in *Good as Gold*, is that really the most mild character is this obnoxious, objectionable father. He's the only one with a conscience, really. He won't forgive Roosevelt and he hates the Rockefellers [laughs]. Gold was aware of the moral ambiguity that he was going through, but old Julius Gold says: "In my generation, we didn't send parents off to nursing homes to die. When they got sick, we kept them at home." And then: "That bastard Roosevelt . . . " [laughs] It's a rare old Jew who would say that.

You also established much of the book's humor through your use of Yiddish. I thought it was funny, and I don't even know what most of those words mean.
I must tell you that I don't know many of them either. I was just hoping that context would convey the meaning. I had to ask friends how to say certain things; they had to spell them.

Having King David call Solomon a putz, *in* God Knows, *was doubly funny because readers have their preconceptions about Solomon.*
See, there is a degree of accuracy in that quote, because if you read the passages on Solomon, there's nothing there—nothing at all—to indicate any intelligence. He was very much a tyrant and a lecher, confused with religion, and it is *said* he was wise, but there's no evidence of his wisdom, except for the cutting of the baby in half, and you can take that any way you want to [laughs].

What made you choose the Bible as a subject for a novel?
I didn't decide I wanted to do it until I investigated it mentally. I had the idea, and I did my research, which was to read the first few books of the Bible, through David. Then my imagination worked, and I saw my ending and my beginning, and I saw my central conflict. Then I began making my notes. I've never begun a book that I didn't finish, because I haven't started writing a book until I knew the beginning and the ending, felt that they matched, and felt they associated with enough of a middle. The journey from the opening paragraph to the end would have to make interesting fiction.

Do you still use notecards to determine all this?

Oh, sure. In fact, I'm doing a novel now, and I have the ending written. I'm not sure how to begin the next chapter, or what order the chapters are going to be in, but I have the ending.

How about Catch-22?
That was the truth with *Catch-22*, although I didn't get the ending for months. I wrote the first chapter and began planning it in my head. When a manuscript is finished, I never have to revise it, other than to cut. I do a lot of cutting. But it's because I do slow revision while I'm writing and I *do* think it through.

Is there anything in humor you won't touch, any subject that's off-limits?
No. This may come as a surprise to you, but I use humor sparingly or judiciously [laughs]. I omit some of the ideas for jokes, dialogue or situation that come with each chapter, because I feel it is gratuitous. In *God Knows*, I deliberately used a number of very bad jokes, very old jokes. I've not written one book in which humor was the intention. It's something I like to use to support or complement the basic approach to subject matter. The humor in *Something Happened*, for example, is so muted. If I wanted, I could read to an audience for one hour from *Something Happened*, and they would be rolling with laughter, just from my picking up the parts that are funny. But in the context of that book, in that personality, Slocum couldn't have Joseph Heller's humor. He didn't have my life; he was not a successful writer. Other than that, the humor is used almost all ironically, and almost in an unhappy way.

That seemed to be the case with Catch-22. *So much of that book's humor was ironic.*
Yeah, but in *Catch-22*, there's farce, there's burlesque, and there's parody—just about the whole range of humor. In *Something Happened*, there isn't. In *Good as Gold*, it's a combination of something, and in *God Knows*, it's still something else.

In Good as Gold *and* God Knows, *you made humorous notations addressing criticism of your own work. In* God Knows, *you have Bathsheba criticize David's psalms with the claim that "some are masterpieces, but, like everything you write, they're flawed by excessive length."*
[laughing] Oh, yeah. And in *Good as Gold*, there's one where Gold criticizes Dickens because he's long-winded and because of all the unlikely coincidences in his books. There's one chapter where I begin the book as a book: "The thought arose that he was spending an awful lot of time in this book eating and talking."

How do those things occur to you?
It's easy to think of; what's difficult is to know not to go

too far with it. I originally had one of the dialogues [in *Good as Gold*], in which either Ralph or Gold says, "it's just like *Catch-22*" [laughs]. It's something somebody else might use, but I felt that I should not do that.

There's even irony to the titles of your books: they're all American idiom or cliche—
With the exception of *Catch-22*.

Which is now cliche [laughter].
After *Catch-22*, I followed that with the four books, from *Something Happened* through *No Laughing Matter*. I'm not going to stick to it, though.

Sometime you had to come to the conclusion that humor or farcical situation was your strong suit in writing. Do you remember when that was?
No, I don't except that it was there in my plan for *Catch-22* without my even being aware of it. I recall writing the first chapter and having a friend read it, and hearing him laugh and say, "this is funny." I was not aware that I was being funny enough, and once I realized that, I began using it. As a child, I was witty and did practical jokes. The practical jokes almost always involved some kind of farcical concept, so it's there in my personality, and I think I have no choice but to use it.

Realism is not my forte. Plot suspense isn't. I would fail if I were going to write a Robert Ludlum book—or even a John Updike book. My imagination does not produce anything like that, and it would be inferior. I have maybe two or three things I do well, and I think I'm astute enough to make use of them and not try to do anything I can't do.

As a writer, do you have a concept of success?
Success is much better than failure [laughs]. I have almost no complaints about writing. As a writer, I feel fairly fulfilled because I write only what I want to write and never have to work with anybody I dislike. To me, that measures the success: to do what I want to do and not associate with people I don't want to.

It's almost inevitable that you be asked about Catch-22 *in comparison to your other books. If one were to see a body of work as one's offspring, you had what might be considered a genius for your firstborn. That puts a lot of pressure on those who follow, and I can't help but wonder about the fates of the others.*
Well, what's happening in the last few years is that more and more people are telling me they think *Something Happened* is my best novel, or that it's become their favorite. It's usually preceded with "Now, I loved *Catch-22*, but *Something Happened* is the one that meant the most to me." Of all my novels, it was the hardest to do successfully, so it has a special place for me. It's hard to write a long book about a man leading a boring life—

knowing it—without making the book boring, yet having the book reflect that personality.

I remember reading somewhere that you wrote Catch-22 *as if it were going to be your only book.*

I also said that I wanted to write the book I would love to read if somebody else had written it.

Did you succeed?
Oh yeah [laughs]. I never read it, but I'm going to . . .

BY BILL STRICKLAND

TOM ROBBINS

Insist on joy in spite of everything.

Tom Robbins leans against the roll-top desk in his writing room. Along the far wall hang prints of his novel covers: *Another Roadside Attraction,* which sold more than 750,000 copies; *Even Cowgirls Get the Blues,* a million-copy bestseller; *Still Life With Woodpecker,* 600,000 sales; and *Jitterbug Perfume,* with half a million copies in print.

But none of that matters right now. What's important is that someone—his housekeeper, probably—rearranged his table-top of toy motorcycles. They all face the same direction now. Straight. Orderly.

"This is terrible," Robbins says. His head quivers just a bit; he might be shaking his head inside his head. "I had them all arranged how I wanted—" and now his hands move, describe crazy lopsided circles and invisible cycles careening away from each other—"in all different directions. And now they're straight."

It might be one of his own wild metaphors—Tom Robbins seating the description of his style on a toy motorcycle: swerve like a madman and never let the housekeeper catch you:

The day was rumpled and dreary. It looked like Edgar Allan Poe's pajamas.

. . . an afternoon squeezed out of Mickey Mouse's snout, an afternoon carved from mashed potatoes and lye, an afternoon scraped out of the dog dish of meteorology.

A noisy unstoppable churning wheel of fear that rolls out of the altitudes like the flat tire off God's Cadillac . . .

A teardrop hung out of each blue eye, like a fat lady leaning out of a tenement window.

The noise at the gates sounded like Cecil B. DeMille's garage sale.

"Bohemian Embassy."

That's how he answers the phone, in the slow, measured tone of his southern Virginia upbringing, inflection leapfrogging syllables to stress the end. "Bohemian Embassy." He might not be joking. If there is such a place, it could be Robbins's Pacific Northwest home—shielded from a small touristy fishing town by an unfinished Zen garden. And if there is such an ambassador, it is Robbins.

Robbins—who produced the only novel with the amoeba as mascot, who wrote the book Elvis was reading in the bathroom before his death—began life in 1936 in North Carolina. While moving through a series of small towns near Richmond, Virginia, he discovered writing through his mother, a nurse who wrote children's stories for small religious magazines in her spare time.

"But no one seems satisfied with that," Robbins says, sitting on his living room couch after the short, yes-no-yes phone call. He leans forward, hands on knees. Sometimes one hand will reach to his close-cropped beard and scratch or twirl, or just rest. "Everybody wants to pin me down on my childhood introduction to magic and creativity, which *I've* never pinned down."

The appeal of Tom Robbins is that he shows us our nosehairs and warts, but lets us have fun along the way. He flips ordinary objects over, exposing the magical underbelly of the mundane. And he does it all in a style that has been both damned ("Oblique, florid, willing to sacrifice everything for an old joke or corny pun"—The New York Times Book Review) and praised ("Mixing the lunatic and the thoughtful—doing a literary watusi up every page and jitterbugging back down"—Publishers Weekly), a style that has taken him from underground classic to bestseller.

In this 1988 romp through his "Bohemian Embassy," Robbins mulls the seriousness of whimsy, the secrets of effective images and the joy of struggling to write.

The comparable adult moment would come more than 20 years later, after several unfinished college careers—including one cut short after being expelled from his fraternity for flipping peas and biscuits down the housemother's cleavage—and jobs with the *Richmond Times-Dispatch* and *Seattle Times.* All of which left Robbins vaguely dissatisfied. "I had taken LSD very early on, in 1963, and I didn't know anyone else who had. I had the sense some immense cultural changes were stewing, but where I was, there was no one to share them with. I was trying to keep my hand in fiction, but couldn't put anything together. Something was missing.

"One day, I had gone to the bank, and was hurrying back to the *Seattle Times,* back to my job. I was walking very fast and very intently, with my coattails flapping and my tie swinging over my shoulder. I was a harried young man, on the way up. And in the distance, I saw a figure approaching—a man with red hair, bewhiskered not like he cultivated a beard, but more like he'd been drunk for four days and hadn't shaved. Wearing a World War II overcoat, the hem dragging the sidewalk.

"And he was singing, walking up the sidewalk singing. When he got really close to me—he was watching me all the way because I was watching him—he looked at me in the face and laughed, burst out in derisive laughter. It was as if he had seen through me, and registered all my areas of discontent, and then laughed at it all. He might have been a mesquilito, a peyote god, a Pan-like figure. I just call him the red-headed wino.

"On Monday I called in to work well. I said, 'I've been sick for a long time, but I'm well today so I can't make it in.' I went to New York."

There, in the momentum of the counterculture, and later in San Francisco, Robbins found the stimulus he'd been seeking. He returned to Seattle to collect his thoughts and took a job writing art columns for *Seattle Magazine.* He married and he and his wife "made enough to live on—almost." By chance, the art columns caught the attention of Luther Nichols, an editor with Doubleday, who arranged a meeting with Robbins to discuss buying a book on West Coast art.

"Without any justification, I assumed he meant a novel," Robbins says. "He told me what he really wanted, and I was disappointed, but I told him I really wanted to write a novel. Then it was his turn to be disappointed. But we both concealed our disappointments, and he asked about the novel.

"I told him all I knew. I said, 'It's about the discovery of the mummified body of Christ in the catacombs under the Vatican and its subsequent theft and reappearance in America in a roadside zoo.' His ears pricked up, and he wanted to know more. I improvised. At the end of our meeting, he asked to see the manuscript."

Fleetwood gets in the car. "Hey dad, have you seen *Manhunter?* This guy specializes in psychotic crimes—"

"He specializes?" Robbins hoots, looking in the back seat, lifting a hand from the steering wheel and offering to shake. "Hi Fleet, I specialize in chain saws . . ."

Fleetwood, who would have been named Kubrick had he been a girl, is Robbins's son from his now-ended marriage. Fleet's freckled and mildly punk-haired, and working summers for a tulip factory.

"They sort tulips here, ship them to Holland, and old people import them back," Robbins explains. Except for tennis shoes the color of faded Yellow Pages, Robbins is dressed in black. Looking at father and son, you might guess 20 years separates them. It's closer to 40, but Robbins has the kind of Etch-A-Sketch face that shakes off lines at will, and his hair, perhaps in defiance to its graying, remains curly-unruly.

On the drive to the tulip factory, Robbins had talked about the writers he's grouped with—Vonnegut, Pynchon, Brautigan, and Heller—and those he feels closer to—Gabriel Garcia Marquez and Gunter Grass. He had talked about the weather and grocery stores. And he had explained the serious side of whimsy.

"Hold on to your questions," he'd said. "What I want to talk about is growing up. A number of people took the last sentence of *Still Life With Woodpecker,* 'It's never too late to have a happy childhood,' to mean that we shouldn't grow up. That's a total misinterpretation. I'm saying just the opposite. It's really telling people to grow up. Have that happy childhood and then get on with your life. Shift that to writing: You have to do whatever it takes to get on with that happier life. There will be a struggle, all writers struggle. If you want to succeed, you'll get through."

Mr. Million-seller. That's easy for him to say, right? It's easy *now.* It wasn't always.

His first book, *Another Roadside Attraction,* was published in 1971, sold only 2,200 copies in hardcover, and was out of print in 1975. Even the paperback edition sold so slowly at first that it barely earned back its $3,500 advance. It was a tough time for Robbins and his wife. His second book, *Even Cowgirls Get the Blues,* was nearly finished, but he received only a meager offer from Doubleday. He seemed confined to midlist success—and midlist advances.

"I got an advance I couldn't really live on. I needed to be working full time somewhere, making a living. But I wanted to finish *Cowgirls.* So we made midnight shopping trips to the produce fields, stole cabbage and cauliflower and spinach out of the fields, and that was the bulk of our diet."

His agent had been tending other fields. She showed a copy of *Cowgirls* to an editor at Bantam, who promptly offered a $50,000 advance—if Robbins could somehow buy back his old contract.

"I wrote Doubleday a sob story, saying I had prostate trouble, I was sitting on a blowtorch and wanted out of the contract. Two people loaned me 25 hundred dollars apiece. I was a success."

That's where he is today, happy childhood and struggling writerhood behind him, in the middle of a fifth novel. He works steadily once he's started a book but takes time between to travel or write an occasional short nonfiction piece. Talk of movies reminds him that he had a bit part, as a toymaker in heaven, in friend Alan Rudolph's *Made In Heaven* (1987). "I got to write my own dialogue," he says, "but they took my best line and gave it to Debra Winger."

Not to worry. There are sure to be more.

When people think of Tom Robbins, they think of metaphors and similes. How do you create images?
Maybe it's in my DNA. My writing pulls me in that direction, but once there, I have to concentrate on evoking images. Usually, it comes from looking at what I want to describe. Either actually looking at it, or forming a picture in my mind. If I look long enough, associations reveal themselves."

But "the sun is an orange" doesn't get it. You'd elaborate on that.
Yeah, something a little more unpredictable, in order to allow a leap of consciousness to take place in the reader. You want to create an image that will surprise a reader, make him remember the story. That can't happen with a predictable phrase.

How do you decide when to use imagery?
Most of it has to do with the rhythm of a sentence. I'm very concerned with the rhythm of language. "The sun came up" is an inadequate sentence. Even though it conveys all the necessary information, rhythmically it's lacking.

The sun came up.

But, if you say, as Laurie Anderson said, "The sun came up like a big bald head," not only have you, perhaps, entertained the fancy of the reader, but you have made a more complete sentence. The sound of a sentence.

Rhythm aside, how do you know if the picture you're evoking is too ridiculous to be accepted?
Well, you know when it doesn't work.

But you don't know how you know when it doesn't work.
No. Anything that works, works [laughs]. Anything that works is good. I don't think there are any rules in fiction.

Rules that can't be broken.

In creative writing classes, one of the cardinal rules is "Don't preach." I happen to preach somewhat in my fiction. Both of my grandfathers are Southern Baptist ministers, so I came by the pulpit naturally. But I always tried to keep the preaching to a minimum, and always felt a little guilty about it. I thought perhaps it was a flaw in my work, even though I was committed to it to the point where I couldn't eliminate it totally.

And then it occurred to me one day: why can't you preach? There are epistolary novels, psychiatric case history novels, stream-of-consciousness novels—why not the sermon novel? If you can make it work. The trick is to make it work. So I very deliberately wrote a couple of sermons into *Jitterbug Perfume*, with the idea that I was going to make them fit into the plot so smoothly that everything would work, add to the book rather than subtract.

So, *make it work* is maybe the only rule.

That freedom to ignore strictures opens up some wonderful techniques. A description in Jitterbug Perfume *of the god Pan comes to mind. Instead of a physical description, you portray him through a litany of titles: "Yes, Mr. Goat Foot . . . you, Mr. Charmer, Mr. Irrational, Mr. Instinct, Mr. Gypsy Hoof, Mr. Clown; you Mr. Body Odor, Mr. Animal Mystery . . . Mr. Bark at the Moon, Mr. Wayward Force . . ." It goes on and on; it's not an ordinary, physical description, but readers get a clear idea of Pan. How do techniques like that occur to you?*
Boy I wish I knew [laughs]. I wish I knew how to make that happen. I would do it a lot more than I do. It's just this fortuitous . . . I don't know. It's a mystery to me. I love it when it happens; I'm happy that day.

It has to do with language. Some days you just get into a particular relationship with language that's a bit offskew yet perfect. It probably started out, I said "Mr. Goat Foot," then I thought "that's not the only way I want to describe him, so maybe instead of Mr. Goat Foot I should say Mr. Shaggy"—or whatever. And then I thought, "Well, I like Goat Foot too, so I'll say Goat Foot and Shaggy" and then, before long, I liked the way that happened, so I started adding all those others. It's quite organic and unexpected.

But other writers might edit themselves at that point, not include so many titles.

> *You have to eat your technique. Digest it. It's in your blood, but you're not concerned with it anymore.*

You have to trust your intuition. You can't be totally spontaneous, you've got to shape your material, but at the same time, if you put too many restrictions on yourself, you're going to produce dull work. Constricted. Anal-retentive.

Isn't there a danger of being too excessive? In Cowgirls, *you stop the story and turn Chapter 100 into champagne so the reader can celebrate that chapter with you. For some people, that's too much.*

Well, I did that for a very sound philosophical reason. I wanted to relate to the audience in a different way than most writers relate to them. But I also wanted to poke through the narrative, pop out of the narrative, to reaffirm the concreteness of the book itself, to remind the reader that he or she was reading words on a page and, yet, it's still valid.

That's your art background showing.

Yeah—to give some substance to the physical object of a book, to call attention to the book's physicality, and say it doesn't have to be escapism. You don't have to lose yourself in it for the act of reading to be totally fulfilling.

So the primary purpose of imagery is not to entertain, but—

To awaken in the reader his or her own sense of wonder. If you get too predictable and too symmetrical, you lull readers into a—not a literal sleep—but you put part of their brain to sleep. Even if they might stay physically awake and finish your book, their imagination, their sense of wonder, is asleep.

Again, rhythm is also a part of that. Language has to exist in an exalted state to awaken wonder. I'm not interested in colloquial language. If something doesn't have that rhythm, it doesn't have the radiance, the luminosity—it doesn't have the angelic intensity. And if you need to be excessive to awaken the reader, okay. A simpler way to do that is with unexpected words.

I'm thinking of a line in Still Life *when you use* peepee *in a serious sentence. The context called for the word* penis, *but the change startled me into a laugh.*

[Nodding] Exactly. But you have to use the right word. You can't just, like a surrealist, throw in *cucumber* when you mean *cat*. It's important to use inappropriately appropriate words: words that once were used a lot and

now aren't, or words that are just kind of goofy, but yet are precise.

It's not some kind of formula I use. I don't say, "Okay, today I'm going to look for words that are too predictable and put in something that's not predictable." But as I reread a sentence, I frequently see words that are just kind of blah, just kind of conventionally sit there, and I'll think of something else. The unexpected word.

The other thing I wanted to say when you mentioned the champagne chapter is that I've quit doing things like that now because it was getting to be too much of a device. At first it was very natural—it still is natural for me to write like that—but it was starting to become like a shtick. My shtick. So I didn't do that at all in *Jitterbug Perfume*.

In Roadside, *you presented yourself as a character writing the story; in* Cowgirls *you were a character; in* Still Life *you weren't a character, but a very intrusive narrator. You were much less visible in* Jitterbug.

Yeah, and equally so in the one I'm writing now.

Is that a progression? Are you growing as a writer?

No, I'm just tired of doing it. I don't think my absence from the book makes it a better book, or a more mature book. It's just different. Not any better, just different.

Is it any harder for you to stay out of the story?

It's no harder at all. In fact, it's probably even easier. To be able to stop the story, break the reader's attention, make him or her think about something, and then convincingly restart the story takes a lot of control.

But you can't keep doing something like that, because after a while it just gets cute. And that's one of the dangers of playfulness. There's a thin line between playful and cute, and there are often times I stray over the line into cuteness. I know I do. But that's a risk I'm going to take, because I have what I think are really sound philosophical reasons for playfulness.

That's the main criticism you receive in reviews. People say you're more concerned about being funny than telling a story.

The word that I get most often is not *cute* but *whimsical*. Well, in the first place, there's nothing wrong with whimsy. Too many people mistake misery for art. You don't have to be somber to be serious about a subject. My

Get yourself in that extreme state of being next to madness. You should always write with an erection. Even if you're a woman.

characters show that. One of my main themes is *joy in spite of everything.* I don't think that I am pollyannish; my characters suffer, they die. They experience pain, alienation, frustration—all the hardships of life that real people experience. But, my heroes and heroines, the characters with whom I most identify and who are most important to me, all insist on joy in spite of everything.

Not that this is the best of all possible worlds—it's a pretty screwed up world—but they insist on being happy in spite of it. They aren't whiners.

Critics also say your characters aren't believable, that they exist only as tools for your philosophy and jokes.
I'm sorry some people are that shallow. The number of people who have identified with my characters astonishes me. So, if the characters are not real, there are an awful lot of people out there who are not real.

Those critics are mistaking dullness for depth. The universe is playful; quantum physics teaches us, among other things, that the universe is made up of irrevocable laws *and* random playfulness. Evolution is playful. It's always going off on adventures, playing games, taking chances. Evolution frequently does things just for the hell of it—why not writers, too?

Another reason some people think my characters are flat is because I don't develop them in the usual way. I don't paint detailed psychological portraits. I squeeze out little bits of information about them like toothpaste out of a tube. A little dab here, a little dab there, and it's cumulative.

I don't always detail motives for their actions, but I give enough clues that any intelligent person can figure out that what they do is not arbitrary. I'm not interested in the dynamics of the psychological novel. It's been done thousands of times, it's been done extremely well by certain writers, and I simply am bored by it. I'm not saying it's not valid—it's extremely valid—but I'm not interested in it. It isn't necessary to peel away psychological layers of characters, the way you peel an onion, in order for the character to be alive on the page. It simply isn't necessary.

But I don't want to give you the idea—[pause] You can't be too concerned, too occupied, with conforming to a style when you write. I think this is the best way to approach writing: first of all, you have to eat your technique. You can't write technique any more than you can speak grammar. So, you develop some technique, and then you eat it. Digest it. Eliminate it so it's a part of yourself; it's in your blood, but you're not concerned with it anymore.

And then all you do is, you write a sentence and see where it takes you. You take a trip on the page. You go where sentences lead you. It's a journey.

It's a longhand journey for you, isn't it? You periodically break into Still Life *to document a feud with your typewriter, but you actually write longhand, right?*
Well, I write both ways. I bought that Remington electric mentioned in *Still Life* as one of my ill-gotten gains from *Cowgirls,* and I just hated that typewriter. I ended up destroying it.

So the running commentary in Still Life *is authentic?*
Well. of course not 100 percent [laughs]. It's based on actual situations. One day I painted it red because I couldn't stand to look at it any longer and it never worked right after that. I ended up beating it to pieces with a 2x4 and throwing it in a garbage can.

Why? Did you feel distanced from the page?
Part of it was the noise. Electric typewriters buzz. And it was like pressure on me all the time. I write very, very slowly, and it was like the typewriter was pressuring me to write faster. Or to write continuously, rather than sitting and thinking for long periods of time, which I sometimes do.

So that was the main thing. I didn't like the color, and I missed the contact with the page. I like the idea of ink flowing out of my hand and saturating the paper. There's something intimate about that. It's more like you're making something than typing is. I'm thinking about going back to raven quill. And writing in lizard blood.

So how's your writing day go now that the typewriter's dead?
My first two books I wrote longhand and then typed. I have an electronic typewriter now, so it's a lot quieter, completely silent. *Still Life,* I wrote the descriptive passages longhand, and then if there was a long section of dialogue, I wrote it on the typewriter. I can write dialogue on typewriters because it comes to me fast.

Then I pasted together the handwritten and the typewritten pages, and hired Wendy the Typist to learn to read my handwriting. She did the copy I sent to the publisher from that mixture of longhand and typing, which is the same way I'm doing this book.

I work five days a week, 10-3, with a goal of two pages a day. Sometimes I don't get two pages, and sometimes I get a lot more. If I'm doing dialogue, which of course takes up more space anyway, I might get five or six pages.

You're writing incredibly slowly, then. You've said before you spend as much as a half-hour on single sentences.
In one of the first interviews I ever did I said that I didn't rewrite, and somebody wrote a snotty essay in which they brought back to life that bitchy remark of Truman Capote's about Jack Kerouac, [Capote imitation] "That's not writing, that's typing," which is probably the dumbest literary remark that has ever been given any credence.

So I don't ever say that anymore. What I meant is that I write so slowly that I am rewriting as I go along. When you're only doing two pages a day, and you're at your desk for up to six hours a day, that's not just typing. I try never to leave a sentence until it's as perfect as I can make it. I'm not one of those people who sits down and vomits out 20 to 30 pages and comes out with 18 rewritten pages.

I never work ahead of myself. I start with the first sentence—usually I start with the title; I write that on one page, then I turn the page and write the first sentence. Then I write the second sentence. It's very linear, very chronological, although the action and the plot might not be.

You must have the story plotted out beforehand, then.
No. Oh no, God, no. Just a really vague idea.

Jitterbug Perfume *jumps from century to century, city to city, and all the incidents are related. You got every loose end to fit without plotting the story out?*
In the beginning, I had no idea what I was doing [laughs]. That's not true; I had some idea, but I was just following a hunch, following the characters.

Before I send sections to the typist, I double-check for accuracy. Contradictions in the act of writing a novel are like mosquitos on the tundra [smiles]. You're constantly swatting at them, they swarm. You're always fighting the battle of contradictions. As I get sections back from my typist—this new book I'm doing is in seven parts, and I just got the third part back; I not only read that through, but I went back to the beginning to get a sense of the whole book. I've gone over the first three parts several times this past week-and-a-half. That's how I remember which ends are tied and which are open.

Do you set aside time for research?
Begrudgingly, yes. I do most of it here at home. I buy the books instead of searching through libraries for some of the more esoteric stuff. So I order them through the local bookstore and write it off on my income tax [laughs]. I guess that's an advantage of success.

But I think the amount of research I do is deceptive. For *Another Roadside Attraction*, I read 17 books on the historical Christ.

But maybe only a hundredth of that actually shows.
Oh, a thousandth. It's there, it's all there, but between the lines. The book is informed by it even though it's not all there in the way that James Michener would put all of it in.

I try to store my information and let it marinate in my imagination and come out later. I hate to sit down one day, or one week, and research and then go try to write about that. I like as long a period as possible to elapse, so it doesn't come out as research.

Frequently it comes out in your books as digressions

or brief asides. You give a history of whale puke in Jitterbug.
[Laughs] Well, like the chapter of champagne, I'm being more quietly excessive now. In *Another Roadside Attraction*, there were a lot of digressions that contributed absolutely nothing to the plot, but they contributed to the book. There was the plot, and there was the book. I described once the structure of that book as being a series of flashes strung together like beads. Some of the flashes illuminate plot, and others illuminate the reader; they weren't intended to illuminate the plot. But that was all part and parcel of the carefully planned structure of that book.

I do that less now. Whatever research I include is part of the book. It informs the plot, and it's a tighter fit. But you might have to read 60 or 70 pages ahead before you see where the information fits into the plot.

Why don't you use your characters to impart such information?
Two reasons really. One is that you eliminate the middleman. You, the author, know more about what you want to say than the character does, and your character will change it, put it in his or her own voice, and it isn't going to come out the same.

The other reason has to do with the rhythm of the book, the flow of information and words to the reader. It's another way for me to orchestrate the rhythm of what the reader is experiencing: Stop the story. Think about this. Back to the story. Some more thought. I still do that. I'm doing it in the book I'm working on now.

One thing I want to stress about research is that, if you write fanciful fiction, fiction that lopes past reality—I don't mean science fiction, although this applies there also—it must be grounded in reality. You need those 17 books on Christ to stimulate your thought. If you're right about the true facts, people will more easily accept your made-up ones. So you need real facts as a base of departure into more fanciful facts. And you need a lot of different sources.

In an author's note in Cowgirls, *you say that no novel is ever written by one person.*
Oh, yeah. I'm surprised at how few people are willing to acknowledge that. I mean, where do they think these things come from? I don't know if there has ever been a novel in history that has been totally invented. Writers are taking stuff all the time. A painter, a landscape painter, looks out the window and paints what he or she sees. Writers create that way, too. They go to a cocktail party, they take home some of the language, they take home a description of a dress that a fat woman was wearing. They're taking things from their environment constantly. It's all a collage creation.

I'm not sure that there's any such thing as plagiarism. There was a man who took a book published in South

Africa and published it in the United States under his own name. That's plagiarism. But to take a fragment from another writer and put it within a completely different context, I don't think is wrong. I don't own language, I just perform with it.

[Silence]

It's hard for me to give advice. There are some writers who talk beautifully about writing, but it's a pretty obscure process to me. One writer cannot tell another writer, or aspiring writers, what to think about or how to write. People have different metabolisms, different body chemistry. Some people write around the clock for two days, then go to sleep for two days. People just have different habits because of their individual systems. Psychological differences.

But there are some concrete things I think I can tell people that would be helpful. All of these occur away from the writing desk, except the first one, which is *always write*. Whether it's two hours a day or 20 hours a day. Or maybe one full day and a day off. People have their own patterns of activity, but always be in a writing mode.

Then there are four things that, particularly, beginning writers should do to make sure they'll be in that mode, ready to write. It takes two hours a day, and it's just as important as the time you spend at your desk:

Spend half an hour every day doing yoga, or aerobics, or playing handball—something physical to keep you in your physical body. Writers tend to live too much in their heads. Too, too many thoughts. You need to be grounded in your physical body.

Two, you should spend half an hour a day reading poetry. It could be prose, as long as it's not something that's directly related to what you're doing. Not research, but something that will get you excited about language. And, again, that can be different for different sensibilities.

Another half-hour a day should be spent looking at clouds, looking at the sky. Not necessarily a cloudy sky; it could be a night sky, a starry sky. The reason for this is that most of the great philosophical ideas of humankind have come from the sky. Our notions of time, our notions of change, of religion, all came from looking at stars and clouds. It's just very good discipline, philosophically and poetically, to look at the sky.

And then you should spend 30 minutes a day looking at dirty pictures. Or thinking about sex. The purpose of this is to get yourself sexually excited, which builds

Whatever it is everybody seems to hate in your first work, that's what you should work on and develop. That's the thing you do best.

tremendous amounts of energy, and then carry that into your work. Get yourself in that intense state of being next to madness. Keep yourself in, not necessarily a frenzied state, but in a state of great intensity. The kind of state you would be in before going to bed with your partner. That heightened state when you're in a carnal embrace: time stops and nothing else matters. You should always write with an erection. Even if you're a woman.

You have the time for the four-point plan, but what about people who don't have at least two hours a day writing time?

Well, maintaining a pitch next to madness also means following Hermann Hesse's advice to avoid the bourgeois compromise. Don't get yourself in a nice, safe, comfortable bourgeois situation where you're afraid or unable to take risks. Don't become too middle-class. If you're starting out, don't go get married and have several kids and get a mortgage on a house, because you're going to get yourself in a situation where you aren't willing to take the kind of risks that really good writers take.

Those are tough words for people already married or settled. Do you mean they can't write?

I'm not saying families are bad. You just shouldn't dull your senses with too much furniture, with all the conventions. The social bars, the societal bars, the government bars, the religious bars, all the things we pen ourselves in with, most of which are really just abstract ideas. Don't get in situations where you can't steal vegetables, or listen to red-headed winos. Originality evaporates.

I own far too many things right now. I've got so much stuff accumulated, sometimes I secretly wish my house would burn down.

If you don't have the two hours a day, clean everything out. Eat dinner off crates. Most writers are, at least, metaphysical outlaws anyway. They don't make a lot of money. They keep strange hours. They're intimidating—eccentric if not neurotic—and the very lifestyle that's dictated by their chosen profession makes for a way of relating to the world that is somewhat outside the social norm. The ones on university campuses—universities are like furniture—don't get too far beyond jail. But a guy living in a house trailer or a room somewhere, trying to do what he loves best, at a typewriter, is kind of put by circumstances into a position of being at odds with much of the culture around him.

One of the hardest things for a writer to deal with is the loneliness caused by that lifestyle. And yet it's absolutely necessary. If you spend too much time with other people, you find that you're having only secondhand ideas, for one thing.

Yeah. If you share your ideas, they become diluted.
You shouldn't talk about your work. I've watched people fall into that pothole. They talk all their juice away. A lot of talented writers just talk their books away, their stories away. They go to bars and talk about writing to the point where they talk all the sizzle out of them. Their work is either flat or never gets finished at all because it's already done; they did what they had to do with it in talking rather than putting it on a page.

Too much input is another danger of that. If you had shared your early work with many people, they might have said it was too quirky, advised you to tone down.
Which would have been a mistake. That's why I say stay away from universities, because too often that's the kind of advice you get.

Whatever it is everybody seems to hate in your first work that's what you should work on and develop. If it's arousing that kind of antipathy, you can figure that that's the thing you do best. That's the thing about you that is unique and special.

But nothing I've said, nothing you do, will make a difference if you can't face the solitude. You can take risks, and be playful, and look at the sky, and find a technique and plot, but it's impotent if you can't discipline yourself. Very few people can write in a crowd. This is a very solitary occupation. I have known people who were more talented than me, who never made it. And the primary reason was always that they couldn't stand to be alone for several hours a day. Any writer worth anything has mastered the art.

The art of solitude.

[Silence]

He said didactically [laughs]. See, that's what happens when you start talking to a tape recorder.

JOHN STEINBECK

I have written a great many stories and I still don't know how to go about it except to write it and take my chances.

ear Writer:
Although it must be a thousand years ago that I sat in a class in story writing at Stanford, I remember the experience very clearly. I was bright-eyed and bushy-brained and prepared to absorb the secret formula for writing good short stories, even great short stories. This illusion was canceled very quickly. The only way to write a good short story, we were told, is to write a good short story. Only after it is written can it be taken apart to see how it was done. It is a most difficult form, as we were told, and the proof lies in how very few great short stories there are in the world.

The basic rule given us was simple and heartbreaking. A story to be effective had to convey something from writer to reader, and the power of its offering was the measure of its excellence. Outside of that, there were no rules. A story could be about anything and could use any means and any technique at all—so long as it was effective. As a subhead to this rule, it seemed to be necessary for the writer to know what he wanted to say, in short, what he was talking about. As an exercise we were to try reducing the meat of our story to one sentence, for only then could we know it well enough to enlarge it to three- or six- or ten-thousand words.

So there went the magic formula, the secret ingredient. With no more than that, we were set on the desolate, lonely path of the writer. And we must have turned in some abysmally bad stories. If I had expected to be discovered in a full bloom of excellence, the grades given my efforts quickly disillusioned me. And if I felt unjustly criticized, the judgments of editors for many years afterward upheld my teacher's side, not mine. The low grades on my college stories were echoed in the rejection slips, in the hundreds of rejection slips.

It seemed unfair. I could read a fine story and could even know how it was done. Why could I not then do it myself? Well, I couldn't, and maybe it's because no two stories dare be alike. Over the years I have written a great many stories and I still don't know how to go about

it except to write it and take my chances.

If there is a magic in story writing, and I am convinced that there is, no one has ever been able to reduce it to a recipe that can be passed from one person to another. The formula seems to lie solely in the aching urge of the writer to convey something he feels important to the reader. If the writer has that urge, he may sometimes, but by no means always, find the way to do it. You must perceive the excellence that makes a good story good or the errors that make a bad story. For a bad story is only an ineffective story.

It is not so very hard to judge a story after it is written, but, after many years, to start a story still scares me to death. I will go so far as to say that the writer who is not scared is happily unaware of the remote and tantalizing majesty of the medium.

I remember one last piece of advice given me. It was during the exuberance of the rich and frantic '20s, and I was going out into that world to try to be a writer.

I was told, "It's going to take a long time, and you haven't got any money. Maybe it would be better if you could go to Europe."

"Why?" I asked.

"Because in Europe poverty is a misfortune, but in America it is shameful. I wonder whether or not you can stand the shame of being poor."

It wasn't too long afterward that the depression came down. Then everyone was poor and it was no shame any more. And so I will never know whether or not I could have stood it. But surely my teacher was right about one thing. It took a long time—a very long time. And it is still going on, and it has never got easier.

She told me it wouldn't.

For two years, John Steinbeck lived and worked with migrant workers from Oklahoma and California. The result was The Grapes of Wrath *and a Pulitzer Prize.*

For 66 years, 1902-1968, he lived and worked with words. The result was this letter, published in 1963.